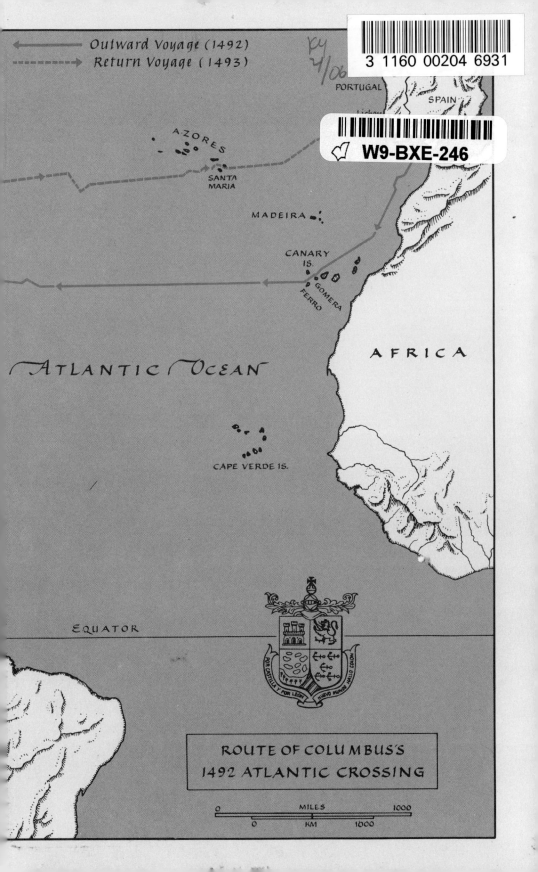

Outward Voyage (1492)
Return Voyage (1493)

PORTUGAL   SPAIN

Lisbon

AZORES

SANTA
MARIA

MADEIRA

CANARY
IS.

GOMERA
FERRO

AFRICA

ATLANTIC OCEAN

CAPE VERDE IS.

EQUATOR

POR CASTILLA Y POR LEON   NUEVO MUNDO HALLO COLON

ROUTE OF COLUMBUS'S
1492 ATLANTIC CROSSING

MILES
0   1000
0   KM   1000

Christopher Columbus

Christopher Columbus

~~~

GIANNI GRANZOTTO

Translated by Stephen Sartarelli

Doubleday & Company, Inc.
Garden City, New York
1985

Library of Congress Cataloging in Publication Data
Granzotto, Gianni
Christopher Columbus.
Translation of: Cristoforo Colombo.
Bibliography: p. 286
Includes index.
1. Columbus, Christopher. 2. Explorers—America—
Biography. 3. Explorers—Spain—Biography. 4. America—
Discovery and exploration—Spanish. I. Title.
E111.G784 1985 970.01'5 [B]
ISBN 0-385-19677-6
Library of Congress Catalog Card Number 85-4387

To my dear wife Carolina,
who saw this book through to the end
before departing.

Contents

Contents

List of Maps

List of Maps

Christopher Columbus

1

The Other Sea

The ninth of July, 1453, was a Monday. The summer had not yet entered the sign of Leo, but already it was blazing white-hot across sea and sky. The old folks said they could not remember a heat wave so intense; it was clearly the hottest in living memory. The city of Genoa, rising up beneath the sun, lay breathless and still. It was not a day to go out of doors. Even the shady recesses seemed red-hot, though no one was about to quit them for the sunlight.

Yet it happened that right around noon, at the hottest hour of the day, the silent city suddenly came alive with noise and commotion, shouts and footsteps resonating amid the cobblestones of the narrow streets, echoing back and forth as if all of Genoa were about to plunge headlong into the sea. Down by Portoria and Piccapietra, the alleyways, with their small staircases and passageways cut into the side of the mountain, sloped almost straight down. Shouting and covered in sweat, the crowd was rushing down toward the bottom. To anyone watching from the beach, it must have looked like lines of ants moving very swiftly through the cracks formed by the streets. When puzzled onlookers at their windows asked what could possibly be happening, the ants, without stopping for a moment, answered, "Curse the day! Constantinople has fallen to the Turks!"

People wanted to know more, to try to understand. A sailing vessel had just arrived from the island of Chios with the news. It was moored at the pier of the Graces, and everyone was rushing there to learn more from those who had heard and perhaps seen the terrible event firsthand. When they reached the water they formed a group around the sailors, who spread their arms in the air in a gesture of fatalism. What had happened had happened, and there was nothing more to be done about it.

But what had happened? All the pressing questions met with the same answer. Mohammed, Sultan of the Turks, had taken Constantinople, the city and the straits. He had also captured Pera, the district of Constantinople that had been governed for two centuries by the Genoese. Constantinople had fallen the morning of May 29. It had gone down fighting, with Emperor Constantine at the head of his troops. All resistance had been thwarted, thousands had been killed. The emperor himself had died in battle. The massacre was so great that his body was never found amid the corpses piled everywhere. The Genoese ships had fled Pera just in time and escaped to Chios, which was still free. They brought firsthand accounts of the defeat and the massacre, leaving the island's inhabitants struck with fear and dismay. Then they set sail for Genoa. The commander had already gone to the doge's palace to inform him of the event.

The crowd on the pier fell silent. A monk who had come from Chios with the sailors, standing tall and black against the door of the Church of San Marco where seamen go to pray upon landing, was crying aloud, in a terrible, monotonous voice, "Never has there been, and never again will there be so terrible an event!" Tears streamed from his eyes, and others cried and despaired along with him. The whole city was stunned.

After the spoken accounts, the written reports began to arrive, confirming the worst. The first to arrive was a letter from Angelo Lomellino, chief administrator of Pera at the time of the fall. The letter was addressed to the Doge of Genoa, Pietro Fregoso. Lomellino had written it in Chios, where he too had been forced to take refuge. He had tried everything possible to enter into the sultan's good graces, and was not ashamed to say so; indeed, he spoke of it as something heroic. He had even sent a representative of the powerful Spinola family, Luciano Spinola, to the sultan's castle on the Bosporus to congratulate him on his "great victory." To Lomellino, flattery seemed the best and shrewdest approach. Mohammed was asked to confirm officially whether Pera would still enjoy the privileges formerly granted it by the Byzantines. "They told me only that the bells must ring no more."

While Constantinople was still under siege, Genoese rule in Pera was abolished, and the district came under the sway of the infidels. With sorrow and regret, Lomellino declared, "No longer will our ships be able to sail toward the Black Sea bearing our goods." It was not so much the military defeat as the commercial setback that darkened Genoa's horizons. Lomellino, in his letter, stated as much with typical Genoese clarity: "The certificates of the trading companies are henceforth worthless."

This is what so disturbed the citizens of Genoa in the torrid summer of 1453. Of course the tears they shed were for the poor Christians "cut down like grass in a meadow," for the holy relics tossed into the sea by the Turks, for the beheaded consuls; they themselves remained gripped by horror for what had happened and fear for what might still happen. But their anxiety and despair were caused by a profound concern for the future of the seas and of Genoa itself. With Constantinople fallen, and Pera along with it, what would happen to Chios, Kaffa and all the Genoese outposts on the way to Smyrna and Trebizond? Would the Black Sea still remain, as many had proudly called it, "Genoa's lake," providing her boats free passage all the way to the ports on the Don, where they entered the land of the Tartars to deal in furs and silks, Mongolian leather and Persian gold filigree? What would become of the treasures of the Levant, which materialized like a victor's garland after the adventure of the Crusades and the Christian conquest of Jerusalem? Genoa's prosperity had sprung from these roots: it was a tree of abundance whose branches bore the rich fruits of her customs, habits, projects, and visions of the future. But the Turks' seizure of Constantinople suddenly changed everything, abolishing all hope of continued prosperity. Nothing would escape the ferocity of their hatred; their vigor was pure and invincible. The road to the Orient had been broken in two, like a valley obstructed by a landslide too large to remove. The idea of recapturing Jerusalem became the stuff of utopia. And the wall now blocking the doorstep to Asia would soon engulf all profits, enterprise and trade, the whole arena of commerce and of life in general. The letters that reached the doge from the scenes of the disaster all bore the same message: "We fear much more serious calamities on the horizon."

Genoa shuddered with the fear of becoming poor from one moment to the next. The Turkish conquest of Constantinople would bring with it a complete severing of the spice route, which for so long had served as the lifeline of the Mediterranean world's economy and politics and shaped its ways of living and thinking. Everything became unstable, uncertain. What kind of life lay in store for Genoa? If Byzantium no longer existed, how would Genoa survive?

For centuries, the spice route had been the stuff of legend. By the end of the Middle Ages, spices had become objects of fascination for the people of Europe, with their seductive aromas and their mysterious, distant origins. The very term used for spices in those days, *merces subtiles,* had an alluring sound. Spices represented a new thrill, a kind of newfound freedom, a thread of light in the darkness, to a world that for generations had suffered through the anguish of such disasters as the Hundred Years' War and the Black Death, which had decimated whole cities and countrysides. Now, from unknown, faraway places came a dreamworld in the form of Malabar pepper, evoking images of the legendary caravans of Hejaz, the mirages of the Straits of Hormuz and the Arabian Sea, and the emirs, sultans and courtesans that inhabited this world. Everything that bore the name of Arabicum or Indicum served to give pleasure and stimulate the imagination, the two things that distinguish life from despair. And since this dreamworld proved for the most part difficult to obtain, those with the strongest yearning for it had to seek it out, or else hope to acquire it by other means. In other words, it was a matter of business. But, as Martin Benhaim, a learned geographer, once wrote, "Indian spices change hands at least twelve times before they reach their final buyer."

Arab ships would first go to India to find them, then transport them across the Persian Gulf to Syrian ports, where the Genoese loaded them onto their xebecs and carracks. The Genoese never dealt in heavy loads, since their business almost always involved expensive items, including herbs and spices used to enhance the flavor of certain wines and foods, such as cinnamon, nutmeg, cloves, ginger, vanilla, the abovementioned pepper (which was in great demand), and saffron; they also bought highly prized dyes for silk and wool extracted from plants not found in Europe, such as indigo for blue colors, gallnut for black, the bark and pulp of the brazilwood tree for reds, not to mention the Eastern cochineal from the slopes of Mount Ararat, the mountain of Noah. New trends in fashion required ever more varied and refined colors, and played a part in the cultivation of exoticism and the taste for faraway places and legends remote in both space and time.

New social classes were already beginning to form, reflecting broad strata of income. During the long period of wars, plagues and famines, they had been too weak to grow and prosper. Now their rise led to a search for refinement, marked above all by the desire for opulence and the allure of exoticism. There is nothing more seductive than the superfluous, which must always be invented and reinvented, like art, entertainment and even love.

But there were still other things. We hardly even need mention silk, or sugar, which was beginning to replace honey as the common sweetener. There was the ivory of the wonders of the East. But above all else, there was gold, the noble metal that helped give the courts their pomp and the churches their magnificence, but whose main importance by far lay in its use in the minting of coins and in all financial dealings. Universally accepted as the

standard of comparison, gold formed the basis of the great international exchanges and commercial transactions which helped Medieval Europe to
emerge from the walls of her cities and towns and take on the dimensions of
nations and peoples. The famous letters of exchange that powerful merchants
used to give as a pledge in their dealings were always guaranteed in fine gold,
the surest, most precious of bartering items. Gold was worth ten times as
much as silver.

The need for gold increased with the growth of commerce and the diffu-
sion of coins. There were wars to finance, ships to launch, moneys to invest.
Gold created wealth, and was at the same time a reflection of the wealth that
was spreading to new classes of citizens. At the beginning of the fifteenth
century, things had gotten to the point throughout Europe where the demand
for gold far exceeded the supply. Some actually took to exploiting ancient
mines abandoned by the Romans in the north. Gold seekers went to the
Pyrenees to sift the sands of the riverbeds. The most substantial acquisitions,
however, were made by the Genoese, who went looking for gold in the Mediterranean ports of northern Africa, from Morocco to Egypt. The gold was
transported to the sea by Sudanese or Arabian caravans. Deals were made in
gestures, with a sign of the hand communicating the difference between ac-
ceptance and refusal. These kinds of exchanges earned the name of "mute
markets," since no one knew anyone else's language.

Thus gold remained a mystery, as did its origins: little was known of the
countries from which it came, and even less was known concerning what
countries it might be found in. The writings of Marco Polo, of which about a
hundred copies were already in circulation by the mid-fifteenth century, told
of palaces with roofs of solid gold in legendary Cathay. But who was going to
risk going there, past the land of the Tartars and Turks and beyond the far
reaches of Christendom? The Genoese Antonio Malfante ventured as far as
the basin of the Niger, crossed the Sahara and reached the banks of the
Senegal. Benedetto Drei "discovered" legendary Timbuktu. Groups of finan-
ciers backed these daring men in the hope that they would find gold. But in
fact, most of them got lost in the desert and elsewhere, and gold remained as
much a mystery as ever.

Of course this surprised no one. Throughout all of antiquity, the image
of gold had always been linked to unknown and inaccessible regions. There
was the gold of Abyssinia, the gold of the Sudan, and now the gold of Cathay.
Ptolemy had warned that gold is found only in torrid, remote and dangerous
lands. Scholars updated this notion when they asserted that man's relation-

ship to gold was marked by a sense of destiny and heroism; gold had to be long desired, sought out, earned: it had to be torn from the bowels of the earth after long peregrinations and many dangers, much as in the epic quests.

Hence, whether the quest was for gold or for spices, it always involved a difficult struggle. But the West was experiencing an ever greater, more urgent need for both things, due both to force of habit and the impetuous violence inherent in the desire for wealth. No price was so high, or sacrifice so great as to discourage those who desired these things from going out in pursuit of them. The emergence of the information contained in Marco Polo's recent book, which raised expectations and held great promise for the future, not only threw into disarray the world of geographers and explorers, but created a great stir in the milieux of finance, government and commerce.

But at this very moment of eagerness and hope, the fall of Constantinople suddenly blocked all roads to prosperity, since they invariably led to the East and only the East, and all eastward traffic was now obstructed. The Crusades, of course, had also been fought for this reason. They had served to tear down a wall, beyond which lay new horizons, options and opportunities. Now everything went back to the starting point, and the East was once again impenetrable, hostile territory. No longer could a Christian ship sail across the Red Sea or the Black Sea unmolested. An impregnable barrier of hostile infidels now stood between the West and the regions of spices and gold. Lomellino's letters to the Doge of Genoa had been right. Within a few years of Pera's fall, Chios, Kaffa and Tripoli in Syria were also submerged by the Moslem tide. One by one, all the markets were shut down.

Of course, this was not only Genoa's drama. It was also Venice's. But Venice was a naval power, a state organized for combat, with military policies to go along with her trade policies. Venice possessed an armed fleet, and did not give ground. She remained as it were Christendom's bastion against the Turks, and successfully defended most of her territories in the Adriatic and the Aegean. She also successfully protected her commerce, which was for the most part Mediterranean. Genoa, on the other hand, was a merchant city, the center of a network of trade which stretched from Levantine shores all the way to France, Germany, Flanders and the British Isles. Genoa dealt in rare goods from the East. When the Turkish conquest blocked her ports of call and finally destroyed the foundations of her economy within just a few years, Genoa was left without resources, like a spring gone dry.

In that summer of 1453, everyone in Genoa understood this harsh fact. It was self-evident. The question was not: How will we get it all back? Genoa, a city of practical people, realized that she could never go back to Chios or Kaffa. That road was not merely closed, it no longer existed. The question was: What other solution will we find?

There were no immediate answers. One of the most pressing problems was finding ways to invest Genoa's accumulated capital. Genoa was rich. If she did not find some alternatives, her wealth would disappear. The choice fell to Spain, which was liberating itself from the Moors after centuries of decadence and seemed to offer the prospects of youth, expansion, and an attractive flowering of trade and commerce. Genoese capital emigrated to Spain—to Seville, Barcelona and other active centers of the growing nation, as well as to Portugal—to Lisbon and the shores of the Atlantic. From here the first convoys left to go down the African coast in search of gold, taking the opposite direction from that taken by Marco Polo, which had quickly become inaccessible. Genoa's gaze, and that of Europe too, had turned away from the East and now looked West, onto "the other sea."

There were still no definite conclusions to be drawn from all of this, even though the conviction that the world was round was by now widespread, especially among cartographers, astronomers, geographers and seamen. But it was these very shores, the shores of the other sea, that were believed to mark the boundaries of the world—and the boundaries of man, according to the wisdom of the ancients, which was part of everyone's cultural heritage. No, there was no definite answer as yet. But the art of commerce contains within itself a spur to movement and change. It leads to endeavor, to change and discovery. Suggestions such as these were also present, mixed in with all the questions and laments, in the summer of 1453, circulating through Genoa from the hills to the sea, not unlike the pollen that begins to float in the air at about the same time of year.

In the summer of 1453, when the pollen was just beginning to rise up into the wind, Christopher Columbus was two years old.

2

The Irrelevant Country

Enter Christopher Columbus, the central figure of our story. He is two years old when he comes onto the scene, at the time of Constantinople's fall to the Turks. Since we first mentioned him in our description of how the news of this defeat reached Genoa in July of 1453, the reader no doubt will have gathered that Christopher Columbus was born in Genoa in 1451, or that I, at least, believe so.

But the reader is probably also aware of the many doubts that have been raised and of the sometimes fierce polemics waged by not only historians but by whole nations over the question of Columbus's country of origin. It is a confusing question often romanticized and perhaps, in the end, unanswerable. Hence the reader may be asking himself why I appear to be so sure of my conclusion.

The subject of Columbus's birth has filled hundreds of volumes. Plunging into this ocean of writing is as risky as taking to sea in a storm without a lifeboat. The various opinions do not merely differ from one another, they clash violently. The only way out of this tumult is to stick to the documentation and to try to select from among the myriad of texts only those based on serious research and study, leaving aside everything merely inspired by flag-waving fervor.

Since this is the approach I have adopted in conducting my investigation into Columbus's birthplace, I tend to reject all hypotheses that smack of fanatical nationalism, patriotic pride or similar forms of obstinacy, which are quick to arouse the emotions but in the end provide nothing concrete. They actually become quite unjustifiable once we consider the historical context in which Columbus lived, and the rather limited importance of questions of nationality and geographic origin at that time in history. Moreover, debates over an individual's birthplace always end up arousing the patriotic itch. The one-sidedness of those who insist on Columbus's Spanish nationality is just as open to criticism as the prejudice of those who would have him Genoese at all costs. Certainties of this sort often come precariously close to resembling enigmas.

But do we know anything for certain about Columbus's country of origin? In taking a general overview of the question, we can discern a few salient points. The first is that the Genoese theory is by far the most plausible and reliable. The second is that if we want to be absolutely precise, a few marginal doubts will always remain, probably never to be quelled. The third is that those hypotheses that ascribe another national origin to Columbus are by contrast all rather feeble, sometimes even laughable or patently false.

What sort of proof do we have at our disposal? It is an indisputable fact that in Genoa, just past the mid-1400s, there lived a man named Christopher Columbus. This is documented dryly and impartially by notarial deeds. Genoa, a seafaring mercantile city, has always placed great emphasis on precision in written records. The notarial deeds concerning the Columbus family are many, more than twenty testimonies recorded by disinterested notaries. Of this handful of records, two in particular shed light on the life of Christopher Columbus. The first is from 1470 and concerns the acknowledgment of a debt—48 Genoese lire—to be paid to a certain Pietro Balessio. The document refers specifically to "Cristoforo Colombo [Christopher Columbus], son of Domenico, an adult nineteen years of age."

The second is from 1479. By that time Columbus had already established residence in Lisbon. But he was called back to Genoa to testify before a notary about a trip he had made to Madeira. The document states that the witness "is about twenty-seven years old." Christopher Columbus attests that he was sent to Madeira to buy sugar on behalf of the commission agent Paolo DiNegro. He declares that the following day he must leave to go back to Lisbon. When asked which of the two litigating parties he thinks should win the case, he answers only, "The one in the right."

These two dry, impersonal public documents constitute the major basis for concluding that Christopher Columbus in all likelihood was Genoese. Though the notarial deeds do not say explicitly that he was born in Genoa, references to his father Domenico, a citizen of Genoa and for many years a resident, abound in many earlier deeds. What it is important to emphasize at this point of our narrative is the reality of this young man named Christopher Columbus living in Genoa, entering onto the stage of life with words, gestures and actions. I would like the reader henceforth to join me in my attempt to separate him from the stick figures of past accounts, the statues of history that render everything cold and bloodless. The notarial deeds reflect a life fully lived, throbbing with energy. Christopher Columbus was as real as you or I. The documents tell us how old he was at the time they were drafted, pointing once again to 1451 as the year of his birth. They tell us how he lived his young life, making trips across the sea and restlessly moving from one place of residence to another. They even give us a clear indication of his character, with their citation of his prudent, pointed reply, May the one in the right win.

A dozen years after the last document mentioned above, the fledgling seaman made his immortal voyage. Rising up from the obscurity of notarial deeds, his name suddenly soared to glorious heights. Who knew him? In Barcelona, in 1493 when he returned in triumph from the unknown, received with full ceremony by the king and queen, everyone wanted to know who he was, where he came from. Columbus himself, during the period of uncertainty and waiting, had, in his few intimate confidences and writings, said only that he was an *extraniero,* a foreigner. After his return from the Indies the whole world began to talk about him, and without exception all considered him Genoese. They continued to regard him as such throughout the sixteenth century and beyond. When identified as anything other than Genoese, he was said to be Ligurian, referring to the region in which Genoa lay.

The most direct testimony comes from his contemporaries. Pietro Martire, a Lombard, the earliest of Columbus's chroniclers and whose accounts were in many ways a precursor of modern journalism, was in Barcelona when Columbus returned. Martire frequented the court, and had a mania for disseminating information; he sent letters everywhere, to his friends in Lake Maggiore, to Florence, to the Vatican court. With his letter of May 14, 1493, addressed to Giovanni Borromeo, he was the first to send news that "a few days ago, a certain Christopher Columbus, Ligurian *[vir ligur],* who had obtained three ships from the Spanish Crown, returned from the Western antipodes." But even before Columbus set out on his voyage we find a reference, dated 1492, to the agreements made between him and the Spanish sovereigns in a miscellaneous register kept in the court during the century's final decade by a scribe named Galindez, where Columbus is referred to as *"Cristóbal Colón, genovés."*

Columbus was also Genoese to the parish priest of Palacíos, Andrés Bernaldez, his good friend and confidant (who wrote in his *History of the*

Catholic Kings: "Columbus was a man who came from the land of Genoa.");
he was Genoese to the Bishop Bartolomé de Las Casas, the major source for
sixteenth-century historians of Columbus's exploits, who asserts his "Genoese
nationality" with certainty in his *General and Natural History of the Indies;*
and he was Genoese, or more precisely "originating from the province of
Liguria, which is found in Italy," for Gonzalo Fernández de Oviedo, who met
Columbus when he was still quite young and recounted his exploits in a
monumental work with the same title as that of Las Casas. Las Casas,
Bernaldez and Oviedo were Columbus's contemporary historians, and they
would serve as authoritative sources for centuries to come. There was never
any doubt in their minds that Columbus was born anywhere but in Genoa, on
Ligurian soil.

Let us look briefly at the Genoese chroniclers of the time. The Republic
of Genoa's rulers were quick to congratulate the Spanish royal family on the
discovery of the Indies. But, alas, they had no idea that the memorable event
had been brought about by a fellow citizen of theirs. In sending their compli-
ments they said only that "your dominion has now spread to parts of the
world unknown to even the Romans." This was a wise and correct observation in itself. For the first time in history a man had ventured beyond the
orbis, the circle believed to mark the limits of the earth. The Genoese of
course realized that this had been achieved by sea. But as limited as Genoa's
commerce and markets were by this point, they had no idea that a Genoese
had performed the feat. As if to atone for such a significant oversight, in the
years that followed, the city's chroniclers were always quick to point out that
the hero of this great discovery came from their city. Antonio Gallo writes
that Columbus "was born in Genoa of plebeian parents"; the bishop Agostino
Giustiniani, in his *Polyglot Psaltery,* states that "the Genoese Christopher
Columbus, with admirable daring, discovered the New World"; the chronicler Bartolomeo Senarega attests to Columbus's "Genoese birth." All these
writings appeared between 1499 and 1516, when Columbus was still alive or
had been dead just a few years.

But what about the hero to whom all these many documents refer, who
himself told the story of his voyages, described his fortunes and misfortunes,
carried on active correspondences, wrote letters of entreaty and letters of
anger—what did Columbus leave us as evidence of the Genoese origins that
everyone imputed to him even when he was still alive?

Strangely enough, almost nothing. In all the texts that can be said to
have been indisputably written by him, only once does he mention that he is

Genoese. There is also another document, which he probably wrote but which for a number of reasons has been put into question, in which reference is made to Genoa as his birthplace. But that is all. Nothing more for forty years, the amount of time that passed between the notarial deed of his voyage to Madeira and his last moments in a house in Valladolid, Spain. If he really was Genoese, as I believe he was, he certainly did not boast of it. Indeed, he seems to have done all he could to hide the fact. Why?

The text that I consider to be beyond doubt is a letter sent in 1502 from Seville, addressed to the friends of the Banco di San Giorgio, the center of Genoese commerce. By that time Columbus had already completed three expeditions across the Atlantic and was getting ready for a fourth, which would prove to be the longest and most troublesome of them all. He was already a famous man, and to a certain degree a rich man as well. The human soul, even when most closed and impenetrable, always has its moments of homesickness and nostalgia; some even have moments of pride when they feel the urge to show old and forgotten friends how much their lot has changed since the day they left those friends and their home behind, how far they have come purely on the strength of daring and will. This is no doubt the motive behind Columbus's letter to the Banco di San Giorgio, in which he lists his achievements and the titles and privileges he has received. But what really convinces me of the letter's authenticity, even more than the handwriting analyses (which leave little room for doubt), is the much deeper correspondence between the writer's feelings and the very natural manner in which they are expressed. "In the city of Genoa I have my roots, and there I was born," says the letter. An unequivocal statement, surely. But listen how eloquently his homesickness speaks: "Though my body be here, my heart is forever there." (The bank wrote back to Columbus, addressing the letter to "the Admiral of the Ocean Sea and Viceroy of the Indies." Is this not perhaps what Columbus wanted from them, a declaration of pride on the part of Genoa for being his "country of origin"?)

The other document in which Genoa is mentioned is Columbus's first will and testament, drawn up in Seville in 1498, but held by many to be apocryphal, starting with the date itself. The text is recognized as a deed of majorat, inasmuch as it names the son Diego as direct heir to the benefits and titles conferred upon Columbus by the Spanish throne in reward for his discovery of the new lands. But rather than go through the labyrinth of contestations that his document has stirred up and continues to stir up, I should like to call the reader's attention to two specific facts: that the first mentions of a testament left by Columbus refer to a text written in 1502, which was lost and of which no trace has ever been found; and that the text bearing the date 1498 is not an original but a copy.

With these two facts in mind, skeptical historians have speculated that the 1498 document was rewritten long after the indicated date and modeled on the real testament, written in 1502. This was presumably done by Columbus's heirs, who used it as evidence during the endless litigations with the Spanish Crown that they began after his death. The document said to be apocryphal was in fact exhibited for the first time in court in 1578.

That the only surviving will is not an original but merely a copy is an unfortunate accident for which, however, Columbus's heirs bear no responsibility whatsoever, even though over the years it helped to support their presumed deceit. Many Columbus-related documents kept in the castle of Simancas, where Philip II compiled the general archives of the kingdom, were lost during the Napoleonic occupation. The emperor's troops set up camp at Simancas and stayed for a while. Finding no straw for the horses to sleep on, they took tons of documents from the archives and improvised beds for their steeds, and perhaps for the soldiers themselves. Hence if blame is to be cast on anyone for the absence of an original document, it must go to Napoleon.

What does the allegedly apocryphal text contain? Among other things, declarations that would be very useful in establishing Columbus's place of birth, such as the following: "Being born in Genoa, I came here to Castile to serve their Highnesses"; or the passage where Columbus assigns to his son Diego and to his successors the responsibility of supporting "a person of our line" in Genoa, saying that "from that city I departed, and in that city I was born."

No one can say—and I less than anyone—that these words were not in the 1502 document. The document clearly was backdated for reasons other than the affirmation or denial of Columbus's birthplace, and most likely any other hypothetical distortions of the original addressed concerns entirely unrelated to this question. But once doubt's shadow falls on a single detail, it eventually darkens the whole, leaving nothing untouched, whether true or not.

It must also be said that Columbus, with his impenetrable silences and the general ambiguousness surrounding most aspects of his life, does nothing at all to help clear the doubts that he leaves in his wake. But I am hardly complaining. People are what they are, consistent even in obscurity. The ambiguousness surrounding Columbus is part of his overall character and cannot be separated from other facts and aspects of his life. I must confess that this very aspect has held a particular fascination for me, leading me to attempt to explore its hidden side, swathed in shadow like the dark side of the moon.

Even less helpful in our attempts to resolve the uncertainty of Columbus's birthplace is the book written by his son Fernando, the *History of the Life and Deeds of Christopher Columbus,* which had a wide circulation all over Europe and first appeared in Venice in 1571, a year before the author's death. Fernando was a rather cultured man with a great passion for books and considerable learning in the sciences of navigation, geography, cosmography, and the study of travel and discovery. He amassed a library of fifteen thousand volumes and published an index of tables of the planet's longitudes and latitudes, considered invaluable at the time. In his youth, when little more than an adolescent, he accompanied his father on his last ocean voyage, sharing with him for more than two long years all the marvels as well as anxieties of that expedition famed for the mishaps, dangers and moments of despair encountered along the way. This beloved son thus would seem to have had all the requirements and knowledge necessary to compile a true and accurate biography of his father, the only one that could have unequivocally won the credence of his contemporaries.

But this was not the case. On the contrary, Fernando's recollections turned out to be full of gaps, imperfections and perhaps even conscious distortions of fact. Here once again, the family's reticence and hesitation was largely due to their litigation with the Spanish throne, carried on for generations and even centuries afterward. Things were written and rewritten with the purpose of gaining an advantage in the debate or disputing the adversary's contentions. Fernando, for example, remained silent on a number of things that he surely must have known about. Other things he took care to wrap in a cloud of uncertainty and doubt. Silence and the confusion of facts are parallel roads, both of which lead away from the truth. Fernando took both roads. Moreover, with regard to our area of concern—his father's native country— rather than helping to clarify the issue, he merely adds to all the confusion.

How can a son so deeply attached to his father write that the greater the man's fame became, "the greater became the doubts surrounding his native country and origins"? Doubts for everyone else, surely, but certainly not for him. And yet in his text he goes wandering from place to place, using absurd quotations and following the trail of mere hearsay and rumor from Nervi to

Cogoleto, to Bogliasco and Savona, and finally to Piacenza. It all points to a birth in Liguria, or somewhere nearby. But the matter remains always vague. If the man's own son is unsure, how can this not open the door to all sorts of other conjecture? Clearly Fernando did nothing but pave the way for all later fantasies on the matter. In essence, he asserted that Columbus's birthplace was open to question. And the resulting void was ready to be filled by all manner of suppositions, however unfounded they might be.

Nevertheless, we find in Fernando's own text one of the reasons why he shies away from naming Genoa as the real place of his family's origins. In looking back to his ancestors—in accordance with the practice, very fashionable at the time, of tracing one's name back to Roman consular families—Fernando asserts, this time with assurance, that the Columbus family descended from a certain Colon of whom Tacitus speaks in his Histories. This Colon was known for having brought King Mithridates back to Rome as a prisoner, whereupon he was made a consul. What a way to add honor and ancient nobility to the family line, and thereby give added weight to the titles first granted by royal privilege to the discoverer of the New World and then cast into doubt with regard to his descendants!

But Fernando was mistaken. The person cited by Tacitus was not named Colon but Cilon (Julius Cilus). And the Mithridates he captured was not Rome's great adversary, who committed suicide rather than let himself fall into enemy hands, but a petty sovereign of the Bosporus with the same name who lived a good century later, during Claudius's reign. This second Mithridates alternated between periods of loyalty to the empire and rebellion against it, and was finally executed for it. All in all, his "captor" was hardly a figure on which to construct an illustrious lineage.

Thus we begin to see whence arises the mist surrounding Christopher Columbus's birth. Father and son both remained silent on the matter in order to conceal their humble origins. Not to hide Genoa in itself, but to suppress the memory of the poor carder who sired Christopher in Genoa. A background so modest constituted an obstacle to Christopher's ambitious desires of higher station and his aspiration to titles and armorial bearings that he might pass on to his descendants. Columbus found the fame that he deserved. But he also wanted a coat of arms, something altogether different with a different set of rules, which nevertheless aroused his yearnings like an enchanting mirage. He sacrificed his homesickness for the past to this dream of aristocratic immortality. And since he was such an assiduous dreamer, to the

point of mixing fantasy and reality by confusing the object of his ambition
with the means of attaining it, who can say with any certainty that Columbus
did not really think that he was descended from fallen noble stock, whose
lineage he was anxious to reestablish? His pride was notorious. He actually
considered himself an emissary of providence. So much for Cilon and Mithridates! Perhaps the key to unlock this mystery lies in the following pronouncement by his son: "My father, apostle that he was, wanted no emphasis placed
on his native country and origins, and he preferred that his parents remain
little-known."

Imagine then what happened when, amid all these intentional obfusca-
tions, Columbus's fame became so great as to tempt other nations to appropriate a bit of it for themselves. At least ten different nations besides Italy
have claimed and continue to claim Columbus as a native son. I shall disre-
gard the more marginal cases, some of them quite humorous from an objective point of view, such as that of a certain abbé Casanova who a century ago
maintained that Columbus was Corsican by birth, thus enabling the island to
boast of having produced two of the greatest men in history, Napoleon and
Columbus.

This abbé Casanova, who was from Calvi, based his argument on the fact
that there had been a family in Calvi by the name of Columbus (Colombo)
since time immemorial. Similar reasoning lies behind most nationalistic
claims such as this one. For example, in France—there being also a case made
for a French Columbus—a certain lawyer from Digne once proclaimed himself a descendant of the admiral merely because his name was Juan Colomb.
Elsewhere, a French privateer by the name of Coullon, much better known
than the obscure provincial lawyer, became frequently mistaken for the real
Columbus because, while only the linguistic transposition of their family
name distinguished them from each other, they had many things in common,
such as having lived at the same time and, more astonishingly, having fought
in the same battle at sea. But Mediterranean Europe was full of such coinci-
dences of names. There were thousands of Colombos in Italy, and just as
many Colóns in Spain, Coloms in Portugal, and Coullons in France. It is not
hard to get them confused. There has been no lack of fanatics in each locale
ready to identify Columbus as their own. But what is always missing is documentation, proof, convincing arguments in favor of such identification.

A few more serious arguments can be found among the Spanish claims,
if only because one of the writers supporting them is a man with some author-

ity, Salvador de Madariaga. Madariaga's book on Columbus is undoubtedly one of the more fascinating on the life of the great seaman. It towers above the hundreds of other volumes of very dry, lifeless inquiry, which García Marquez once referred to as "the most detestible of all writing." Madariaga had great powers of expression, imagination and style. He is not a historian limited to his own field, he is a writer. But when he discusses Columbus's origins he suddenly falls prey to an irresistible desire for fictions and sidesteps like a thoroughbred shying before an obstacle. According to Madariaga, Columbus is a converted Jew of Spanish origin whose family was forced by racial persecution to emigrate to Liguria, where it subsequently embraced the Catholic faith. For him, the history of Spain's converted Jews is like a spiderweb that extends everywhere, even to the levels of power, as far as the antechamber of the Catholic kings. Madariaga alleges that Columbus was part of a conspiracy of this sort and belonged to a sectarian band of *conversos,* converted Jews. His entire book flows from this single spring of interpretation, following the course of Columbus's life as it branches out into a thousand different rivulets and cascades.

It is an imaginary spring. In the fifteenth century Genoa had no Jewish community as did Marseilles, Venice and other cities. None of the public or private records of 1450 known to us today shows that there was a single Jew in Genoa who declared himself as such. Columbus's father, as we shall see, was a keeper of one of the gates at the city walls. The city of Genoa would never have entrusted him with such a responsibility if he had been of Jewish descent. Madariaga nevertheless continues his argument by describing Columbus's aquiline nose, his fondness for gold and money in general, the mystical, nearly fanatical spirit in which he carried out his undertakings. These, says Madariaga, are typically Jewish traits. But they are also typical of the Genoese temperament, if fanaticism is one aspect of stubbornness. Arguments of this sort prove nothing. The only thing that enables us to pardon Madariaga for this clearly farfetched part of his book is the depth, human richness and freshness with which he paints the figure of Columbus and the lively background of the Spain in which he lived.

The theory of a Spanish Columbus has also had other, less prestigious exponents. In the late nineteenth century a notorious falsifier of documents, García de la Riega, succeeded in drawing attention to the city of Pontevedra in Galicia as Columbus's probable birthplace. It was later ascertained that the documents he produced had been forged.

As we can see, the contestations of Columbus's presumed Genoese birth are numerous, so numerous that one cannot avoid talking about them. But they all hold little substance—not even enough to warrant making any serious arguments in response. All of which ends up giving more weight and credibility to the Genoese assumption, the only solid one still standing. So little is it affected by the others' desires for posthumous fame that Antonio Ballesteros, the Spanish historian and author of the most complete collection of studies on the life of Columbus, after devoting about a hundred pages to the question of Columbus's birth—marshalling scores of quotations, texts, documents and hypotheses regarding the beginnings of the man who transformed the world's geography—concludes with the unequivocal assertion, "No one can any longer foster even the vaguest shadow of a doubt as to the Genoese birth of Christopher Columbus."

This may even be too strong. The ambiguities surrounding Christopher Columbus continue to cast a light mist of uncertainty around his birth, if for no other reason than that the designations of Genoese and Ligurian correspond to different geographical limits, the former being a subset of the latter. I have already said that for my part I believe Genoa to be Columbus's birthplace, and it is certainly the least fictionalized of all the places hypothesized. Hence I began my narrative with Christopher as a child amid the alleyways of Genoa, on the day that the fall of Constantinople was announced to the city.

And so? Would history have been any different if Columbus had not been born in Genoa? Of what importance is birthplace to a man who left it so early in life and never went back? He ceased caring about those he left behind there and continually concealed the name of his native land, never once boasting of having been born there. It almost seems as if he wanted to renounce Genoa forever. Columbus knew very well that if he had remained in Genoa he would never have been able to realize his dreams of discovery, his great and glorious adventure. He went knocking at the doors of the European courts to ask for the means and support for his voyage, yet never once thought, even remotely, of turning to Genoa. He actually reached a point where he believed that his being Genoese was more of a hindrance than a help in his climb to success.

Obviously the notion of native country, as we understand it today, mattered very little to him. And in my opinion it is wrong to overestimate its importance in his regard, which is precisely what so many seem to do all too impetuously, in every camp. But this I say not out of disdain, disapproval or desire for controversy. We must not, however, forget that this story's protagonist is Christopher Columbus, a man who built his whole life on a dream. And dreams have no native country. To dreams, after all, all countries are irrelevant.

3

The Genoa Years

Be that as it may, Christopher Columbus did not spend many years of his life in Genoa. He left the city for good before his thirtieth year, turning his back on Genoa from that point on. He went to sea for the first time at the young age of thirteen or fourteen, and thereafter was constantly sailing off, using the city and his family merely as ever more tenuous home bases for his restless existence.

When we think of Columbus as Genoese, as I maintain we can, we must take into consideration that any real connection between the man and the city, between Columbus and Genoa, was limited to his childhood and early adolescence. Antonio Gallo, a contemporary of Columbus and chancellor of the Banco di San Giorgio, who became a diligent chronicler of Genoese events after 1477, wrote that "although [Columbus] had little education during his childhood, when he reached the age of puberty he devoted himself to navigation." Gallo adds that Christopher "was born of plebeian parents, who made their living working with wool."

These few lines summarize all of Columbus's brief youth: the setting of his birth, his environment, education and later decision to break away from his modest roots, which had not been able to sustain his growth. The Colombo side of his family came from Moconesi, in the valley of Fontanabuona, which lies parallel to the coast about a dozen kilometers from the sea, surrounded by steep mountains. His mother, Susanna di Fontanarossa, also came from a mountain village, this one in the Bisagno valley. The sea was a foreign, distrusted element to these "chestnut-eaters." But the city beckoned. The closed circles of the Middle Ages were beginning to break, and the peasants came down from the mountains like tribes in migration, cautious and united before venturing off into the new and the unknown. The first

Colombo to leave Moconesi was Christopher's grandfather Giovanni, at the beginning of the fifteenth century. He settled in Quinto, which was then a village at Genoa's eastern gates, at the foot of the hills that he had just abandoned. He chose weaving as his trade, weaving wool—a rather crude art that demanded no special skill or qualifications, as did that of weaving silk, for example.

Nevertheless, working with wool must have provided sufficient earnings to the newly citified provincial, since Giovanni persevered in that line of work. He found a job for his son Domenico as an apprentice with a Flemish weaver who owned a shop in Genoa. The apprentice—following the formula *pro famulo et discipulo* (part servant, part pupil)—had to work for five years and was guaranteed room and board, clothing and footwear, and a bit of pocket money now and then. At the time, Domenico was eleven years old. All these facts and developments—including names, origins and trades—are known from a notarial deed of 1429, the first document containing information of the existence of the Colombo branch from which Christopher would issue.

Let us follow momentarily the movements of the young Domenico, who twenty years later would father a son destined to become one of the most famous men in the world. The flow of emigrants from the mountains continued gradually toward Genoa. They often all had the same trade, belonged to the same religious brotherhood, married amongst one another and moved about together. And all things considered, they did it rather rapidly. Domenico was barely twenty-two years old when he left Quinto to settle in the city itself, on the very edge yet inside the Genoese walls, in the district where other woolworkers like himself lived. His identification with the place and the trade was now complete, and all his ties to the mountains broken. From the friars of Santo Stefano, Domenico rented a house and a small piece of property on vico dell'Olivella, and went there to live.

Vico dell'Olivella, located in the Portoria district, was a little lane that Genoa later swallowed up over the course of its urban expansion. At the time, however, it was a lively little street that joined the city's new wall, built a century earlier, to the ancient wall within which Genoa had first developed into a nucleus of population, from the port up to the first of its steep inclines. Between the two walls, the city had spread and grown denser. The Olivella was at the edge of the outer walls and had gardens running along the city's fortifications, as well as a few vestiges of the rural countryside remaining between the houses. The house that Domenico moved into was surrounded by a small band of wooded terrain. It was not far from the Olivella Gate, one of the new gates of Genoa opened after the city's expansion. It was there that Domenico married Susanna in 1445. And it was there that, in all likelihood, Christopher was born in 1451. (A few have observed that the amount of time between the marriage and the birth of their first child seems a bit long for a young couple. This has led some to suspect that Christopher was not the firstborn. But we have no evidence of the existence of any brothers or sisters who may have preceded him. In all the notarized documents in which Christopher is mentioned he always appears as the eldest child.)

Several years after moving to Genoa, onto the friars' property, Domenico Colombo made another great stride, a qualitative leap in terms of his standing as a citizen. He was appointed keeper of the Olivella Gate by the doge himself, Giano Fregoso, in 1447. It was essentially a political act, a partisan appointment. In those days there was a struggle for power in Genoa between the Adornos and the Fregosos, the latter being vaguely Ghibelline and allied with the Fieschis and the Spinolas. They drew support from the French, that is, the Anjou dynasty; whereas the Guelph faction benefited from the protection of the Spanish, that is, the Aragon dynasty, which by now was very strong in the Mediterranean, having taken Sicily and entertaining thoughts of taking Naples as well, with the help of the pope. Caught between these forces and intrigues, Genoa led a difficult, unstable existence. On Christmas Day of 1446, the year before Domenico became guardian of the Olivella, the Fregosos, with a sudden and fierce attack, occupied the city and came to power. Domenico had fought in their ranks, and was rewarded immediately.

He remained gatekeeper for about four years, his guardianship being renewed three consecutive times. The final renewal, made in 1451, the year of Christopher's birth, was granted him by Pietro Fregoso, the doge in power at the time of Constantinople's fall. He had succeeded Giano, the old party head, upon the latter's death. At the funeral, listed among the 229 citizens and men-at-arms who followed the coffin in a solemn procession of those loyal to the clan, was Domenico Colombo himself. He was thus an activist with ambitions for self-distinction and equally strong tendencies to partisanship.

As the fortunes of the Fieschis began to wane in the years that followed, Domenico's climb slowed down as well. Doubt and uncertainty began to grow in Genoa, and poverty struck the lower classes, brought on by the instability of commerce with the East and the raids of Catalonian pirates, who would come ashore unmolested and sack, pillage and burn, then leave with arms full of booty. The Adornos came back to power with foreign support.

Life became very difficult for Domenico. He had to hide out in his garden and pretend nothing was happening. He experienced financial troubles and could get no help from anyone. Wool was selling poorly and at very low prices, just like everything else in periods of upheaval and change. He began to sustain losses in his trade.

He changed homes, moving to a place on the vico Diritto di Ponticello, only about a hundred meters away from his previous house and still on the land of the friars of Santo Stefano, but a bit further inside the urbanized area near the gate of Sant'Andrea. Anyone who visits Genoa today will notice that these areas, which at the time were situated on the city's outskirts, are now lost in the downtown traffic that circulates around the bustling axis of via Venti Settembre. Behind the line of green buses swarming across the asphalt one may notice an imaginary "home of Columbus," perched under the cylindrical towers of the gate of Sant'Andrea, or the Soprana Gate. This "home" is the product of a patriotic fantasy. Nevertheless, the vico Diritto used to pass through there, and it was on those slopes, the steep slopes of Ravecca, that Christopher Columbus spent his childhood, running, playing, looking at the world around him and listening to people tell about their hopes and disenchantments.

In 1459, when Christopher was eight years old, Fregoso and Fieschi attempted to recapture the city. The battle raged in the very area between the old and new walls that the symbolic "home of Columbus" indicates to have been the real neighborhood in which he lived. In this same area Pietro Fregoso was felled by a mace blow, his forehead gashed open, and in his agony took shelter beneath the Sant'Andrea gate, hunted down like a beast. He died several hours later at the doors of the ducal palace. Young Christopher had probably taken refuge with his mother and younger brothers in the back rooms of their house, and may even have heard the dying man's shouts and wails and the frantic galloping of his horse as he was chased through the district's narrow streets.

The vico Diritto di Ponticello, where he now lived, and the via Madre di Dio were the two main streets of the woolworkers' quarter and comprised the setting for Christopher's everyday activity, the experiences that were slowly becoming a life. His friends were sons of weavers and sons of gardeners who each day brought to market fruit, vegetables and herbs grown near the walls.

Christopher spent a good deal of time with the friars, as was the custom in those days—the friars of Santo Stefano and Santa Caterina, who were connected to the Bianchi (or Cappucciati) brotherhood to which the mountain emigrants belonged. In their sacristies, Christopher learned the basic rudiments of reading, writing and spelling, as well as those of the seafaring art, considered in Genoa to be indispensable to all trades. His son Fernando relates: "He studied just enough to be able to understand the cosmographers. He took up astrology and geometry as well. And since Ptolemy once said that no one can be a good cosmographer without being also a painter, he also practiced drawing, in order to be able to trace the contours of the land and shape the cosmographical forms three-dimensionally."

Thus he already showed a clear-cut, well-developed predilection for the representation of the earth with land and water. And though he was learning to render it along conventional lines, behind these rough drawings his imagination was already waiting to burst forth. The dream was taking shape. It was his way of escaping life's tedium, the doubts and hardships that his family had to combat in its new urban situation. Christopher kept to himself. He had little enthusiasm for looms, wool, comb dust and the patches left out in the fields to dry. What interested him in his father's shop was instead the bookkeeping, the management of the business, the basic principles of enterprise, for which his talents seemed much better suited.

He also, no doubt, often went down to the seashore. It was a place where news was always arriving from people of every sort, where he could observe the different manners and costumes of many different nations, where he could sense the presence of adventure and faraway places. There he could get a taste of the unknown. And it all became part of the dream.

His father had become estranged from politics and after Fregoso's ouster lived the life of a defeated man. Poverty's oppressive shadow once again fell upon the house on vico Diritto. Now there were problems with debts, and Domenico even spent a few days in prison for not always paying them on time. Christopher, now a full-fledged adolescent, was growing up. The family needed him to go to work. But he wouldn't let himself be drawn into his father's trade. He refused to follow the rest of the flock. His father, in an attempt to break out of his financial straits, had started a small traffic of wool and textiles between Genoa and Savona, also transporting shipments of wines and cheeses in both directions. Downstairs from their house, Domenico had also opened a kind of tavern. In several notarial deeds he is referred to as a *tabernarius* or innkeeper.

The road that Christopher chose to follow was that of accompanying his father's shipments across the sea, negotiating the transactions and bartering for other merchandise in exchange, to be resold in turn. Of course these trips were made on little coastal vessels, with the shoreline always in view. They took Christopher to Savona, with stops at Voltri and Varazze. The farthest they went was to such places as Noli and Albenga. Later they ventured as far as Italy's eastern coast, to Camogli, Sestri, Lérici. The going was slow. Christopher would be away for whole days and nights. He began this sort of work at a very young age, around thirteen. In 1492, Columbus wrote that he had been "at sea for the good part of twenty-three years, the only exceptions being insignificantly brief periods." In another letter, this one cited by his son Fernando, he asserts that he first started sailing at fourteen years of age. And in a 1501 document Christopher Columbus, by then Admiral of the Ocean Sea, proudly remembers the fact that he has been "navigating for over forty years, having sailed across everything that to this date has been navigated."

In my opinion, it was probably not that easy getting his father to approve of his seafaring. It was a step away from tradition and from authority as well. There probably were many arguments and disagreements. It no doubt took a great deal of effort on Christopher's part to get a father as stubborn, ambitious and quarrelsome as Domenico to accept his choice. Their relationship was always a difficult one. This is proved by the absence of written correspondence between the two during the father's later years, when Christopher was in Spain being showered with honors, having conquered not only the seas but his poverty as well. It appears that he never once sent his father any financial assistance after his rise to fame. He had built his life alone, facing the future. He took a devoted interest, on the other hand, in his children and their fortunes. His father belonged to the past.

Domenico, meanwhile, moved to Savona. The money problems persisted, now with his son-in-law and brother-in-law, as did the debts with other artisans and merchants. Business was going badly, and he must have realized, perhaps reluctantly, that Christopher had not been entirely mistaken in taking to the sea for a living. Domenico's few remaining contacts with the Fregoso party were put to use to obtain for the young navigator routes more profitable than his humble coastal run. Several patrons from warring times— the Centuriones, Spinolas and DiNegros—helped Christopher to widen his range of activity by giving him business assignments and allowing him to sail on larger ships with farther destinations as a "man of passage." The Centuriones, Spinolas and DiNegros were all shipbuilders of great importance. The

Centuriones were the ones who financed Antonio Malfante's voyage into the Sahara in search of African gold. The Spinolas controlled all surviving trade with the Levant after the Turkish tide engulfed Constantinople and the eastern seas. The farthest point to which Genoa could still venture in that direction was the island of Chios. The businesses operating on the island had agreed to pay taxes to the sultan, which were increasing rapidly. They could continue to benefit from their commerce only if they turned over part of their profits to the Turks. In this way Chios saved itself, amid loyalty disputes and financial crises, for another fifty years. It was all alone off the Smyrna coast, in enemy seas—a kind of prisoner paying its own ransom day by day, for the sake of its business, but not without courage.

Columbus managed to make a journey to Chios before the tottering bastion was finally engulfed by the Moslem invasion. He did it in 1473, with the assistance of the Spinola family. He sailed on a tall three-master that bore the name of *Roxana,* in memory of a beautiful Ligurian woman who had been kidnapped by Turkish pirates, made a slave and then freed by the love of a prince who later became sultan and proceeded to marry her, making her a sultana. In Istanbul, next to a mosque, her tomb is still honored.

The voyage was a memorable one for Christopher, who was just over twenty years old at the time. We find mention of it in a note written in his hand in the margin of a book, where he describes the view of Mount Etna while passing through the Strait of Messina. It was the first time he had sailed that far from home. The size and dimension of everything had changed. The ships, with their masts thirty meters high and more, seemed to him like floating fortresses. Navigation itself had become a whole new experience. The *Roxana* wasted no time stopping at small, intermediate ports, as the boats had done on his short Ligurian runs. The helmsman decidedly abandoned the coast and took to the open seas, studying the patterns of the major winds, which it was useless to fight against. It was better to submit to them and exploit their force to one's advantage. All this was new to Columbus, and served to enrich his experience and test his character. The *Roxana* navigated by reckoning, using winds and water currents. This required constant attention, a spirit of observation and a very keen sense of the route. The voyage to Chios, which was followed by many others, left a more precise impression of the sea in Columbus's mind, and of the virtues and risks of navigation.

Landing at the island was like crossing a border. Genoese mixed with Turks, Greeks, Circassians, Arabs. Asia, with all its gulfs, mountains, rivers and forests, lay visible in the distance, just a few miles away. It seemed a quiet place, accessible. Beyond its coast the continent stretched for thousands of miles, and somewhere in that distance lay the Indies: the spice and silk routes, and perhaps the gold route as well, began not far from there. Though the voyage across the Mediterranean may have seemed long, they still were only at the doorstep to the East.

Such were the sorts of images and reflections that formed in Christopher Columbus's mind, which youth kept open to every kind of stimulus. Chios was close to Constantinople, which in turn was not so far from Jerusalem. Christopher must at some point have cast his gaze toward Palestine. The fall of Constantinople had awakened a new religious fervor in him. New orders and congregations had been founded. The hope of recapturing the Holy Land was seeming more and more an impossible dream, a utopia. But utopias inspire people, and their ideals spread more rapidly than resignation. The friars of Santo Stefano and Santa Caterina had left a strong impression on young Christopher when they predicted the return of heroic times for the soldiers of Christ. While other myths fell, this one was being resurrected. In the desert of ideals, faith became something to fight for, an oasis of salvation, the only thing still capable of moving the spirit. Chios, as a place and an environment, lay at the very heart of these currents.

Columbus stayed in Chios for about a year, which seems a bit long if we consider that the sole purpose of his voyage was to acquire sailing experience. By now Columbus had rejected for good the path of weaving, and in so doing had ceased living with his family. His new profession as sailor/merchant had already proved profitable enough to allow him to live independently, and even to help pull his father out of some of his financial difficulties. Several notarial deeds from 1470, one of which we cited above, prove this point, though in later years Columbus's ties with his father's business and with the family home in Savona would become weaker and more sporadic, until they vanished altogether.

In a sense, Columbus went to Chios to seek his fortune. He started with nothing, and had no clear idea of what he wanted to do. He was ready to try anything just to create his own life, since this was his most obvious goal. In Chios, he began to acquire and deal in mastic, a very profitable substance. Mastic is an aromatic resin obtained from a small Mediterranean evergreen tree, and in those days it was very often used in making varnishes, adhesives and medical applications. The island was covered with these shrubby trees and with forests of pine. Columbus relates how he first saw mastic being extracted from the trees in Chios. He did not, however, make his fortune there as he had hoped. He left Chios in 1474 and probably went back to Savona, but only to plan for new adventures on the open sea, which was where his future lay.

And indeed, sometimes they were precisely that—adventures. I shall mention only two such cases, which, though they take him in an opposite direction from his later fame, are nevertheless important to this period of Columbus's life, when he was still trying to find himself. They will help give us a clearer sense of the time and place of his first attempts at navigation, the risks involved, and the manner in which a man of the seas in the late fifteenth century had to steer his own course in order not to remain their subject but to become, as later happened, their absolute master.

The first of these adventures was a warlike act of piracy in which Columbus supposedly took part in 1472, at a mere twenty-one years old. If this story is true, it happened before the voyage to Chios. On this piratical mission, then, Christopher supposedly served as commander. But something seems not to fit here. A man's life never unfolds in haphazard fashion, with sudden and unforeseeable deviations. There may be unforeseeable opportunities and circumstances, which then produce unexpected turns of events which not even the person living right in the middle of them could have conceived; such is life's variety, its perpetual capacity for change. But there is no corresponding variety in man himself: an individual's fundamental and personal unity is what it is, and is not inclined to total transformation from one day to the next. It is like a key that can enter only one keyhole. How is it possible for a very young man at the threshold of adulthood to become commander of a ship engaged in an act of war, and then several months later set off for Chios as a mere passenger barely tolerated on board a merchant vessel, on which he was allowed passage solely because of favors obtained from powerful protectors of his family? Life's logic, like that of human nature, makes an aberration of this sort rather unlikely.

What is, then, the source of this adventure story? How much historical truth and falsity does it contain? The story was first told by Columbus's son Fernando, not always the most accurate chronicler of his father's life nor the most believable, given as he was to making equivocations and creating confusion. To authenticate his account, Fernando cited a letter sent by his father in 1495 to the Spanish royal family. But as there was no remaining trace of the original letter, the letter quoted had been rewritten in Fernando's hand. Bishop Las Casas, a somewhat more dependable historian, had free access to the papers that Fernando had collected or was still collecting. He says that he saw with his own eyes the text drawn up by Fernando, and then copied it. Hence Las Casas repeats what Fernando says, even though his *History* was written first. (To provide the reader with a few dates: Las Casas's work was completed in 1550, Fernando's *History* in 1564. Columbus died in 1506, half a century before the biographers began to trace his life, bringing the letter in question to light.)

Does Columbus reveal anything of importance in his letter to the royal family? He tells of something that happened in his youth, when the Aragons and Angevins were fighting each other for control of Naples. Columbus's protectors, the faction consisting of the Fregosos, Fieschis and Spinolas, were allied with the Angevins. But more generally speaking, popular sentiment in Genoa had always regarded the Catalonians and Aragons as enemies. Many times they had come and laid waste to the Ligurian coast, and moreover they competed with the Genoese for the routes to the eastern Mediterranean. The head of the Angevins at this time was René d'Anjou, who supposedly entrusted Columbus with the task of sailing to Tunis to capture the Aragonese galleass, the *Ferrandina*.

Columbus carried out his orders. He set sail from Genoa in a swift vessel, heading directly south. When the ship reached Sardinian waters, near the island of San Pietro, Columbus and his crew were informed that the *Ferrandina* was not alone, but in the company of two other ships and a galleon. The crew got frightened and wanted to turn back. As hard as Columbus tried to persuade the sailors to proceed on their mission, he could not get them to change their minds. Thus, says the letter cited by Fernando, "I was forced to resort to subterfuge." He pretended to give in to the crew's desire and change direction towards Marseilles. Instead, he spun the compass in such a manner that the needle pointed north while the ship was in fact heading south. "I had them unfurl the sails shortly before nightfall, and by sunrise we were passing the Carthaginian headland, all firmly convinced that we were arriving at Marseilles."

The letter says no more than this, being merely a pretext for showing the royal family how easily one can be deceived about changes in a ship's course. What eventually happened was that the *Ferrandina* was no longer in Tunis when the Genoese arrived to capture it, hoping to aid the cause of the Angevins under siege at sea near Barcelona.

All this happened in the fall of 1472. It happened, that is, as far as the war between the Angevins and the Aragons is concerned, as well as the fate of the *Ferrandina*, which the chronicles of the period talk about. But did Columbus's mission also happen? I have tried very hard to glean some truth from the episode. I know that numerous illustrious historians have given credence to the letter quoted by Fernando, accepting it without question as authentic. Others, however, in greater number, have raised doubts as to both the adventure itself and the existence of any letter written by Columbus resembling the one reconstructed by his son.

The arguments against it are many. First of all there is the unlikelihood that a young man barely twenty years old, without any real sailing experience, would be entrusted with the command of a ship on a mission of such importance. It is true that by 1472 Columbus had already been sailing for a number of years. But he had sailed as a transporter of merchandise, a kind of cross between a messenger and a small business agent. He himself later acknowledged never having served as a ship's boy, never having been employed for any work, however subordinate, related to the arts of navigation. The voyages he had made were limited to his coastal trade near home.

Then there is the incongruity of the great distance covered in the short time between the sun's setting and rising. It is true that November nights are long and can last up to thirteen and fourteen hours. But the island of San Pietro is 180 nautical miles away from Carthage, and only under absolutely ideal circumstances could a sailing vessel have averaged thirteen miles per hour along that route, from beginning to end. But there's more. René d'Anjou, under whose orders Columbus supposedly acted, was a sworn enemy of the house of Aragon and of the very same King Ferdinand to whom Columbus ostensibly addressed the letter. Thus such a letter would have revealed to the king that Columbus had once fought against him and his men. Why would Columbus have done that? Among the various explanations given for Columbus's puzzling silence on his Genoese origins, one of the more accepted ones has been the political conflicts that had long existed between Genoa and Spain, the hostility between the Genoese and the house of Aragon. Why would Columbus so suddenly, and only in this single instance, have revealed such a thing?

I return to my initial observation that a man's life does not change radically from one day to the next; it never leaps forward or backward without warning. The doubts raised as to the *Ferrandina* affair only convince me further of this truth, which seems to apply especially to men of great character and valor, such as Columbus was from a very young age. In my opinion, the episode never happened. Nor do I believe that Columbus could have written such a letter. Fernando's reconstruction, assuming good faith on his part, was probably based on stories and accounts that his father told him regarding the various adventures of his life as a sailor, or those of his friends, episodes that became vague and indistinguishable in Fernando's mind with the passage of time, especially given his propensity for confusing dates, places and circumstances. In the absence of any other supporting documents, I am entirely unable to give credence to the questionable and highly improbable account that Fernando presents in this instance.

The second adventure of Columbus's early years of navigation is instead quite plausible, to my mind. Not only plausible, but borne out by a large number of documents from Spain, Italy and Portugal. Fernando, who of course recounts this episode as well in his *History,* this time gives us a fairly credible account which he heard from his father's own lips.

In August of 1476, some time after the Chios voyage, Columbus took part in a commercial convoy of Genoese ships headed for Flanders and England. There were five ships in all, most of them flying the Genoese flag, with its insignia and red cross against a white background. Only one flew the oriflamme of Burgundy—a large white transport vessel which the Flemish called the *Orca.* Many of the ships belonged to the Spinolas and DiNegros, and the entire convoy was carrying out their business. Columbus sailed on board a whaler belonging to Nicolò Spinola. His patrons in Chios had great faith in him. He had acquired skill through experience and was now fairly well versed in both sailing and trade. Although once again he did not serve as a seaman on this voyage, it is likely that the responsibilities entrusted to him were of greater consequence than those he had borne in the past when in the service of the same trading companies. The expedition was in fact of much greater importance and was much longer than any previous one. For the first time in his life Christopher Columbus would gaze out onto the horizons of the Atlantic, the Ocean Sea whose Admiral he was to become.

The five-boat fleet sailed in convoy, in the manner of merchant expeditions. But each vessel was equipped with heavy cannons and other, smaller firearms to defend itself against pirates, who were known to frequent those waters. The convoy met up with pirates shortly after passing through the Strait of Gibraltar, the outer limit of the ancient world. At Gibraltar, the entrance to the ocean, the fearsome French pirate Casenove, known as Coullon (the French analog for Columbus), lay in wait, spying the passing ships for a worthy prey. As we have already seen, over the centuries a fair amount of confusion has arisen between the names Coullon and Columbus. The chronicle recounting this very event translated the name of Coullon into its court Latin analog, Columbus. In the eighteenth century Leibniz read this document, and the great rationalist did not hesitate to identify Columbus as the pirate, rather than consider him among the victims.

And Columbus was indeed a victim of the battle that broke out in the waters off the Cape of St. Vincent, where Portugal projects farthest out into the ocean. The Genoese, on the verge of being overpowered, began to launch pots full of burning substances at the enemy ships in an attempt to set fire to the wood. But the vessels had been brought so close to one another after the boarding maneuvers that the flames spread quickly from deck to deck, mast to mast, until the fire engulfed honest and criminal ships alike. The pirates lost four ships, the Genoese three. The other ships fled the site of the disaster. The men caught in the flames, however, had no choice but to dive into the sea, and only those who knew how to swim and were not weighted down by heavy armor managed to save themselves. Five hundred Portuguese nobles clad in cuirasses (though the figure may be exaggerated, as is usually the case in the chronicling of great adventures) perished in those waters. Many other sailors and merchants were drowned or burned to death. The ship that Columbus was on was full of Savonese, who were seafaring, mercantile men. Nearly all of them died, so many that someone at the time wrote that in Savona "the women make a world out of their tears."

Columbus survived "because he was a prodigious swimmer," as his son likes to point out. He saved himself by swimming for two leagues, the equivalent of about six miles, holding onto an oar that he had found floating amid the wreckage. He himself wrote many years later that he had managed to reach the Portuguese shore "by miracle." He landed at the fishing village of Lagos so exhausted that he needed many days to recover his strength. The ocean that was to bring him glory had nearly, at first contact, brought him death. There could easily have been no later adventure across the same waters. The life saved in Lagos was to make him immortal.

Not long thereafter he set off again for Lisbon, where the Spinolas and DiNegros had offices, houses and representatives. Lisbon was the first step in the climb toward his dream. For all intents and purposes, he did not leave the city for many years. This was a decisive turning point, part desired, part unintentional, and in any case fateful. For if Columbus had remained in Genoa, his Atlantic undertaking would not even have been conceivable. Not only did the political conditions in the republic prevent all serious consideration of maritime expansion, there wasn't anyone even thinking of such things. Genoa was not in a position to take on an enterprise like the one that its native son, by now emigrated to Portugal, was perhaps already devising in his mind. Genoa was merely the first stepping-stone in Columbus's existence. His life as America's discoverer begins in Lisbon, at the very moment he leaves Genoa behind him.

4

The Lisbon Years

Christopher Columbus came to Lisbon almost accidentally, as though led there by fortune, like someone who falls down a hill expecting to land in a tangle of thorns and briars but ends up in the middle of a meadow instead. Call it survivor's luck. What better place could fate, never a stranger to human existence, have brought the ocean's future conqueror than to Lisbon, at that time the key and the door to all seafaring adventures?

When Columbus landed in Lisbon he was twenty-five years old. He remained in the Portuguese capital until 1484, when he was thirty-three, having spent eight years of his prime there, a period of young adulthood when everything seems new and more intense than it ever will again. During those eight years Columbus sailed to the North and South Atlantic, from Iceland to Africa, from the Arctic to the tropics. He sojourned on islands in the middle of the ocean, at the farthest known reaches of the world. He immersed himself in the study of those who had surveyed the world, voyagers who in their writings described the lands and seas that he had learned about through geography. He listened to the tales of sailors who had gazed out onto Atlantic routes. He was charmed by the afterglow of legends that flashed from the unknown. He began to fantasize about them, and they became the constant subject of his thoughts and dreams; he thus learned to travel the invisible roads that lay between wisdom and exaltation.

Lisbon transformed Columbus entirely. It broadened his spirit, opening up dimensions he did not know existed. When he first arrived in Lisbon, the young Genoese knew very little about the world. His education was of the most rudimentary sort, since he had never had any formal kind of training; his knowledge of the seas was limited to the Mediterranean, "on whose edge," says Socrates, "we all sit and stare, like frogs on the banks of a pond." Eight years in Lisbon opened Columbus's eyes, as well as his mind. He began to form an image of the globe with its vast expanses of continents and oceans. At first these new ideas took shape in rather vague and confused ways. As these notions grew and expanded, he was faced with the additional problem of weighing their potential for truth and falsity. In the end what prevailed was his will—tenacious, stubborn and, from a certain point on, totally indomitable—his will to extract a meaning from everything he had read, heard and pondered. He knew what had been done up to the present. What was needed now was to calculate what might have been done if man had just pushed farther. Columbus, at this point, was stepping beyond imagination. He was entering the realm of invention—a thrilling, rarefied, solitary realm.

This was how Christopher Columbus, when living in Lisbon, conceived his plan to find a route to the Indies by sailing westward across the Atlantic. *Buscar el levante por el poniente:* to reach the East by going west. By the time he left Lisbon, the undertaking that would make him forever famous was only another eight years away. What sort of notions did his fortuitous stay in Lisbon inspire in him? How did it spur him on?

In those days cities did not all resemble one another, as is so often the case today. There was a world of difference between one place and the next. Each city had its own flavor, its own aroma. Genoa, on the Ligurian Sea, was a far cry from Lisbon, which had that great breath of ocean that filled the port and the streets—a sharp and lingering odor of salt, ocean breezes, and boundless solitudes. The smell of the sea is never the same as that of the ocean, which tells of its hidden force, throbbing like a huge, distant heart. The Atlantic's pulse enters Lisbon through the mouth of the Tagus, where the river opens up and mixes with the ocean. Between these two bodies of water Lisbon shines like a diamond. It is a bright, clear city, and a bit mutable as well: everything in it and around it is always in motion—the skies, the waves, the winds, the horizon.

A series of hills runs along the river's curve. Today there is a long row of villas and mansions there, but when Columbus lived the coast was still wild and fragrant. Rustic odors drifted down from those heights and into the city, which was aflame with the colors of nature—yellow brambles, scarlet geraniums, and the eccentric branches of fig trees leaning on the slopes. The façades of the houses, painted red and green with different colors for the walls and window trimmings, festively announced the city's presence from across the Tagus. In the city's lower section, there was the maze of narrow streets lined with shops and overflowing with people frantically bustling about as though trying to find their way out of a labyrinth. It was a symbol of life, of its pleasures and mysteries.

A colony of Genoese emigrants had settled in this district, around a textile market of which a few ruins still survive in the area near the port. Bartholomew, Christopher's youngest brother, had a shop there, a kind of store in which he sold maps and perhaps books as well. The maps, intended for use by seamen, were designed by Bartholomew himself, with intermittent help from Christopher, when he was not at sea. They were both good cartographers, and good calligraphers as well when it came to writing in the names of cities, ports, islands, seas and continents. Bartholomew probably came to Lisbon at his brother's prompting, after Christopher had gotten back in contact with his Genoese patrons and obtained permission to continue the northward voyage that had been interrupted by the pirate attack. Christopher noticed that sailors in Lisbon seemed impatient for longer routes, new destinations, and clearer, more legible maps. They eagerly seized the maps as soon as they were finished; the cartographers worked day and night. All Portuguese navigation was by now along the Atlantic coast. Lisbon was possessed by the idea of the Ocean Sea.

It didn't take long for Columbus himself to fall under its spell. He arrived in Lisbon probably in September of 1476. Already by the first months of 1477, sometime in January or February, he had set sail on a convoy loaded with merchandise that the Centuriones and the DiNegros had once again prepared for sale in Flemish, English and Icelandic ports. He was thus headed toward the top of the world, so to speak. Iceland was the farthermost of known lands, the Thule which for the ancients marked the edge of the globe. Even Ptolemy had doubts about situating it anywhere but in a vague, remote region, as misty as the northern skies unknown to most men on earth.

Columbus made it to Iceland, crossing the water that used to be called *Il Mare Tenebroso,* "the Dark Sea." He may even have ventured farther beyond, if we are to believe a note cited by Las Casas in which Columbus says, "In the month of February I sailed a hundred miles beyond the island of Thule." He even gives his latitudes, just as he had measured them. They do not correspond with those that Ptolemy gives for a ten-degree deviation to north. Nor, says Columbus, "is this island situated inside the line marking the end of the Occident, but much farther west." He was struck by the tides there, the magnitude of their swell. "When I arrived there the sea was not frozen, though there were very big tides, so big that in some areas they rose and fell by as much as 25 fathoms twice a day." This is equivalent to about 12 to 13 meters, whereas in Iceland the most the tides ever rise is 4 or 5 meters, on days of the full moon and the new moon. Columbus was thus confusing Iceland with somewhere else, perhaps Bristol, a port where he landed before continuing on to Iceland. The figures he mentions would not be exaggerated if applied to the waters at Bristol.

On this voyage, perhaps on the way back, Columbus also stopped in Ireland. At Galway he was told the story of "two people clinging to two planks from a shipwreck, a man and a beautiful woman," who had one day appeared on Irish shores. It was said that they came from Cathay, the Orient. But Columbus's conversations with Irish sailors were always in Latin and hence must have given rise to many inaccuracies and misunderstandings. Nevertheless, this strengthened Columbus's almost morbid fascination with anything that might reveal the secrets of the Atlantic. Everywhere he went, he sought out information of this sort. In Iceland the existence of more westerly lands, Greenland and Labrador, was common knowledge. The memory of the prodigious Viking explorations still survived in Nordic sagas. As it was clear that these legends might contain some element of truth, it is more than likely that in Iceland as well Columbus went about asking people, listening to people, trying to separate the fantasy from the reality. (Even though, deep down, fantasy was his preferred realm.) One testimony to his investigations in Iceland appears in a book by Lord Dufferin, *Letters from the Northern Latitudes,* in which the author relates: "It is said that in the month of February, 1477, there arrived in Reykjavik, on a ship coming from Bristol, a Genoese sailor with a long face and grey eyes who took a singular interest in everything related to the subject of the Viking discoveries."

It may be an obvious point, but in order to avoid any confusion as to the exploits of the Vikings, it must be said that at that time no one had ever spoken of a new continent. The Vikings were great seamen who had gone in search of new seas for fishing. They ventured far out into the Atlantic, perhaps reaching American coasts in specific cases, like someone groping in the dark and finally bumping into something. But they never imagined that they had discovered anything, nor had they had any such intention. One thing is certain, they left no trace of any documents. The memory of what they did, or did not do, does not belong to the realm of history. It remains within the confines of legend and folk tradition, as merely an indication, an image in the void.

Did Columbus learn anything that was of use to him in all this? He teemed with desires and new ideas, but was not yet aware of himself as a maker of history. But how, when hearing people speak of other lands west of Iceland, could he not have thought that over the vast stretch of ocean there was always a point "beyond," past the horizon, where the sun set westward just as it did in Lisbon, Reykjavik and Ireland, and as it presumably did in the remote lands reached by the Vikings?

Columbus was at that stage in life when we often secretly feel that the best is yet to come. But he did not leave his future to fate or chance. He sought to understand it and create it himself. He sought feverishly, like someone digging for a treasure that he knows to be buried in a certain place but is not sure exactly where. Columbus's treasure lay past that point "beyond," to the west, across the Atlantic. But he didn't know exactly where, or how he should go about searching for it. At the start of his quest he didn't even know if it was possible. But he had time to wait and see, bolstered by the youthful conviction of better days ahead. All around him teemed fertile Lisbon, where in a sense everyone had temptations similar to his. Just living in Lisbon in this period was like a wild adventure. Never before had a single geographical location bolted at such a dizzying pace to the forefront of human history. Everyone who had anything to do with the sea—sailors, scientists, astronomers, merchants—was involved in a kind of hand-to-hand combat with the ocean. For them, too, the best was yet to come, for the world was beginning to break out of its age-old insularity and take to the sea. The Portuguese and the others living there were the first to believe that somewhere beyond the ocean, unknown lands existed. In Lisbon this was all anyone talked about. It was the reason that maps were continually being remade and revised to conform to the new developments and discoveries made by cosmographers and navigators. What can be more contagious than excitement? Like flocks of birds in migration, some of the sharpest minds in the world—German, Italian, Jewish and Arab mathematicians, geographers and scientists—gathered in Lisbon. They were inventing the future. And amid all this excitement, Columbus's own imagination thrived.

He had always had a passion for the seafaring arts. And he had learned a thing or two at school in Genoa and during his Mediterranean voyages. But the vastness of the world, as it appeared to him from Lisbon, and the vastness of the ocean gave him a sense of just how limited the extent of his knowledge actually was. The scholars who frequented his brother's shop seemed to have scaled mountaintops unreachable to him. The head of that particular group was Mestre Vizinho, a student of the celebrated Jewish astronomer Abram Zacuto. They had plans for establishing the true dimensions and forms of the earth, sky and sea. They used the Bible and the ancients as their spring-boards. They closely studied the writings and descriptions of men who had traveled to the most remote parts of the globe—men such as Marco Polo and seamen who had ventured farther than the rest. From all of this data they formulated their hypotheses.

Columbus felt rather disarmed before so much knowledge. But he never gave up. Just as he had once cast himself out to sea, he now immersed himself in books. He read a bit of everything that was available to him. He studied, took notes. The shadows of ignorance were dense—as they are for everyone—but not impenetrable. He was able to venture deep enough into them to spot a specific goal where the treasure lay hidden.

What did he read? We have fairly reliable indications in the books that Fernando preserved in his own library, which were later passed on to the Columbian archives in Seville, where one can still read the volumes annotated by Columbus himself. There were four or five books in particular, however, which he carried with him throughout his entire life, even when crossing the ocean; they are: the *Historia Rerum* by Cardinal Piccolomini, who later became Pope Pius II; the *Imago Mundi* of Cardinal Pierre d'Ailly, rector of the Sorbonne in the first part of the century; *The Book of Marco Polo,* also known under the title of *Il Milione;* Pliny's *Natural History;* and Zacuto's *Perpetual Almanac.*

The most important of these for Columbus was Cardinal d'Ailly's text, which was actually a rather elementary compendium of ancient texts, but which for America's discoverer constituted an invaluable sampling of Greek and Latin thought on the world's geography, a kind of recapitulatory digest of things he had to know. Without having to resort to other texts, he thus gained some knowledge of Plato, Aristotle, Theophrastus, Cicero, Seneca, Pomponius Mela and Macrobius, the authors most often commented on in the margins of the d'Ailly book, where the cardinal makes reference to them.

All this notwithstanding, Columbus's main source remained the Bible. A text that he certainly must have been familiar with was a much-consulted handbook of sorts put together by a fifteenth-century Spanish luminary, which brought together all the Bible's various passages on cosmographical and astronomical matters, providing all the proper concordances. Over the centuries, the custodians of biblical truth for Christendom had been the church fathers. Among them Columbus seemed to favor St. Augustine. But in the end the most essential author, on whom all geographical knowledge was based, was Ptolemy. Ptolemy was Columbus's passion and his torment, a source of both knowledge and perplexity. If he had believed blindly in everything Ptolemy says, he never would have discovered America. Yet without Ptolemy he never would have been able to discover it.

In the Ptolemaic system there was only half the world, half an earth in terms of its description and surface. The medieval world remained enclosed within these limits, like a prison within its walls. For Ptolemy, as for all the ancients, the ocean was unnavigable. It represented the infinite, a limitless space within which, somewhere, lay the earth's confines. One could explore the unknown; but to travel the infinite was impossible, even sacrilegious. Working within these limits, which in time came to be accepted as both logical and religious, mixing precepts of faith with those of science, traditional theory posited a tripartite world divided into contiguous regions not separated by oceans: Europe, Africa, Asia. They were not yet called continents. And other lands did not exist.

Lisbon no longer believed in such tidy, immutable schemata. There was not a single sailor—not to mention scientist, geographer or mathematician—in Lisbon who did not entertain the idea that the world was round. This in itself enlarged the world, removing the sense of infinity from the ocean whose waves broke on Portuguese shores. There had to be other shores where those same waves also broke, across the expanse. But how far away, and in what direction? No one knew. A few daring men had attempted to find out, or so people said. But none had returned to tell about it. The fear prevailed that an undertaking of this nature was beyond man's capabilities.

By this time all of Columbus's letters, notes, marginalia and textual comparisons were centered around this dilemma—the limits of land and ocean, what lay or might lie beyond the ocean. He saw flashes of hope from time to time. Macrobius spoke of a "fourfold earth," presuming the existence of a "fourth" region of the world. Plato, in relating the legends of the Island of Atlantis, saw a "hidden land" larger than Asia and Africa. Pomponius Mela alluded to an *alter orbis,* another world beyond the known ones. Cicero maintained there were two habitable zones on earth. These were glimmers in the dark. They would appear, then disappear. In the d'Ailly book, Columbus underlined Anchises' famous lines to his son Aeneas in the *Aeneid:* "There are lands beyond the signs of the zodiac, beyond the course of the years and the sun." Beyond. Even the great master Virgil believed in it.

Other notes that Columbus made in his copy of *Imago Mundi*—and it really is exciting to sense the life, the human presence, anxious and full of doubt and hope, still perceptible in that yellowed parchment in the Seville library—give an indication of the progress of his thought in Lisbon. For example: *"Mare totum navigabile,"* all seas are navigable. Or: "all seas are peopled by lands"; "the Ocean Sea is no emptier than any other"; "every country has its east and west." Columbus was remarkably swift to intuit, in everything he read and heard, allusions to the future events toward which his life was heading with increasing momentum. He cast himself headlong in that direction, though unsure of the road. Intuition guided him in applying inventiveness to the stimuli that reality provided, yet remained suspended between that which knowledge teaches and that which the imagination creates. His marginalia—anxious and excited, yet always written with an eye toward his hopes—show his entire investigation to be imbued with a nearly prophetic sense, under whose spell every word, every argument rises up and becomes something very close to poetry. Invention, imagination, prophecy and poetry, with an occasional mad leap away from reality: it all pointed toward his goal, like an arrow already in flight and trembling in midair as it shoots toward its target.

Columbus's years in Lisbon were not all spent reading, studying and staying up late listening to sailors and scholars in his brother's shop. His day-to-day existence included other activities as well, such as leisure, casual conversation, and love. Christopher Columbus was married in Lisbon, one year after his long voyage to the North. He met his future wife when frequenting the All Saints' Church, which was connected to the very powerful order of Santiago. The two young people would go there for Mass and for vespers, first casually and then with the added incentive of love. The use of the church as a place for rendezvous between men and women was a practice begun in the closed society of the Middle Ages, when there were precious few opportunities for mingling. Fernando Columbus, who was not born of this marriage, described how the Portuguese woman fell in love: "She became so familiar and friendly with my father that she became his wife."

Apparently Christopher, then twenty-seven years old, was an attractive man. Of course we cannot know what he really looked like, since there are no authentic likenesses of him, no paintings or descriptions portraying him from life. No painter of his time set down his features for posterity, and the first authors to write about him began rather late, decades after his death. The portraits that we always see reproduced in books about his exploits—the most famous being the one by Sebastiano del Piombo—are all products of the imagination. They usually endow him with a Christlike aura, long hair blowing in the wind, as perhaps was only proper for the man who brought Chris-

tianity to the new, unknown half of the world. In 1892, for the fourth centen-
nial of America's discovery, an exposition was held in Chicago, featuring
seventy-one different portraits of Columbus. No two were alike: some had
mustaches, some did not, some were fair, some dark, some had long faces,
some had oval faces.

Going by the very brief descriptions of him provided in the notes of
those who knew him, Columbus probably had fiery reddish-blond hair, which
turned white at an early age, and a fair, somewhat freckled complexion, quick
to flush. He was a man of some height, "taller than the average" according to
Las Casas and Oviedo. He had bright eyes, blue or in any case light in color
(the fishermen of Iceland described them as "grey"), and a rather hard, intense gaze. His forehead was high and his bearing noble and marked by a
certain solemnity and willfulness. As he was a stubborn, silent man, his appearance as a whole must have seemed rather inscrutable. But when he so
desired he could be very persuasive, and expressed himself with ease. This
was usually when he wanted something. No doubt this was also the way he
won the affections of the young woman who frequented the All Saints'
Church.

Her name was Felipa, Moniz on the mother's side, Perestrello on the
father's. We know nothing of her physical appearance. Usually when a
woman is very beautiful, many will say so, leaving behind some token or trace
of their admiration. Such was not the case with Felipa. We may assume that
she was not strikingly beautiful. She was probably younger than Christopher.
One thing we do know is that she came from a family with some claim to
nobility, which had contacts with the court and enjoyed a certain influence in
Portuguese society in general. Perestrello descended from Italian ancestors
who had emigrated a century earlier from Piacenza. He was a man of the sea
with a solid education, one of the enterprising young men trained by Henry
the Navigator at his famous school in Sagres Castle, overlooking the ocean.
Together with Prince Henry's men, he had taken part in the discovery of the
Madeira Islands, forty years before Columbus married into his family. One of
the islands in the archipelago, the little island of Porto Santo, he had taken
himself with an expedition in his command. As a prize, he was given the title
of governor and the right to rule. The island, however, was tiny, devoid of
resources and for the most part without water. It was not the best of arrangements. Felipa's father returned to Lisbon and became a town councillor. At
the time of his daughter's marriage he had been dead a few years, and the

family fortunes were left in the hands of Christopher's mother-in-law, Dona Moniz.

She was of a noble stock, but the island's troubles and her husband's death had left the family laden with problems, fallen in terms of both rank and patrimony. Nevertheless, for Columbus the marriage represented a step upward in Portuguese society. It was hardly a common occurrence for a young immigrant just settled in Lisbon to marry the heiress to an aristocratic name. There is no reason to believe, however, that he didn't marry out of love. To be sure, he derived certain advantages from the arrangement, which he had perhaps anticipated. But then his whole life was one long, single-minded calculation. His marriage to Felipa was no doubt consistent with any number of aspects of his character.

Of his married life with Felipa we know almost nothing. We know that it lasted little more than five years, since Felipa died in 1485, and that, from all appearances, the widower was not overly grief-stricken. They had one child, Diego, who was later to inherit every title and privilege bestowed upon his father after his discovery. There were, in any case, a number of important events in Columbus's life linked to his marriage which deserve some mention here, first of all his long sojourn in the Madeira Islands in the middle of the ocean, six hundred miles from Lisbon.

Immediately after their wedding the two young newlyweds went to Porto Santo as guests of Felipa's brother, then governor of the island. It was not a honeymoon, however, seeing that Columbus and his bride stayed there for two years, moving only as far as it took to go from Porto Santo to Funchal, in the largest of the Madeira Islands. Their ostensible reason for staying was to arrange a situation that would provide some relief for the family's financial straits by creating a business headquarters for Columbus from which he could work half as a sailor, half as a merchant. Less apparently, it also provided Columbus with an observation post for his future plans, which were still uncertain and unformed.

As had already happened on other occasions, Columbus's business abilities proved to be rather scant. He had been to Madeira before, prior to his marriage, on voyages involving the transport of sugar and other goods. He tried to establish himself more firmly in this line, but with little success. What was considerably more important about Columbus's years in Porto Santo, and perhaps even a determining factor in his later years, was his direct contact with the ocean, upon which he could gaze for long days and nights as though looking out from the balcony of his dream.

Felipa's mother, who had accompanied the couple on their trip, gave Christopher access to all the maps and papers that her husband had left in Porto Santo, which contained invaluable information on ocean navigation. Fernando, no doubt having been told by his father, wrote: "Dona Moniz turned over to him all the navigational writings and charts of Perestrello, a great sailor who owned a collection of maps, pilot-books and handwritten notes about Atlantic routes: those along the African coast, those to Madeira and those to the Azores." In Perestrello's day the island of Madeira had been an important base for all subsequent Portuguese discoveries in the Atlantic. Later on, as a stopping place and port of call, it became a center for news and information brought by sailors over the course of their voyages. For those who actually lived there, it also provided a wealth of direct observations on the patterns of the winds, waves, currents, and the flight of marine birds: information indispensable to the art of sailing on the open sea along solitary, unknown routes far from familiar reference points.

This was the "informational" aspect of Columbus's stay in Porto Santo; there was also a "mythic" side to it as well. Everyone in those days believed in the islands. The successive discoveries of the Canaries, the Azores, Madeira and the Cape Verde archipelago had revealed an Atlantic strewn with islands, just as the greats of antiquity had imagined it—Plato with his Atlantis, Pliny with his "floating islands" and, more recently, the "lost islands" of the medieval era. Every now and then, out of the mists of nothingness, one of these fragments of earth would emerge in the middle of the ocean, looking like a copy of paradise, covered with virgin forests, bright green palms, untouched meadows. The islands were pristine, innocent. Very soon all the sea charts and world maps began to dot the Atlantic with other, imaginary islands and archipelagos. Such charts and maps were drawn up on the orders of powerful patrons, or else on the orders of people who wanted to make gifts of them to powerful patrons. The ocean's empty spaces were no longer appealing. Mapmakers feared being accused of ignorance if their maps had no islands in the Atlantic. Thus, in addition to the real islands, false ones began to sprout up: Antilia, San Brandano, the rocks of Brazil. Many of these inventions were so reluctant to die out that it wasn't until the second half of the nineteenth century that they disappeared once and for all from the maps of the British Admiralty.

The islands were like strange voices that called from the sea. In Porto Santo there were even people who claimed to have seen new ones looming on the water, "out there." Columbus spent hours and sometimes whole days on his seaside "balcony," under the ocean's spell. The rhythm of the waves resounded without respite; the Atlantic's presence was very vivid, haunting. It dominated the senses with odors and rumblings come from far away: from the West, Columbus must have thought. The wind, too, constantly blew from west to east, an invaluable observation that Columbus made at Porto Santo. He noticed that the sun set two hours later in Madeira than it did in Genoa. He must have asked himself: If the world is truly round, how many hours of difference are there between Madeira and the outer reaches of Asia, or between Madeira and the Indies? I am fully convinced that for Columbus, Porto Santo served as confirmation of his earlier intuition that it was possible to *buscar el levante por el poniente,* to reach the East by sailing west. The East was Asia, India, Cathay. Nothing even vaguely resembling America ever entered his mind. America was more than unforeseeable: it did not exist. The Atlantic between Europe and Asia was empty. Empty except for those islands that fed the dream. Is this not perhaps how America came to be discovered, because no one, not even Columbus, knew it was there?

I am purposely giving little attention to the wild tales, some of them perhaps even true, about the flotsam and jetsam that Atlantic storms would sometimes wash up onto the shores of islands such as Madeira and the Azores. On the beaches people would find such things as pieces of wood and large reeds of unknown plants; on the island of Flores the tide supposedly once washed ashore two corpses "that seemed to have very wide faces, of a shape different from those of Christians." Most such accounts were either stories that came out after Columbus's discovery, or else sailors' tales that had become exaggerated in being passed on by word of mouth.

Among these I would also class the still well-known story, even to this day believed by some to be true, of the unknown helmsman. As the story goes, a sailing vessel dismasted by an ocean storm and left to the mercy of the waves one day landed by chance at Porto Santo when Columbus was living there. All the ship's sailors had died at sea except the helmsman, who, when he came ashore, was utterly drained of his strength and at the end of his rope. Columbus put him up in his house, and just as the dying sailor was breathing his last he told Columbus that on the other side of the ocean were other lands, toward which the dying man's ship had been pushed by hurricanes. Columbus supposedly asked the unknown helmsman to draw him a map of his journey. This the man did and then died, leaving Columbus alone with the secret.

The first Columbus biographer to mention this story was Oviedo, around

1535. But after recounting it he says, "In my opinion, none of this is true." Around the same time, the story of the unknown helmsman was sung by the poet Garcilaso de la Vega, who handed it down to posterity after filling in every detail, down to the helmsman's name. He told the story as though it were a romance, and as such it was very well liked and reached a large audience. What's more, it was widely exploited by all of Columbus's adversaries during the long ordeal of the inheritance trials. Over the decades the story was further transformed and elaborated by yet other inventions: Columbus was said to have "extorted" the maps from the helmsman, then killed him to ensure that the knowledge remain a secret. There were some who, more than a century after the legend's birth, identified the helmsman as the Andalusian navigator Alonso Sánchez, a native of Palos or its environs. The most obvious error in all these fictions is the idea that Columbus came upon the notion of a westward route all of a sudden, as though at one specific moment he suddenly knew what to do, having been told every last detail by the unknown helmsman. Indeed, the latter functions a bit like the *deus ex machina* of ancient theater, a form of which was used traditionally for centuries to solve enigmas of this sort through fictive constructs, especially in the tall tales of seamen that so often whisper of extraordinary occurrences.

By contrast, the great Atlantic voyage that Columbus made in 1482 or 1483, shortly before his wife's death, along the African coast as far as the equator, was anything but imaginary. At the time the Portuguese, great explorers of the African Atlantic, had just finished building the fortress of Saint George in the gold-bearing region of La Mina, in that part of the African continent which at the time was generally called Guinea and which extended from Cape Verde to the Niger delta, where the large mass of western Africa begins to bend toward the south. The La Mina fortress was in what is now Ghana. There is a spot on Ghana's coast where one may still find a fortress, built in a later era on top of the ruins of the old one. The place bears the evocative name of Elmina.

The Portuguese found a lot of gold at La Mina and believed they had made an incredible discovery. In reality, the gold had been accumulating for many generations and did not reflect a production of any great magnitude. All the promise of the first few years proved to be illusory. Columbus took part in the excitement all the same, and it was his voyage to Guinea that first awakened the attraction to gold that would obsess him for the rest of his life. In a certain sense, discovering new lands was in his mind equivalent to discovering gold or hidden riches, the buried treasure. This feverish desire, also

medieval in nature, was offset in his own conscience—and thus morally justified—by his exaltation of the Christian faith. The expeditions to Guinea all
flew banners of the Cross and preached of the Holy Sepulcher's liberation
from Mohammedan dominion by means of the gold found in Africa, which
would serve to finance a holy war. The pope even granted plenary indulgences
to those who died along the way. The theme of recapturing Jerusalem with
the gold discovered in the new lands would arise again repeatedly during
Columbus's Atlantic adventures. For the present, he was ascertaining for
himself what it was like to navigate in tropical waters, in the middle of the
ocean that already dominated his thoughts.

It was not easy for a foreigner to gain passage on ships headed for
Guinea, along a route that the Portuguese wanted to keep secret in order to
maintain exclusive access to it. But here the ties to the Lisbon court that his
mother-in-law (with her noble lineage) and his father-in-law had established
became very useful to him. It was this network of contacts that enabled him
to make this much-coveted voyage. It was his first colonial experience. He
sailed under a star-laden sky whose constellations shifted as the ship moved
to southern latitudes. The North Star had almost vanished from sight by the
time the ship reached the fortress. In his stops along the way he saw men,
plants and animals that neither Greek nor Roman geographers had ever described. He was rather relieved to discover that the torrid regions were inhabitable, and that there one encountered neither monsters nor God's scourges.
The ships did not burn up in equatorial fires. Reality belied "his" Ptolemy.

He took note of everything—everything he saw and everything that
aroused his interest. In the writings that he left to posterity, especially in the
narration of his great crossing, he very often cites examples and memories
from his Guinea experiences. Apparently they constituted a kind of connec-
tive tissue between the years of waiting and the years of success. Iceland,
Madeira, Lisbon and Guinea—all had a direct, unbroken line of contact to
the dream: the Ocean Sea, which Columbus had now learned to sail, to
understand and to love. The Atlantic had become his frontier.

5

The Courage to Make Mistakes

In the late fourteenth century at a gathering of scholars in Paris, a French bishop by the name of Nicole Oresme, who was also a theologian and writer of mathematical and astrological treatises famous in their time, proposed a difficult riddle to his learned colleagues. It went as follows: "Suppose that Plato leaves Athens heading westward on his way to circling the world, and Socrates does the same heading eastward. Exactly three years later Plato and Socrates return to Athens, each of them coming from the opposite direction. Now, did Plato, Socrates and the other Athenians who stayed put during that time all age three years, or did time pass differently for each?" Very few knew how to respond. Most were in disagreement with one another. Oresme solved the riddle in the following manner: Plato, when he came back to Athens, had lived one more day than those who had stayed in the city; Socrates one day less.

All the French bishop had done was to anticipate the time zones and the international date line, which today are quite familiar to anyone who has flown by airplane from one continent to another. But coming as it did at the end of the Middle Ages, one century before Columbus's undertaking, Oresme's riddle had great significance. It contained, in synthesis, the two propositions that formed the basis of Columbus's project. That of reaching the East by going west, and that of crossing the Atlantic as the shortest route to the Indies. The first proposition concerned the earth's roundness. The second contained the inference that in traveling over the round surface of the globe one could reach any point from both east and west.

These concepts were no longer new by the time Columbus put his plan into effect. All the European princes had globes in their libraries, and Christian, Jewish and Arab scientists all believed that the earth was round. But such ideas were theoretical; they remained achievements of the intellect. It never occurred to anyone to apply them, except perhaps to cartographers when making their maps and to scholars when trying to represent them with images of the globe. Columbus's bold step forward lay in considering this new, general information on the shape of the earth as elementary, incontestable truth from which one could derive concrete hypotheses to learn more about the various parts into which the world is divided. The globe's spherical shape already contained the unexplored regions. It was now a question of acting, of going and discovering them.

On Columbus's return from Guinea in 1483, his mind was swimming with ideas. He had accumulated a great store of experience, adventure, reflection, research and reading which formed a kind of labyrinth of fancy in which he risked getting lost. For years and years he had done nothing but fantasize. But now he had gauged the ocean, had sailed it far and wide. His mind was no longer filled with only illusions. He had experienced direct physical contact with the objects of his fancy. The time had come to unwind the skein, to unravel the thread that would lead him past the frontier separating dream and reality.

And this frontier—there was no more doubt—was the ocean. The basic theory of the earth's roundness, from which everything else followed, always brought him back to the same point, the ocean. On this particular matter Columbus was very sure of himself. The goal toward which he was reaching seemed to him so sure a thing that he needed no other explanations to justify his confidence. He was untroubled by doubt. Unfortunately, however, he was the only one. But the practical side of Columbus's intelligence realized that an undertaking of this sort could never be carried out privately. Only the cooperation and patronage of a sovereign or prince could guarantee him the necessary means and support. He would have to present such sovereign or prince with a concrete plan of action, explain to him why the ocean was the most favorable route, and prove to him that it was possible to cross it successfully. To do this he needed a persuasive, logical, coherent argument.

The first part was easy. The very globes sitting in the private studies of the powerful plainly showed that in crossing the earth's round surface it was possible to reach any point in the world departing in one direction or its opposite. Let us suppose that this point is the Indies, or the Cathay that Marco Polo tells about. Up to now everyone had always approached these regions, with their gold, spices and gems, by going eastward. After the fall of Constantinople this route became extremely difficult, in some places impassable. Why not try the opposite direction, the western route? The earth's roundness guaranteed that the destination could be reached just the same.

So much for the easy part. Now the thread began to get tangled. One had only to name the two different routes to know that they were marked by one essential difference. The road to the East had always been overland, and was a well-known, time-tested route. The road proposed by Columbus, the western one, was entirely over water, over the ocean in fact, the least known part of the globe. One immediately had to wonder whether an Atlantic expedition was even within human capability. How great a distance had to be covered? How much time would it take? No maritime enterprises, up to this point in time, had ever been known to go beyond certain limits. Or those that had, such as the expedition of the Vivaldis of Genoa a good century earlier, had vanished into nothingness. Would the sailors be able to endure such a long period of isolation? Would the crew have enough provisions for a voyage that would last many weeks, even months, and then still have enough left for a return voyage in the case of failure?

These were not merely theoretical questions. They had a very practical side to them. Princes did not like to entrust their chances to hope alone. If they were going to pledge money and ships, they wanted reasonable guarantees that their money would not be wasted and that their ships would return home safely. The men were of less concern. Perhaps the saying was true that people are divided into three groups: the living, the dead and the men of the sea. The fate of seamen was always suspended between life and death. They themselves knew this, but chose their lot just the same.

Underlying many of these questions was the darkness of the Middle Ages, the fear of nature and of things unknown, always ready to spring to the surface like a latent disease. Rational assumptions and science's support were of no avail in such instances. Though things were moving ahead and people were facing the future, they had to struggle against the weighty memory of the past. Christopher Columbus succeeded in overcoming the contradictions of the Middle Ages precisely because he chose the ocean as the means to his dream. Interest until then had been limited to land. Columbus situated his goal across the water. It took courage even to suggest such a thing.

As much as mathematicians and astronomers might have discovered by then, most people living during the final decades of the 1400s had still not abandoned, deep down, the ancient image of the ocean as a vast space of water surrounding all land, a "sea outside the world," outside of life and knowledge. The continents lay at the center of the globe, and the ocean stretched all around them like a fixed boundary, an outer limit. It had never occurred to anyone to try to cross it or even take a good look out onto its vastness—except for a very small handful of adventurers deemed mad and remembered only as lunatics, as examples of presumptuousness and folly. The ocean was "infinite." How could anyone reach the end of something infinite? The ocean was unknown. How could anyone chart a course through something unknown? The infinite and the unknown have in themselves something sacred about them. And what is sacred must not be violated: it is inviolable.

Such were the mental barriers separating man from the ocean—the "Atlantic abyss" whose boundlessness seemed monstrous because of the association of infinity with nothingness. The Portuguese, for example, gave the name of "Cape No" to the westernmost headland on the Moroccan coast, near the Tropic of Cancer. From that point outward one entered nothingness, and eventually got lost in it. From Cape No, one never returned.

Columbus sought to debunk these myths and quell the fears that they aroused—fears that he himself did not feel. On the contrary, the infinite filled him with a sense of fascination for its invisible labyrinth; it had the allure of an uncharted road that dares you to find it. Columbus's question regarding the whole matter was of a much more modern nature: Is the unknown that which we cannot know, or simply that which we do not know? He seemed to have little doubt about the answer.

But there were still the sovereigns and princes to convince. He had to prove to them that the distance between Europe and Asia was short and therefore practicable, within the range of normal ships and available means. He tackled the problem first by calculating the known distances. The overland route from Europe to Asia had already been much traveled, and measurements of the globe's circumference existed. The oceanic crossing from Europe's westernmost point and Asia's easternmost point was the difference between the two figures, two known figures. It could no longer hide beneath the mantle of the unknown.

What sort of calculations had the illustrious geographers of the past made? Ptolemy was always the starting point. According to him, the surface land from Cape St. Vincent, Europe's westernmost extremity on the Atlantic coast, to Cape Cattigara, which he considered Asia's easternmost extremity, covered approximately 180 degrees of longitude—half the world in other words, since the earth's circumference had been measured at 360 degrees since the earliest days of antiquity. Half of the earth therefore was covered by land, according to Ptolemy; the other half by water—by the ocean.

These figures did not sit well with Columbus. In his estimation, Ptolemy had exaggerated the ocean's vastness. So he decided to research the matter thoroughly, closely studying the texts of other sages, searching for any indication that might point to a more reassuring assessment of the Atlantic's size. He read such thinkers as Marinus of Tyre, a Greek from the second century A.D. and the founder of mathematical geography. For Marinus, whom Columbus first learned about in Cardinal d'Ailly's book, the earth's land area extended for 225 degrees, a considerably larger surface area than that indicated by Ptolemy, which naturally implied that the water surface was diminished accordingly, to a mere 135 degrees. Ptolemy's estimate of half water, half land had thus been reduced to a ratio of three-eighths water and five-eighths land, a ratio much more favorable to Columbus's purposes. Moreover Aristotle, Pliny and Seneca had also all estimated the globe's marine surface to be three-eighths of the whole. Columbus diligently brought together all these references but failed to point out that Ptolemy's figures were not an alternative estimate that carried the same weight as the rest. Ptolemy lived after Marinus of Tyre, and was well aware of his predecessor's calculations. He had refuted them and corrected them with new measurements. Columbus neglected to mention this. He admired Ptolemy, but as far as the ocean was concerned, he preferred Marinus.

Nevertheless, he did not consider Marinus entirely favorable to his designs either. Though reduced with respect to Ptolemy's ocean, Marinus's ocean was still too large. Thus to Marinus's 225 degrees of land surface Columbus added 28 more degrees to account for Marco Polo's discoveries, which d'Ailly didn't know about but which had since revealed to Europeans a vast extension of the Asian continent previously unknown. The 28 degrees that Columbus added were in fact derived from some rather confused notes made by the Venetian traveler, and were supposed to correspond to regions included by Marco Polo in his general description of "all of India beyond the Ganges."

Another 30 degrees of longitude were added by Columbus as an estimation of the distance between Cathay (China) and Cipango (Japan). The ships that would cross the ocean in the direction of the Indies would land first at Cipango. Thus the most unknown and solitary segment of ocean was further reduced. Another 9 degrees were subtracted when Columbus decided he would call at port in the Canaries, and from there head out across the Atlantic. Altogether, of Ptolemy's original 180 degrees only 68 remained, slightly more than a third. In one final modification, this one totally arbitrary, Columbus subtracted another 8 degrees, bringing the total distance to the almost ludicrous figure of 60 degrees. He based this final change on the hypothesis that Marinus of Tyre, his main inspiration, had overestimated the globe's actual size!

Whether conscious or not, the error was a gross one. But it was not the only one. Sea voyages are not measured in degrees, always a rather vague reference in the practice of navigation. They are measured in nautical miles. When sailors estimate the speed with which their vessel is traveling they measure it in miles. And by knowing in miles the distance to be covered, they can calculate how long it will take to complete their voyage. This is what Columbus had to do: translate his estimate of degrees into miles, to give a linear measurement to his projected course.

Here, too, several different hypotheses presented themselves to him. The length in miles of one degree of latitude on the earth's circumference was measured at its widest point, the equator. But there were various estimations, each formulated differently. Columbus, who had to secure the support of princes, naturally chose those estimates that pointed to the shortest route. For the present-day navigator, a degree has a specific length equal to 60 nautical miles or about 111 kilometers. For the purposes that Columbus had in mind, such a measurement would have been problematic. And he couldn't very easily manipulate it as he had done with the degrees. As extraordinary as it may seem, Aristotle had given the degree almost exactly the same length as our modern electronic apparatuses do today. The difference between Aristotle's estimate and the computer's is barely a few dozen meters. Some of the most sophisticated machines do little more than repeat what the human mind discovered twenty-three centuries ago!

Better suited for Columbus's purposes was Ptolemy, who estimated the length of the degree at around 50 miles, using Marinus of Tyre's calculation though this time without correcting it. As if this weren't good enough, Columbus went rummaging through d'Ailly again and found the even more favorable hypothesis of the Arab cosmographer al-Farghani, Alfragano in Italian. For a while now, the great European centers of learning had taken to studying and translating Greek and Arabic texts, ignored for centuries in their dusty sepulchers. Ptolemy himself had only recently regained the attention of scholars. The same was true of Alfragano, especially of his treatise *On the Stars and Celestial Movements.* In this text one finds an estimate of 56

Arabic miles to the degree, a figure more or less the same as Aristotle's. Columbus, however, erred once again and assumed that the Arabic mile was the same as the Roman mile, which in fact was much shorter. On the basis of this mistaken assumption, Alfragano's degree was then estimated to be only 45 miles at the equator, and considerably less still at the latitude at which Columbus intended to make the crossing. Alfragano thus provided the shortest estimate of the distance that had to be crossed. Columbus of course chose it for this very reason, thus completing by far the grossest underestimation of the length of the geographical degree that history has recorded since Eratosthenes. Columbus's earth, based on these erroneous figures, was at least one-fourth smaller than the real one.

This, then, is why he wrote, in the margin of a page of *Imago Mundi,* that "Between the edge of Spain and the beginning of India the sea is short and can be crossed in a matter of a few days." He elaborated even further on this idea in a report written after one of his voyages, using Aristotle as a reference: "The master of Scholasticism tells us that the world's waters are few, and as they are all joined together, the space that they occupy is quite small. One can easily cross from Spain to the Indies; Averroës confirmed this, as Pierre d'Ailly points out."

Thus Columbus's undertaking was born of two huge blunders of geography: the calculation of the earth's size as much smaller than the reality, and the exaggerated estimate of Asia's eastward extension. When the two errors were put together, the remaining distance that had to be traveled to cross the ocean was reduced to a minimum. This was supposed to be encouraging to those who ultimately had to decide, and perhaps even to those who had to make the journey. But since it was the only way Columbus could offset people's fears of the unknown, this grossly inaccurate estimation should not be considered only the result of error—in Columbus's mind, misunderstanding sometimes mixed with hallucination, that companion of folly, and combined they worked with genius to make possible the impossible.

I have tried to find an explanation for the colossal errors on which Columbus based all his projects. Clearly the confusion existing among all the imprecise and sometimes contradictory geographical information at the time was so great as to resemble a state of delirium. It was quite easy for one to rave nonsensically on these matters without even realizing it. I have taken into consideration the fact that Columbus was by and large self-taught, with many gaps in his education and an insufficient foundation on which to build. It is often typical of self-taught men to insist stubbornly on their mistakes, believing blindly in things they think they have discovered. Moreover, the knowledge that Columbus managed to acquire was medieval in nature and derived from the classics, which were mediated and interpreted in the Scholastic spirit and thus rendered not very illuminating. The geographer George Nunn, who fifty years ago wrote what I believe to be the definitive book on Columbus's conceptions of geography, came to the conclusion that "given the circumstances, Columbus *had to make* the mistakes that he did."

Does this really explain it? In my opinion, no. It was more luck than intuition that brought him—firmly convinced that he was headed for India—to America, whose existence he had never even dreamed of. If there had never been any America, his misjudgment of the distance between Europe and Asia would have kept him at sea for many more months. He would never have reached his destination. Nothingness, which he was not afraid to confront, would inevitably have swallowed him up, making him just another explorer who vanished into the unknown.

I have a different interpretation. What saved Columbus was not geography but his courage, the very same that we encounter in his refusal to conform to that which everyone believes to be true. To geographical error, Columbus added enthusiasm's deceit. He deliberately broke the rules and tampered with the figures. But this was not at all a medieval manner of behavior. Columbus's feet may have stood on the ground of the Middle Ages, his physical world and environment, but his mind rose above this world and looked beyond known truths to the future. What was new about Columbus was his passionate spirit of inquiry and the quickness with which he managed to explain facts and phenomena that hitherto had not only gone unexplained, but had been accepted and unquestioned. He had a complex mind and his thoughts sometimes vacillated. But his will remained always unmovable, and this too is a kind of courage.

He was a stranger to doubt. The lack of a critical sense is characteristic of the Middle Ages. In Columbus's case, however, it helped strengthen his stubbornness, and this itself may explain, at least in part, some of his errors—that is, those that he made unknowingly. As is true of so many men touched by greatness, his mind was a mix of the rational and irrational. His thirst for knowledge and his need for discovery, for example, were rational. His certainty of success, on the other hand, was irrational. Las Casas wrote that Columbus "had developed in his heart the unshakable conviction that he would find what he said he would find, as if he had it locked away in a trunk somewhere."

Columbus felt predestined, chosen for a mission. He had an uncanny prophetic sense of the things that lay in store for him. In the end he looked past the geographers, astronomers and philosophers and sought interlocutors among the prophets. The Bible came to his aid. In the book of Esdras, where the story of the days of Genesis is told, he found the following passage: "And on the third day Ye united the waters and the earth's seventh part, and dried the six other parts." It was a decisive illumination. Esdras was considered a prophet by St. Augustine. And Columbus never stopped quoting him to suit his purposes, waving him about like a banner during an attack. "Esdras asserts that the world is made up of six parts earth and one part water," he wrote. He looked to Esdras even more than to Ptolemy, Marinus of Tyre or Alfragano. Esdras symbolized faith, the medieval belief that doctrine is inseparable from truth. Faith is the poetry of life, the past that maps out the future. How can we fail to see Esdras as the sign from heaven that Columbus was waiting for? He would take to the sea, by God, but neither Ptolemy nor Aristotle would be his guide. He would sail by the light of Esdras, with the Old Testament in his heart and in his hopes. And this too was a kind of courage.

Once he had laid out the plans for his undertaking, in a manner designed to inspire the most confidence possible and protect them from the fear of the unknown, he resolved to present them to the King of Portugal and ask him for the necessary vessels and funding. This happened in late 1483, shortly before the death of his wife Felipa. We have to assume that it was his wife's family's contacts with the court that facilitated his access to the throne, which would not have been so easy to obtain for a foreigner of common birth with no reputation as either a geographer or a seaman. The Moniz had social ties close to the king, and were probably related by blood to one of the more influential men in the Lisbon court, the canon Fernando Martins, who later became a cardinal.

Martins had his own reasons for showing interest in Columbus and his plan of discovery. In his youth he had been to Italy on numerous occasions, had frequented the papal Curia and had established friendships with certain figures of the scientific communities in Rome and Florence. In Florence he had known Paolo Toscanelli, humanist, codex researcher and scholar in mathematics and geography, all in all a kind of eminent dilettante who studied the sciences as a hobby. A physician by profession, one of his many responsibilities was drawing up horoscopes—as doctors often did at that time —for Cosimo de' Medici and his family. Toscanelli was therefore an astrologer as well, and in his spare time a cosmographer, a sketcher of seas and continents. He must have had many talents, since Regiomontanus, who consulted him, spoke of him as "one of the greatest scholars" of his day.

Martins, upon returning to Lisbon, told the king about Toscanelli and his novel ideas on how to reach the Far East. The king, then Alfonso V, was impressed enough to have Martins ask Toscanelli the following question: What, in his opinion, was the shortest route to the Indies? This was in 1474, when the theory of the two different routes—the eastern and the western—was beginning to get some attention. Toscanelli answered the query with a letter written in Latin and a fairly detailed map on which he had traced the oceanic route all the way to Cathay and Cipango, adding descriptions and facts regarding distance, information on the possibility of encountering islands along the way—the same old Antilia, object of so many medieval fantasies—and references to reports made by sailors and voyagers. Toscanelli concluded by saying that crossing the ocean was the quickest way to reach Asia: *"brevior via ad loca aromatum"*—the shortest road to the spice regions.

By the time Alfonso V received Toscanelli's reply he was already involved in expeditions to Guinea and attempts to sail around the African continent, in the opposite direction from Toscanelli's proposed voyage. Toscanelli's suggestions were forgotten, his correspondence locked away in the state archives. It is quite likely that Martins himself, whose probable relative Columbus had become through marriage, allowed America's future discoverer to consult Toscanelli's papers under a pledge of secrecy. Columbus probably even copied them, since they can be found reproduced in detail on the flyleaves of his copy of Pope Piccolomini's *Historia Rerum,* which Columbus took with him on all of his voyages, and which today is in the library of Seville.

(The biographer Las Casas and Fernando Columbus both maintained that there had been an exchange of letters between Columbus and Toscanelli, and that this had been decisive in setting Columbus's project in motion, which was still in the planning stage. To my mind, the story is a bit too complaisant and overflowing with the praise that Toscanelli supposedly showered on Columbus for his boldness. Moreover, it adds nothing to what Toscanelli said in his letter to the king, a letter whose existence Columbus knew of. I do, of course, believe that Toscanelli's letter, and especially his map, elicited an ardent enthusiasm in Columbus. Las Casas in fact writes that "That map set Columbus's mind ablaze." But more than anything else, the map served to confirm some of the realities that Columbus had already grasped. Toscanelli gave a certain aura of scientific precision to the products of his imagination. The two hypothetical voyages, that of Columbus and that of Toscanelli, are by no means identical. Both are geographically erroneous, but Columbus's proposed voyage contains a greater number of mistakes that made the crossing seem much simpler than it could ever be. And despite his enthusiasm for Toscanelli, Columbus was careful not to correct those errors that conflicted with the other's findings.)

The Portuguese king who granted Columbus an audience in 1483, almost ten years after Toscanelli's letter, was Alfonso V's eldest son, who had only recently succeeded him to the throne. He ruled under the name of John II, and like his predecessors had a keen interest in seafaring matters. "His mind was always wandering beyond all frontiers," the court historian Ruy de la Piña wrote.

The king and Columbus did not come to an understanding. Columbus used all the arts of persuasion that he knew, and indeed seemed a master of them. He explained his project, conjured up the tantalizing prospect of gold, and recalled examples of other great sovereigns who had inspired discoveries: Alexander the Great, who sent the philosopher Onesicritus and a fleet to Taprobane, the island of Ceylon, to explore the antipodes; Nero, who assigned two centurions to the court of the Ethiopian king to study the sources of the Nile.

John II listened to his argument, giving no indication of his opinion. Many years later Columbus described their encounter in a letter: "The Lord closed King John's eyes and ears, for I failed to make him understand what I was saying." João de Barros, a faithful chronicler of Portuguese events of the time, wrote that to the king, Columbus seemed "more fanciful and imaginatively inspired than accurate in what he said." John "gave him little credence," as Columbus's argument seemed "meaningless" to him.

Can we really fault him for acting this way in the face of a stranger who sought to prove his assertions by quoting Esdras and other passages from the Bible? John was an experienced navigator. In his youth his father had once given him the task of drawing up a chart of all the discoveries believed to be possible. He had at the time examined Toscanelli's map, and had decided that his project was not feasible. Now Columbus had come to him suggesting the same folly. The king was ready to refuse right then and there, but chose a more courtly, drawn-out manner of rejection. He solicited the opinions of several luminaries—the Bishop of Ceuta, Don Diego Ortiz, who was a cosmographer, and the Jewish scientists José Vizinho and Rodrigo, both experts in nautical geography. They unanimously judged Columbus's calculations to be erroneous and recommended rejecting his request. The king then issued his official refusal.

Lope de Vega, in a play long consigned to oblivion—his theatrical works number well over a thousand, and it is impossible to protect them all from time's ravages—gives his own version of this episode. The play is called *El Nuevo Mundo,* and was first performed one hundred years after Columbus's meeting with King John, which constitutes the play's first scene. Lope de Vega's king is much more biting than the King of Portugal was in reality. Though in the play as well John lets Columbus speak at length, the king finally responds by saying that "the radius of a circle traced on the map is not the path of the sun." Then, sending Columbus away in defeat, he cruelly tells him, "Get your head examined!" In the original Spanish, this insulting statement has grotesque tones as well: *"Procura cura para to locura!"*

Columbus, hence, was judged a madman, an obstinate fool who persisted in his desire to reach Asia by crossing the ocean. In the final analysis this was his real virtue, the thing that distinguished him from the Toscanellis, the d'Aillys, Regiomontanus, and the other masters of astronomy, geography and mathematics in his day. They all theorized in their books how one might reach the Indies, from the east or from the west. Columbus did not theorize: he wanted to do it. And in doing it, he wanted to conquer the ocean and its myth. Was he mad? Or was he just reckless? We shall probably never really know exactly what he felt in his own mind, Columbus lived in a world whose ideas were drastically unlike our own. We do know that he wanted to break free of that world. And no one has ever blazed a trail without running the risk of appearing foolhardy.

6

Beatrice and Isabella

It is sometimes easier to halt a charging bull than to stop a thought from completing its course. Columbus's thoughts had raced through the Lisbon years. Now King John's scientists were telling him that he was wrong about the whole thing, that his calculations led nowhere. And, naturally, the king had refused his requests.

Columbus's disappointment was, to say the least, profound. Imagination had met face to face with power, and power had banished it from its hallowed rooms. Had he erred in his calculations? Was his project impossible to carry out? Columbus could not allow himself the luxury of doubt. It was those stuffy savants and their prudent sovereign who had erred. But all those years, those eight years in Portugal, had come to nothing. Failure remained the only tangible result of so many expectations and hopes. It was all rather discouraging.

Columbus, however, did not get discouraged. The willpower that had always driven him did not rest for a moment. He examined his situation coolly and rationally. What had caused his failure? He had gotten trapped in the theoretical side of his project, especially the mathematical propositions. These were small details compared to the transformation of the world that he so vividly envisioned. But it was precisely in such details that his judges were experts. He should not have agreed to fight them on their own ground. Another error on his part was not having come up with a dream of glory to present to the king. Establishing a new route to the Indies was not enough to justify a project that everyone thought mad. He needed a plan with a loftier appeal, something to arouse the nobler sentiments and raise them to exalted spheres beyond the reach of the theoreticians' attacks.

This was the lesson to be learned from Lisbon. Columbus would bear it

PLACES IN SPAIN
AND PORTUGAL
IMPORTANT IN
COLUMBUS'S LIFE

FRANCE

ATLANTIC
OCEAN

BAY OF BISCAY

Bayonne

GALICIA

Burgos

Carrión de los Condes

Barcelona

Valladolid

DUERO R.

Tordesillas

Segovia

TORMES R.

Salamanca

SIERRA DE GUADARRAMA

Madrid

TAGUS R.

CASTILE

Guadalupe

SPAIN

Valencia

PORTUGAL

Sintra

Lisbon

Badajoz

Santa María
de Trasierra

Cascais

CAPE ROCA

ALGARVE

Córdoba

ODIEL R.

TINTO R.

GUADALQUIVIR R.

Pinos Puente

Granada

Huelva

Seville

Santa Fé

Lagos

Palos

SIERRA NEVADA

Sagres

La Rábida
Moguer

Cádiz

CAPE
ST.VINCENT

Sanlúcar de Barramada
Puer to de Santa María

MEDITERRANEAN
SEA

Medina-Sidonia

ATLANTIC
OCEAN

AFRICA

N

W   E

S

0   MILES   200

0   KM   200

in mind next time around, to avoid failing a second time. Rather than desist, he refined his approach. He was well aware that his undertaking needed a prince behind it, and that the most difficult step in his plans—perhaps more difficult than the undertaking itself—was convincing a prince to support it. But what prince could he turn to? Aside from Portugal, there were only three kingdoms in Europe—all with shores on the Atlantic—powerful enough and presumably interested enough in such projects to warrant consideration. They were France, England and Spain. Columbus chose Spain. It was the closest of the three countries and was part of the Mediterranean world that he had known since he felt his first longings for the sea. It was also the only country, aside from Portugal, situated along the route that he had by now deemed the one suited to his plans. For several decades now Spain had been colonizing the Canary Islands, out in the middle of the ocean, some 500 miles from European shores. He would set out from there. Who more than Spain was likely to support him? (Not once did he think of turning to Genoa. It never even occurred to him to go back to Genoa to recover from the pain of failure, to get away from the feeling of always being an obscure foreigner, which was becoming his own personal torment. Genoa was already a closed chapter in his life.)

Spain, therefore, was not an arbitrary choice, nor was it, as far as I am concerned, a destination to which he came unprepared. After his Lisbon experience Columbus would never again leave anything to chance, until his dying day. The common depiction of Columbus going around holding his little boy by the hand, dressed in tattered clothes and knocking at the door of the Palos monastery to ask for help like a hungry and desperate beggar strikes me as rather ludicrous. Illustrations of this sort have hung on the walls of houses and buildings everywhere, and their common idiom has managed to deceive whole generations, for whom a hero must always be a man at odds with fate. This image of Columbus seemed right; before victory one must always suffer long and hard, assuming there will even be a victory. Countless books over the centuries have sung this same false song, telling of a luckless Columbus abused by fate yet undaunted by misfortune—undaunted, however, as a blade of grass carried away by the waves.

Columbus was not like that. He never sat back and let things take their course, passively awaiting the results. He learned of the King of Portugal's refusal in late 1484. By the following spring he had already crossed the border and shown up in Palos, an Andalusian port just a few miles from Portugal. It was a conscious, well-thought-out choice. Given the goals he had set for himself, he could not very well just show up in Spain without points of reference, throwing himself at fortune's mercy as he had done after landing on the Portuguese coast eight years earlier. Time was passing, inexorably, and Columbus had learned that one does not get ahead by chance. The future itself is a destination, toward which one must beat one's own path.

Whom did he know in Spain? Two of his brothers-in-law, married to sisters of his wife Felipa, lived there. One of them was Pedro Correa, who had inherited the governorship of Porto Santo in the Madeira archipelago. Though Correa was content with his title and the meager income that the island brought him, it had been years since he stopped going there. He lived in Huelva, just across the Portuguese border in the region of Castile. Columbus's other brother-in-law, a Fleming named Muller (transcribed in Spanish as Muliar), also lived near Huelva. Huelva is the first Spanish city across the Portuguese border on the southern coast of the Iberian Peninsula. It is a maritime city that faces the Atlantic and lies right next to Palos, which is separated from it only by a branch of water formed by the confluence of the Odiel and Tinto rivers. Columbus also had other friends living in Palos, sailors he had met in Lisbon or in the course of his travels. Palos was a seafaring city, and its sailors were famous for their skill and spirit of adventure. They were the kind of men that Columbus had always liked to converse with; they understood him. In Palos, on a hill overlooking the sea, there was a Franciscan monastery quite familiar to anyone accustomed to sailing along the coast, the monastery of La Rábida. Columbus himself had Franciscans in his background: the friars of Santo Stefano in Genoa, who had owned the land on which his father made his home, and those of St. Catherine, who had been his first teachers. Columbus saw St. Francis as his own sort of tutelary god and he remained devoted to him throughout his life. From what we can tell, it would appear that America's discoverer had actually entered the Franciscan order as a tertiary. Las Casas maintains that he already knew a few of the friars at La Rábida when he arrived, and that he was aware that among them there were a number of scholars of astronomy and a confessor of the queen, who was said to have a great deal of influence at court.

Hence relatives, friends and Franciscans, all in a small area a few miles wide around an ocean port. Already it seems a conscious arrangement, a convenient mosaic. It is quite plausible that Columbus carefully studied the situation beforehand, establishing step by step the necessary contacts. He certainly did not arrive there all of a sudden, on a lark. Those expecting him knew when he would come and what he would need. But he was hardly a man without means. He had not lived poorly in Portugal, having married a woman of aristocratic background with some inheritance. Now his wife was dead and Columbus was left alone with little Diego, who at the time of their move to Spain must have been about six or seven years old. The child, however, could only be a hindrance to the sort of plans that Columbus had in mind. Hence he had to find a place where the child could be cared for. It is possible that Columbus initially considered one of the boy's aunts in Huelva. In the end, however, he decided upon the friars of La Rábida. His appearance at the door of the monastery, child in hand, was not, in any case, a desperate man's cry for help. It was, quite simply, a prearranged appointment.

A number of overly insistent historians maintain that Columbus crossed the border secretly. They base this conclusion on a sentence in Fernando's book stating that his father left Portugal *"lo mas secreto che pudo,"* as secretly as possible. What does this mean? First of all, it is quite likely that Columbus did not come to Spain by the difficult and tortuous land route, but by sea. But did he do it clandestinely? It is difficult to say. Traveling through Europe was considerably easier in those days than it is today, in terms of border control and security. But there were many possible reasons why a man might have to leave a country furtively. In Columbus's case, some say that he was deeply in debt and in danger of being sent to prison. According to this theory, his behavior copied that of his father, who had moved from Genoa to Savona to escape his creditors. But in the father's case we know the whys and wherefores. There is no documentary evidence, on the other hand, of Christopher's ever having been insolvent.

Others have argued, somewhat more convincingly, that Columbus feared being punished by the king for having copied or perhaps even stolen Toscanelli's papers. They were locked away in the royal archives and constituted the kind of information usually considered a state secret. Kings in general and Portuguese kings in particular were always very strict and suspicious in such matters. Sea routes were keys to prosperity and security. If any were considered secret, one was not supposed to talk about them; and foreigners were forbidden to see them. This reasoning would have some validity if in fact Columbus had taken advantage of his contacts at court in order to seize possession of those papers, and the king—assuming Columbus took them—had found out. But these are conjectures within conjectures, and a bit too complicated to warrant belief.

Another possible motive for Columbus's departure may have been politics—that is, the alliance of the Moniz family with the Braganza party. The

Braganzas were a bastard branch of the Portuguese dynasty, springing from an illegitimate son of John I who had been given the title of Duke of Braganza. Like all neglected heirs, the Braganzas aspired to the throne. And the discontented factions of the aristocracy, which one always finds whispering in the shadows of every dynasty, did not hesitate to support them. Did the Moniz belong to this branch? History does not really say. But what are we to think of those two brothers-in-law of Columbus, husbands of the Moniz sisters, who both happened to be living with their noble consorts just across the border in Spain, a few miles from their homeland, as though waiting for fortune's call? They did not frequent the court of the king, which would have been the best, most suitable place for men of their position. On the contrary, they had abandoned it and apparently taken refuge in Spain, where they had a boundary behind them. Had they fled out of fear of reprisals? Had Columbus secretly gone the same route for the same reason?

I shall leave the reader to wend his own way through these speculations, which are in any case of secondary importance. Moreover they are all rather dubious, with little to back them up. The most plausible is perhaps the last, yet it still has very little bearing on the path that Columbus had in any case chosen of his own accord. He had wanted to go to Spain, and he went. Whether he went secretly or openly is only of relative interest to us. We know for a fact that he was concerned with establishing a useful network of contacts in Spain. He did not go there by chance. He stayed for a while with his brothers-in-law, then made contact with the friars in Palos. He arranged for the care of his child and then, once he knew what to expect, went to the monastery at La Rábida, which he planned to use as a springboard from which to present his project to the Spanish throne.

At La Rábida there were two persons indispensable to Columbus's aspirations. One was Father Antonio de Marchena, a cosmographer and humanist well known at court, who had a passionate interest in nautical studies. Columbus noticed immediately that Marchena was very interested in his project, so interested that he gave credence to the very arguments that made it seem impossible. Columbus decided to take him into his confidence, as Franciscan to Franciscan. More than a century earlier, the Franciscans had spawned a school of cosmographical teaching, founded by Duns Scotus, which maintained that the earth was round and the equatorial zones inhabitable, contrary to the teachings of St. Augustine, a great theologian and saint but not the most convincing of geographers.

The other person was Father Juan Perez, the monastery's prior. In his youth he had belonged to the office of the *contadores* of the Crown, the state accounting office. Queen Isabella had retained him as a page. But then Perez decided to become a friar, and Isabella granted him the privilege of being her personal confessor, a largely honorary position which nevertheless conferred a lot of prestige on the friar because of his long-standing familiarity with the court and the extraordinary flair for politics that he showed in his new position. Perez was fascinated with the marvelous things that the monastery's guest had to say. The friars' religious fervor would be aroused when they heard Columbus talk about divine predestination and saving the souls of the people living in the new lands that he would discover. It seemed like another miracle of St. Francis.

Opinions were exchanged, plans of action weighed, advice given. They held very wide-ranging discussions, aided by consultations in the monastery library, that lasted well into the night in silent, empty rooms. Sometimes they invited expert navigators from the region to join in, such as the old Castilian captain Pedro de Velasco, who thirty years earlier had taken part in an expedition to the Azores under the Portuguese flag. Velasco was familiar with the ocean. He said that many of the archipelago's islands, those farthest away, had been discovered by following the flights of birds, who are always "heralds of land" when at sea. Observing nature was one of Columbus's favorite pursuits, especially as he was by nature more inclined toward intuitive perceptions than precise reasoning.

These nights of conversation were full of wonder, full of hope. I myself have visited the monastery, walked beneath its cross-vaults and down its shadowy corridors to the lovely little courtyard that the hospital gives onto. Many things are the same today as they were when Columbus saw them, starting with the portal of red and light-yellow stone at which he first came knocking. One gets a strong sense, no doubt stronger in Columbus's day, that the Arabs once passed through here and stayed quite a while. The monastery's style shows the mark of their influence and the customs and habits they propagated. The white plaster of the walls, the strong pillars, the ornate bricks, even the color of the stone express a nostalgia for the East. But from high atop the monastery, as though looking out from a marine headland, one sees the blue ocean rolling in the distance. In the evening the sun sets into those waters, in the opposite direction from where the Moslem conquerors came. Columbus would direct his prow toward that horizon, where the sun goes down.

The brainstorming at La Rábida finally led to a plan of action. Friars and sailors both suggested that Columbus try in his first sally to win the patronage of the Duke of Medina-Sidonia, who had castles in the area. At the time, the Duke of Medina-Sidonia was the most powerful grandee in Spain, and the richest as well. His properties were centered around the port of Sanlúcar, at the mouth of the Guadalquivir. Their long white walls could be seen twisting across the countryside for miles, along the slopes of the hills. Rows of fig trees and myrtle bushes bathed them in shadow. Behind every wall lay the lands and villas of the Duke of Sidonia, Don Enrique de Guzmán. Would he be able to finance Columbus's expedition?

This was not a problem in itself. Don Enrique had always had a great interest in Atlantic voyages, had sent vessels of his own to Guinea without royal permission, and owned shipyards of his own at Lepe, near Palos. He liked Columbus's idea. But the time was past when he could allow himself everything that his wealth made possible. He had to discuss it with the court, and they did not take too kindly to the plan. Since he was not a man accustomed to being refused, he insisted. He did so repeatedly, resorting to the arrogance proper to his character and his fortune. The sovereigns, who at the time were staying in Seville, slammed the door in his face.

Isabella of Castile and Ferdinand of Aragon had brought together Spain's two crowns, but their realms remained distinct. The Aragons focused their maritime interests on the Mediterranean, on the very lands over which they exercised their sovereignty, which now included northern Spain and Barcelona and stretched as far as Levantine shores. The Castilian throne, on the other hand, preferred the Atlantic. Isabella heard the ocean's call. She had tried to gain a foothold in the routes to Guinea, on which Portugal considered itself to have an exclusive monopoly. There had even been a war over this question some ten years earlier, the first colonial war between European countries. Isabella did little to curb it. With the treaty of Alcaçovas in 1480 Spain promised to refrain from making African expeditions. Nearly all of the caravels that dared to sail along the African coast, in near-piratical raids of thirty and forty ships, were from Palos and Sanlúcar and were financed primarily by the Duke of Medina-Sidonia.

From that point on, Isabella extended the privileges of the Crown to include oceanic routes as well. The idea of launching an expedition across the Atlantic without the Crown's official approval, as a private, independent undertaking, had become an unrealistic proposition. Sailing the high seas had now become an affair of state.

Columbus found this out for himself when, having failed in his attempt

with Sidonia, he turned to the other grandee of the region, the Duke of
Medina Celi. Celi was not as rich as Sidonia, but he certainly had enough
means to make the financing of a small fleet of the size needed for Columbus's
purposes—"three or four well-equipped caravels, since he asked for no more
than this"—seem almost trifling. The Duke of Medina Celi, don Luis de la
Cerda, had his naval base in the port of Santa Maria, not far from Cádiz. His
caravels numbered in the dozens. Though he did not surpass the Duke of
Medina-Sidonia in wealth, he did rank higher than him at court, being a
direct descendent of the first kings.

Columbus was received by the duke at Cádiz in late autumn, 1485. He
came equipped with recommendations from the Franciscans of La Rábida
and the story of his life to tell. His fantastic plans ended up seducing Celi, to
the point that he promised Columbus every kind of support; boats, crews,
lodging and money for anything he might need during his wait. For several
months Columbus did little but live in the duke's shadow, spending whole
days at the Santa Maria port watching old sailing ships come and go and
witnessing the construction of new ones in the shipyard behind the port. He
was dreaming of what lay ahead.

Though the Duke of Medina-Sidonia had decided it wise to inform the
queen of his projects, not daring to proceed against Isabella's wishes, Celi was
too loyal to the throne not to go about it in an even more irreproachable
manner. He wrote to the queen describing the plan and stating his own
willingness to lay out four thousand ducats for the construction of the caravels and a supply of provisions for one year. He asked for the queen's permission to put his plans into action.

Though Isabella's reply was not quite as peremptory as her refusal of
Medina-Sidonia's arrogant demands, it was not the unequivocal "yes" that
Medina Celi perhaps expected. In a letter written after Columbus returned
from his first Atlantic crossing, the duke remembers: "As I saw that this
project was so important as to warrant the decision of our lady the queen, I
wrote to Her Highness about it. She replied by telling me to send this man to
her." "This man" was Columbus. The queen wanted to meet him. His dream
had itself become an affair of state.

Columbus left immediately for Córdoba, where the court was then residing. He presented himself to Alonso de Quintanilla, who managed the property of the Crown. Father Juan Perez, rector of La Rábida, had worked in
Quintanilla's offices in his younger days, when still a *contador*. Quintanilla
and Perez hence knew each other, and among the credentials that Columbus

brought with him was a letter from Perez giving his recommendation of the project.

Columbus was well received. He was officially presented to the court on January 20, 1486. From that day on, Columbus was considered to be "in the service" of the Crown. Quintanilla gave him a small sum of money to serve his needs until he should be granted an official wage. This had to be done by the queen, and at the moment she was not in Córdoba. She had gone with her husband King Ferdinand first to Madrid, then to other parts of their respective realms to prepare for a final assault on Granada, the last Spanish emirate still in Arab hands. When Granada fell, the *reconquista* of the invaded country would be complete and would bring it everlasting glory. The Arabs had seized Spain seven centuries earlier, and Columbus's lifetime spanned the final years of this chapter of history.

Medieval courts customarily moved around a lot, from castle to castle, city to city. This was largely due to the limited resources of any one locale, which could never support for very long the needs of all the guests, nobles, warriors, clerics, secretaries, scribes, idle friends, endless courtiers and their families. Once funds and victuals were exhausted, the "flight of the locusts" went elsewhere. Ferdinand and Isabella's movements had the added military incentive of war. The siege of Granada was at this point their primary objective, and took precedence over all other concerns. Columbus could wait.

Thus began the great discoverer's long years of waiting. He had already used up eight years of his life in Portugal, and was to spend another six in Spain before knowing whether his plan was to become a reality or not. He went through periods in which it seemed that all hope was lost, and others in which hope was suddenly reborn. All in all it was a time of anguish and restlessness for Columbus, who was like the man in the desert for whom the mirage vanishes every time he is at the point of reaching it.

The first months of waiting in Córdoba were not too difficult. Columbus began to make acquaintances among people of the court and spend time in their antechambers. He was admitted to a conference with the Cardinal of Spain, the Archbishop of Toledo Don Pedro Gonzáles de Mendoza, who was so powerful and rich that he was considered "the third king," a sort of unofficial prime minister. Having access to him meant having access to the nucleus of power. Mendoza was not antagonistic to Columbus. But he too, perhaps more than anyone else, was "in the service" of the Crown. He limited himself to explaining to the foreign guest that the crusade against the Moors had created serious financial problems for the Crown. The treasury was nearly exhausted. All the money being collected across the country was going toward financing the war. Columbus had to understand that this was not the best time to ask for support that would be burdensome under any circumstances.

The explorer listened to these arguments and prepared himself to rebut them. They irritated him more than they really worried him. How could there be any question of money for an undertaking that would lead them to the sources of gold, silver and the most precious stones on earth? This response left the cardinal a bit puzzled. There was something very attractive about the designs of this foreigner, who was so eloquent when asserting the advantages to be gained and the reasonableness of his proposition, yet became reserved and nearly distracted when listening to doubts and concerns that the project raised in the mind of his interlocutor.

Amid all this coming and going from and to the royal palace, which had now been continuing for several months, Córdoba became Columbus's first adoptive city in Spain. Córdoba was a beautiful city. Perhaps more than any other city in Spain, it had remained an Arab city—a city of caliphs, Moslem and secretive, sun-baked and silent along narrow streets as uneven as a dried-up riverbed, with tree-lined piazzas and high white walls that looked like sepulchers. The nucleus was the cathedral, now transformed to the Christian faith within the gigantic edifice that the Arabs had built with the intention of making it the largest mosque in the world but one, second only to the mosque in Mecca. It had a thousand columns of green and purple marble, twenty aisles giving onto the orange-tree patio, and all around it the walls of yellow stone that encircled the city like a giant nest.

Columbus felt good in Córdoba. Among the great influx of foreigners who had seen Córdoba as a good city for business, being away from the front and near to the throne, were a good number of Italian merchants and busybodies: one finds among its inhabitants at the time a Joria, a Battista Aulo, as well as the Solaro, Morandi and Gentile families. Among these there was no lack of Genoese emigrants, who made up a rather large group. Most lived in the district of the Hierro Gate on the left bank of the Guadalquivir, between the Synagogue and the Church of the Savior. Columbus often wandered those streets, looking for compatriots with whom to make conversation. He would often stop to visit two brothers, Genoese by origin, who were druggists and had shops in that quarter. Their names were Luciano and Leonardo Barroia. The pharmacy in those days was a kind of meeting place where one made casual friendships with people of every stripe. At the Barroias' shop Columbus happened to make the acquaintance of a certain young man named Diego de Harana, a great spendthrift who was always merry, not to mention disorderly, very sociable and as eccentric a hidalgo as Spain has ever seen. Columbus on the other hand was by nature rather reserved, talked little and generally kept to himself. Nevertheless the whimsical young man managed to arouse the interest of the silent Columbus, perhaps joking with him in the process in that affable manner that often forms the basis of friendships. He brought him to his house and introduced him to his wife, Costanza. They prepared a sumptuous dinner for him, in the manner of well-to-do families, and then introduced him, along with the others sitting at table, to their cousin Beatrice, a girl of twenty.

Córdoba was famous for "its fragrant blossoms, its sturdy mules, and its pretty women." Beatrice corroborated this image of Córdoba. Columbus was not the type to become obsessed with women. Other passions enchanted his heart and held it captive throughout his life. He did have a certain charm, however—a kind of stoic nonchalance toward the opposite sex that usually let women make the first move. He was the pursued, not the pursuer, the prey of desires not exactly his own. Such was the case with Felipa, to whose desires for marriage he eventually gave in. After her death he was still a robust young widower and had no trouble winning women's favors, which from time to time he accepted. Much has been said about his affair with the Marquise de Moya, an intimate friend of the queen, whom he met at court and perhaps used so that he might be painted in the best possible light to Isabella. Now he saw before him a fresh young girl who was dazzled by his warm words, his bright imagination, and the dream of wealth and glory that emanated from his conversation. She found him fascinating, and soon became his lover.

Of this relationship, surely an important one in Columbus's life, we know very little, almost nothing. The same is true of the lovely Beatrice herself. She was the mother of his second child, Fernando, who was born in August of 1488. He never married her, however, despite his strict observance of religious customs. We don't know why. Columbus's life is full of such gaps, unexplained occurrences, dubious dates. It is like one of those rivers that flow along for miles out in the open, then suddenly disappear into hidden caverns, leaving it up to the speleologists to discover the course of their underground passage. But sometimes even the experts are unable to do so, and this is almost always the case with Columbus's life.

Who was this Beatrice? Why didn't Columbus marry her? Beatrice Enríquez de Harana came from a family of wine producers who owned land in

Santa María de Trasierra, some twenty kilometers from Córdoba. It is safe to assume that they were a well-to-do family. Indeed, Beatrice had a certain amount of education; she knew how to read and write, something quite uncommon in women not of the aristocracy. She was orphaned at a rather young age and taken into the care of her father's brother, Rodrigo Enríquez de Harana, father of Diego, the young man who had become Columbus's friend and introduced him to Beatrice. Though Columbus and the young woman forged a bond like marriage in every way, they never tied the knot. But theirs was not, on the other hand, a clandestine affair hidden from Columbus's circle of friends in Córdoba. Beatrice, a full fifteen years younger than he, had complete faith in him, listening to and believing everything he said. Columbus's dreams became Beatrice's dreams. It was a most solid relationship, a desirable thing for a man always surrounded by the doubts of others and enclosed within the limits of his own self-confidence. Beatrice's love, moreover, lent him support during what was probably the most difficult period of his life, as he waited with his future in the balance, tormented by uncertainty. It is also possible that Beatrice, not without some means of her own, helped support her lover when his resources began to run dry, after the Duke of Medina Celi had ceased lending him a hand and before the court treasury began its own subvention of Columbus, which did not happen until the spring of 1487. Columbus, left to himself, was a poor man. But he always managed to choose women of some means—first his wife Felipa Moniz, then Beatrice.

Though specialists in Columbian studies may have succeeded in reconstructing, however sketchily, the figure of Beatrice, none has been able to present a valid reason why Columbus never took her to the altar. It remains a mystery, one of the many clouds of ambiguity that we encounter so often in the life of the great discoverer. A number of hypotheses have been ventured, such as that he didn't marry Beatrice because he was already married; or, amazingly, that she was a tavern waitress whose job was to pour wine. Others have brought up Columbus's affair with the Marquise de Moya, saying that he did not want to arouse her jealousy for fear of losing a contact with the queen. None of these theories is very convincing or credible. And when there is no authoritative information or verifiable documentation of an unclear matter, it is always best to stay within what is known.

After her time in Córdoba with Columbus, however, Beatrice disappears from the scene. We can find no other trace of her, and she is absent from all the later experiences that were to change Columbus's life. She did not even come to his funeral, or at least no one saw her there. Yet she was still alive when he died. In a 1505 letter to his son Diego containing various testamentary codicils, Columbus exhorts him with unaccustomed warmth to "take good care of Beatrice Enríquez, for she weighs heavily on my conscience, though I am at present unable to tell you why." At another point he asserts that "she is the mother of Don Fernando, my son." She was given an annuity on top of the benefits she already enjoyed from Columbus's first discovery as registered holder of the special prize given by the king and queen to the first sailor to sight land, for the duration of said sailor's life. Columbus claimed the prize as his due, then turned the benefits over to Beatrice. The throne obtained the required money from the rental of a few butcher shops in Córdoba. Beatrice thus lived supported by Columbus, who perhaps hoped thereby to repay the money that his lover had sacrificed for him during leaner times. But the break between the two was never mended.

In early May of 1486 the king and queen returned to Córdoba and Columbus was finally received at the royal residence, probably by both king and queen, at least at the start of his audience. Then Ferdinand, as he often did when he lost interest in the discussion, took his leave and left Isabella to carry on. Their respective realms, which at the time were said to be still separate, also had separate jurisdictions. As the ocean belonged to Castile, this whole affair was Isabella's concern. Andrés Bernaldez, a confidant of Columbus, in his *History of the Catholic Kings* (who at the time were not yet called so, but were soon to be granted the appellation by the pope), recounts Columbus's meeting with the sovereigns in the following manner: "He told them his dream, but they remained skeptical. He spoke with them and said that what he was saying was true. Then he showed them a map of the world. In this way, he aroused their desire to hear more about those lands."

This is probably how the interview began. But it was Isabella who carried it through; undoubtedly she was the one who desired to "hear more about those lands." And so Columbus told his story, eloquently and persuasively. The simple and natural manner in which he expressed himself hinted of shrewdness. Can someone be shrewd and sincere at the same time? Columbus was, since he was sincere by nature and shrewd from experience. He was aware of the doubts in the queen's mind that he would have to overcome and he did not want to appear overly eager and enthusiastic—nor too self-confident, since this often arouses mistrust. He kept the tone of his voice, more than the stress, soft and warm, taking refuge in sincerity, which is always a way to win someone's attention. He was affable. Las Casas described his talent at conversation by saying that "The Lord blessed Columbus with a special grace, which always induced others to look on him with love." It is said he had a certain melancholy in his bearing, and that he was rather noble in appearance. He found the right approach for Isabella when he began to paint her a picture of all the countless peoples who had yet to know the true faith, and were just waiting to enter the arms of the Church. He spoke of new lands, of course, but more than anything else he described, for this devout queen's sake, the new souls that could be won over. The queen listened to the stranger. She shared his desire for a new world, a vaster Christian universe.

The interview lasted well into the night, in that Moorish room in the Alcazar, which served as the royal palace. The small windows of the room in which Columbus was received gave onto the river, which was spanned by the sturdy Roman bridge built by Augustus in the early days of the empire. There were water mills beneath the bridge's arches. Columbus kept talking; it seemed as if he would never stop. Everything was rather strange, unreal: the long soliloquy, these fantasies wearing the clothes of truth, that man and woman alone in the room. It was already the middle of spring. The gardens were in bloom, and May's still green aromas reached all the way to the Alcazar's massive walls.

Isabella was the same age as Columbus, thirty-five. She had blond, honey-colored hair, a full face, fair skin and clear eyes. Not very tall, she was somewhat round in physique. Her overall appearance had something both gentle and arrogant about it. The line of her lips softened when she smiled, though there certainly was nothing delicate about her strong, almost peasant-like limbs and the aura of command that she, like most women, knew how to convey when showing indulgence.

The queen looked fixedly at Columbus as he spoke, seeing in his face the signs of boldness, ambition and willfulness. He promised the impossible, but did so in a fascinating manner. Isabella was a woman of cultivated mind, more refined than the king and more appreciative of the power of the imagination. She loved music, and lent her support to the little bit of poetry that saw the light of day in those hard times. Perhaps she saw flashes of brilliance in the plan that this foreigner was unfolding before her. Aroused by the charm of his intelligence, she felt a sudden sympathy for him, a kind of intellectual solidarity in the face of all the war, ignorance and vulgarity around them. Deep into the night, Columbus came back to his theme of reconquering Jerusalem with the gold that they would find in the Orient. He realized that the queen was very sensitive to this issue, and might be willing to grant his dream of discovery in exchange for a dream of redemption. They reinforced each other's sense of devotion and vocation. Columbus succeeded in making Isabella believe that deep down she nourished the same hopes as he.

The currents that pass between a man and a woman always have something veiled and mysterious about them. There is nothing ambiguous about this, since mystery is not ambiguous but merely concealed and inaccessible. Anthony Burgess, a great Catholic writer of our time, has spoken of the "irresistible, deceptive charms that hide in the primal darkness of all women." Isabella too had her dark, unexplored regions. And from this darkness, bit by bit, emerged her extraordinary, unexpected willingness to believe in Columbus, which would change the course of his destiny. Like Beatrice, she had faith in him.

7

The Battle of Salamanca

After the meeting with Isabella, things moved slowly. As soon as Columbus fell silent and the night's fragrances faded, everything became nebulous and uncertain again. King Ferdinand, as Isabella's husband and fellow sovereign, came back into the picture. No decisions could be made solely on the basis of impressions and suggestions that had yet to be examined and tested. It was thus decided to turn Columbus's project over to a committee of experts who would be chosen for this purpose. This was already a victory for the unknown foreigner. But might it not turn out to be a repeat of the Lisbon experience? There, too, Columbus had had to contend with the experts, and they had defeated him.

In Lisbon he hadn't had Isabella behind him. The queen immediately gave Columbus an advance from her own purse, in the amount of about fifteen thousand maravedis (about 400 gold ducats), and continued to do so well into the following year, 1487. Columbus certainly had nothing to complain about. He had become a protégé of the Crown, like all the astronomers, scholars, philosophers and chroniclers, and at the same time had established a kind of exclusive claim to his project. He was henceforth in the service of the Crown.

The task of heading the committee was assigned to Father Fernando de Talavera, the superior of the Prado monastery and a private confessor of the queen. He belonged to the order of St. Jerome, and was a man of great learning. His interests focused mostly on matters that served to propagate the faith. In this respect Columbus was in the right hands, and his arguments right on the mark. The Jeromites in Lisbon, who had a monastery on the Tagus, had also paid a great deal of attention to him for these very same reasons. The goals of these clerics and Columbus's ambitions had many things in common. Talavera, however, was a man of rational mind and always suspicious of anything new. He found someone like Columbus both fascinating and frightening. The psychological tension between the two men reached the breaking point on numerous occasions; of the disputation that went on for six years between Columbus and his judges, the real battles were fought between him and Talavera.

The examination committee usually met at court, in whatever the city the court happened to be residing at the time. Hence in 1486 they met in Córdoba until Christmas; the following winter it was Salamanca, as the sovereigns had by then moved there. Popular accounts of Columbus's story refer to the "sages of Salamanca" as his judges, depicting them as harsh and implacable in their long persecution of Columbus, and obtuse in their inability to appreciate the greatness of the man before them. But it was not at all like that.

For one thing, Salamanca was merely one of the panel's meeting places. And there were no committees other than the one presided over by Talavera. There was no "Córdoba committee" or "Seville committee" as distinct from the "Salamanca committee." The panel moved around, traveling from one part of Spain to another along with the rest of the court. But the judges remained for the most part the same, with only rare, incidental substitutions. Columbus followed them around from place to place, so that he could be available to answer their questions. He accompanied them from one city to the next, bearing on his shoulders the weight of his hopes and disappointments, which grew heavier and more burdensome as time wore on. It should also be said that he was not continually consulted, nor was his relationship to the committee such as we so often find it represented in paintings and prints over the centuries, with dour, dramatic judges brought together in a kind of tribunal and Columbus before them pleading his case like a defendant.

The debate opened with Columbus explaining his project to the panel. This probably took place in Córdoba. After this initial motion, the various members of the committee—sometimes individually, sometimes in groups—would meet from time to time with Columbus to ask him for clarifications or else to present some objection of theirs. The proceedings often came to a halt or were suspended for periods of time, among other things, to allow the various members to practice their usual professions, whether teaching at a university, researching or writing books, or fulfilling religious duties in the case of those who were members of the clergy.

If the name of Salamanca has remained prominent in history it is because for a long time the city was the most celebrated center of learning in all of Spain. At the time, the University of Salamanca was one of the four great universities of Europe together with Paris, Bologna and Oxford. Its fame traveled over mountains and seas. The plateresque portal through which one enters the University of Salamanca, which is made of a pinkish, gilded stone, symbolized the entrance to the realm of knowledge. Coats of arms, figures and various fantastical ornaments are sculpted into its façade, as though implying that imagination goes hand in hand with learning. This little detail probably did not escape Columbus's appreciation. He too must have gazed upon the famous door just as we do today from a distance of centuries, and spotted a striking little curiosity amid all the other bas-reliefs: a croaking frog atop a bald man's head, symbolizing lust. Columbus, still bearing the fresh imprint of Beatrice's charms in his mind, must have looked upon it with humility.

Humility and anxiousness were no doubt the emotions he felt most keenly in Salamanca. One of the more illustrious men teaching at the university at the time was Abram Zacuto, author of the *Perpetual Almanac,* which for Columbus was a kind of Bible. The sharpest, most learned minds of the age were concentrated in this place, and Columbus feared them. Oftentimes the language they used was unfamiliar to him. As had happened in Portugal, the scientists opposed his ideas with their theories; the memory of his Portuguese failure and the slow manner in which it all came to pass was still too fresh in Columbus's mind for him not to feel anxious and awkward as he relived the very same kinds of disputes.

What was Columbus compared to the scholars of Salamanca? He tells us himself: "They say that I am not learned in letters, that I am an ignorant sailor, a mundane man"—in other words, a man of the common herd, totally unversed in matters of science. López de Gómara, who told the story of Columbus's exploits some forty years after his death, described him as follows: *"no era docto ma bien entendido"*—he was not a learned man but quite knowledgeable all the same. It is an unbalanced statement: on the one hand we have those who really "know," on the other those who are merely "knowledgeable." The learning that Columbus did have meant little if he kept insisting on those two points: the earth's roundness (which most accepted as likely), and the shortness of the distance between Europe and Asia (which was obviously untrue)—points which, moreover, Columbus was unable to prove in any convincing manner. In the replies that he made to his judges' questions he was always quite brief. Apparently he wanted to mask the limits of his knowledge, and for this reason often responded in mysterious fashion, as though hiding some secret of major importance. One thing Columbus knew was that he was dealing with people infinitely more educated than he. He was merely trying to hide his ignorance.

But who were these judges who failed to understand him? We have neither names nor lists to consult. Aside from Talavera, the only one about whom we know anything for certain is one Rodrigo Maldonado, a very learned man but apparently more skilled in law than in cosmography. In fact, as far as we can gather, Talavera's committee as a whole had not nearly as many cosmographers and astronomers as it did theologians and jurists. Hence they expended a lot more energy delving into the project's theoretical aspects than evaluating it in any practical manner. Already somewhat inhibited because of his sketchy education, Columbus found himself at an even greater disadvantage in this kind of argumentation.

The Salamanca meetings—which were only one part of the committee's series of sessions, though probably the most important—were held in the Dominican monastery of St. Stephen, situated between the cathedral and the university. The predominant gold color of this complex of buildings—called "Salamantine" because of the rocks taken from a nearby quarry—today still glows in the walls of the churches and palaces perched like eagles on the city's high ground, from where one can see the bright blue waters of the Tormes below, the river that wraps the city in its coils. Outside the monastery one is struck by all this brightness of color and sunlight; but once inside, everything is cloaked in shadow, silence and darkness. The capitular hall in which the committee's sessions were held is a solemn, imposing room. The walls are gray, the ceiling wooden and blackened by time. Columbus was lodged by the Dominicans and spent his days in this environment. He waited and waited, trying to anticipate what sort of turn the judges' arguments would take next; he was admitted into their presence less and less, his answers growing more and more brief and cautious.

The Dominicans assigned him his own cell, and allowed him admission to the refectory. Occasionally, when the weather was good, they took him with them to Valcueva, a spot in the country where the order had a dairy farm. In this haven of nature, far from the pressures of the city, Columbus opened up a bit. He knew how to talk to friars. With them there was no danger of getting lost in a jungle of theories. They were men of faith, sometimes men of poetry. Columbus charmed them. He described the distant lands across the ocean, conjured the image of new multitudes of souls to be converted, an unknown mass just waiting to be taken into Christ's arms. He spoke like a man of destiny, someone whom divine providence had chosen for such an undertaking. He too had an unshakable faith—in himself. Would he succeed?

The prior of St. Stephen's was Father Diego de Deza. He was a professor of theology at the University of Salamanca and was considered something of a luminary in the interpretation of divinity. Diego de Deza probably was not a member of Talavera's committee, at least in any strict sense. But Talavera often consulted him on the matter, telling him his misgivings and the difficulties that the committee was up against, trying to judge a project that was in certain respects rather preposterous. Diego de Deza, however, found it instead "reasonable." He embraced Columbus's cause for a number of reasons, not the least of which were human sympathy, the fervor with which this foreign guest explained his plan, and the heady prospects that it offered for propagation of the Word. Deza was to remain Columbus's friend for life. He was the first among those in Salamanca to take his side.

The debates of these savants were of a decidedly Aristotelian stamp, like their education and the dominant school of thought at the time. Age-old inhibitions strengthened by doctrine reigned in their minds. They were always quoting St. Augustine, to the point of boredom. Augustine believed that the rest of the world was uninhabitable, that emptiness lay beyond the antipodes, that the earth's torrid zones produced heat so great that it would burn up anything that came near them—men, ships, and all forms of plant and animal life. Columbus told them that the Portuguese had already explored these regions some time ago, on their African expeditions. But the judges questioned the validity of his assertions. God created the world many thousands of years ago, they said, and no one has ever known anything for certain about those mysterious regions. They could not accept the possibility that this Columbus could suddenly appear out of nowhere and know more about these matters than all the great minds past and present. What sort of scientific proof did he have?

The committee's cosmographers maintained that the world was so vast that not even three years would suffice to reach the Orient. Columbus countered this claim with his calculations of the length of the degree, the testimony of Marco Polo, and the researches of Toscanelli. He even quoted the Book of Esdras, which may have saved him from accusations of impiousness and defiance of the Holy Scriptures. But he could not justify this scientifically.

Popular legend, which always ignores the subtleties of thought, paints the scholars in charge of Columbus's case as backward and behind the times. This clearly was not true. In Salamanca in particular, some of the most advanced and scientifically certain theories concerning the size of the globe were being worked out at the time. It is true, however, that the majority of Columbus's examiners were, as Washington Irving called them in his nineteenth-century biography, medieval mandarins. They made no distinction between an opinion and an article of faith. It is difficult for us today to understand them, to imagine the sort of debate that took place between Columbus and his judges. (Many exaggerations of the whole affair originate in the book written by his son Fernando, who, in order to exalt the image of his father, decided to denigrate those who opposed him.) Many elements of the debate were part of the reigning dialectics of the time. Some of them seem incomprehensible to us, such as the spirit of contradiction as an oratory skill, an excellent mental exercise that could be applied to even the clearest and most incontrovertible of arguments. It was an almost abstract sort of obstinacy, whose basic rule was to counter anything that was said with its opposite. The burden lay with the main speaker to provide evidence that what he said was true. And within this intellectual framework, this exercise of the purest form of logic, Columbus was almost totally defenseless.

In the meanwhile, the tension between him and Talavera had increased. Columbus played up his own self-importance by appealing to his sense of predestination and the mission for which he felt he had been chosen by the highest of authorities. Talavera, however, had no taste for self-importance. Personal stubbornness irritated him, and put him on his guard. For Columbus, the defense of his project had become a labyrinth. Two main things were working against him. The first and most essential was that he was not explaining himself successfully, not making himself understood. A number of issues in the dispute were related to religious questions, to theological interpretations which Columbus did not dare challenge. Las Casas tells us, "He always remained silent on the most important of matters." As for more technical concerns, his weapons were vastly inferior to those which his adversaries had at their disposal and could use with the greatest of confidence. He always ended up losing, or at least remaining misunderstood. A large number of the judges were unable to determine exactly what he wanted, not because of any prejudice against him but simply because of the differences between the languages used and the manner of confronting the issues.

Another fundamental incompatibility lay in the vast distance between the two different levels on which the debate took place: for Columbus it took place on the level of the imagination, for his judges on the level of scientific validity. The committee members, continually led astray by the foreigner's sibylline words, began to lose their patience. "They thought my project was some kind of joke," Columbus later wrote. Derision was the only way the judges knew how to deal with imagination, which for them was a mystery. No one is more vulnerable to malice than a man hounded by ridicule. Sarcasm and mockery began to follow Columbus around, often accompanied by insults. He suffered a madman's fate.

But who "knew" anything for certain in those days, and just what did they "know"? Of what use was this science that these learned men took such pride in possessing? Columbus was not the only one who did not "know." Nobody really "knew." They were all equal in the face of the unknown. But in the face of the unknown, science could do little; whereas intuition, courage and the much-maligned imagination could do a lot. Columbus had all these qualities, the others did not. If I had to limit my description of the Salamanca debates to just a few lines, I think that this brief observation would suffice.

This is not to say, however, that the committee was monolithic in its skepticism. It consisted of a variety of casts of mind and opinions. Columbus did have some vigorous supporters such as Deza; but he also had resolute adversaries such as Maldonado. The group, moreover, lived in too close a contact with the court not to be affected by its various moods and inclinations. First there was the queen, who in spite of everything believed in Columbus, or was at least inclined to put her trust in him. Other members of the court wavered in one direction or the other. The tentacles of the friars of La Rábida, particularly those of Juan Perez, reached as far as the palace gates and perhaps beyond. Talavera, who had to decide just when to call an end to the debates and issue a verdict, was inclined to drag his feet. A man of great intellectual honesty, he was absolutely impartial on the matter. But he was also a prudent man, and attentive to the consequences that any decision might bring. Hence international relations had to be considered as well: At the moment, Spain was all wrapped up in making its final assault on the Moors' last stronghold. Giving Columbus the go-ahead might have meant risking a hostile reaction on the part of Portugal, which to Talavera seemed even more dangerous than the mere fact of letting themselves be persuaded by an insane project.

Thus the months and years went by, with the flock of savants following the militant king and queen from city to city and Columbus following them, filled with anxiety and a long-frustrated enthusiasm. Fourteen eighty-eight came, then fourteen eighty-nine. Still no decision. But Columbus was not about to give up. Riccardo Bacchelli, in a now forgotten writing entitled *Why I never wrote a biography of Christopher Columbus (Sulle ragioni per cui non scrissi una biografia di Cristoforo Colombo)*, put it very aptly when he said that "Columbus's battle was a human battle waged with desperate passion." (Lope de Vega, in his play, has Columbus say, "I am like someone who has wings on his hands and a stone around his ankle.")

Columbus was a singularly persistent man. He did not give up when Talavera, in the final weeks of 1490, decided to come out with the committee's long-deferred judgment. The rather cruel verdict, addressed to the king and queen, went as follows: "We can find no justification for Their Highness's supporting a project that rests on extremely weak foundations and appears impossible to translate into reality to any person with any knowledge, however modest, of these questions." Columbus's plans were torn to shreds. The decision called his hypotheses "mad" and pointed its finger at his "colossal" errors: The distance between Castile and the Indies was far greater than that calculated by Columbus, and the majority of the earth's surface did not consist of "dry land" but of water or zones that were in any case uninhabitable, as the undisputable authority of St. Augustine clearly stated. The verdict also repeated the conviction that, so many millennia after the creation of the world, it was extremely unlikely that there could still be lands of any sizable magnitude whose existence was still unknown. The committee's emphasis on appeals to theology and Scholasticism was to an extent due to the events of the time. The Holy Inquisition was just getting into full swing. The infamous Torquemada—also a confessor of the queen!—had assumed the powers of inquisitor general, and the campaign to expel the Jews had begun. Faith was not allowed to waver, and hence could not be discussed. Anyone who dared cast the Holy Scriptures into doubt would bring upon himself the wrath of the Creed. Columbus himself ran this risk, since Talavera and the other scholars of the committee did not want to raise any suspicions about their orthodoxy. Of course this was merely one factor leading to their denial, and was unrelated to their scientific judgment. But it played a large part in the choice of arguments cited and in the severity of tone with which the decision was rendered.

As for Columbus, the only people he could count on any more were the queen and those few influential figures who had remained his friends. In all likelihood, Isabella was the inspiration behind the message that broke the news of the committee's denial to Columbus. Apparently a minority within the group did not agree with the verdict, even though it was presented as a unanimous decision. It is possible that Isabella weighed the differences of opinion in an attempt to leave the door open to future reconsiderations. What is certain is that the decision was communicated to Columbus in such a manner as not to destroy all hope of a reexamination of the matter "at a more convenient time." Which meant: when we sovereigns are less wrapped up in matters of war, which at the moment prevent us from thinking about anything else. There will be time to discuss it later.

Further proof of this is that in the meantime Columbus was granted the special privilege of continued admission to the court, as someone "coming to deal in matters concerning our service." This already was an encouraging postscript to the judges' decision, even though Alonso de Quintanilla, head of the depleted public treasury, had stopped giving him money some time since and had no further orders to give him. This was the period of Columbus's life that he later called the "years of great anguish." In Seville the Infanta Isabel, eldest child of the king and queen, was married to the heir to the Portuguese throne. A cheerful atmosphere reigned at court, bringing with it a spirit of indulgence and goodwill that managed to soften the blow of Talavera's decision. The prospects for the war also seemed to be good, and Ferdinand and Isabella planned to return to Granada by the end of the summer of 1491. Since that was to be the "more convenient time" alluded to by the queen, Columbus could once again entertain hopes of resuming pursuit of his dream as his period of waiting grew shorter with each passing day. Anguish was thus tempered by hope, something of which Columbus in his stubbornness seemed to have endless reserves. He was a very restless man by nature. But he knew how to be patient, and in the end this was the key to his victory, which was in a sense a triumph over himself as well.

But by late 1491 all hope seemed lost again. The war was dragging on, the sovereigns inextricably entangled in it, and the coffers of the treasury were empty. Columbus's persistence was becoming bothersome and inappropriate. He was no longer received at court: there were orders to keep him at a distance and not to waste time with him when there were much more pressing matters that needed attention. The future discoverer's situation was getting desperate. He no longer received any money aside from an occasional trickle from Beatrice, who had herself depleted her resources. He had two sons to support, a two-year-old and the older boy he had left at La Rábida. Everyone seemed to have forgotten about him. To earn some money, he started designing geographical maps. Apparently he also sold some books, treatises on astronomy and geography. He was following his brother Bartholomew's example. But it was a downward trail.

In autumn he made a brief visit to La Rábida. He wanted to see his son Diego again, and may have wanted to take the boy to his aunt in Huelva. Apparently Diego was tired of the monastery after all these years. And his father was growing tired of Spain: he wanted to flee, to go elsewhere to seek the fortune that kept eluding him in Spain. He was forty years old now, and life was slipping away. While the battle was raging in Salamanca he had already sent out feelers to Charles VIII in France and Henry VII in England. To no avail. The messenger he had sent was his brother, who then decided to stay for a while in Fontainebleau, working in the French court as a cartographer. There had even been an exchange of letters with the King of Portugal, John II, who was quite cordial and a little concerned. In his reply he called Columbus "my dear friend" and urged him to come see him at once, promising him support. But very shortly thereafter Bartholomeu Dias returned from one of his expeditions around the Cape of Good Hope, thus opening up a sea route to the East and the precious Indies. The problem of reaching them seemed resolved, and by taking the exact opposite direction from the one that Columbus believed in so firmly. He was no longer needed in Lisbon. (A few late chroniclers have speculated that Columbus went back to Lisbon to enjoy again the protection of John II, and was there when he learned of Dias's successful attempt, supposedly meeting with Dias at some point. But there are no testimonies to support any such hypothesis.)

How does one describe an unexpected change of fortune, that phoenix always ready to rise again from its ashes in the most desperate of moments? For this is how it was for Columbus, who was at the end of his rope. In a way, his story is the quintessential fairy tale of the misunderstood, scorned genius who suddenly rises to glory on the wings of fate. By the eve of 1492 his mad proposal was already dead and buried, his cause already lost. But in January of that year Granada fell to the Spanish and the war against the Moors was finally over, after centuries of struggle. People's minds were opening up again, thinking about the future. Spain now had vast perspectives before her, the shadows of the past fading fast behind her. The first to understand the new opportunities that were starting to present themselves were the businessmen. Columbus had a few friends among them who had remained silent and cautious during the years of waiting, but who were now anxious to be the first to seize new opportunities. The old Genoese business connections with the shipbuilding Centuriones and DiNegros reemerged. The Duke of Medina Celi reappeared, years after giving way to the queen in an affair that he had enthusiastically supported. These ties had been maintained in secret at Córdoba and Seville, antechambers to the victory in Granada. The direct line to the court had been kept alive by the monks of Palos, the same who had established it six years earlier. The queen had not forgotten the conversation at the Alcazar, nor the face of the foreigner who had opened his heart to her, nor the promises made. After an unending winter of despair was spring about to reappear, unexpectedly, almost unhoped-for, for Columbus?

It was unquestionably on its way. The change of fortune began precisely when Columbus was at his most dejected, when he returned to La Rábida to see his son and experience again some of the human warmth and friendship he had previously known with the friars, who had been the first to take him in upon his arrival in Spain when his hope was still burning strong. The Franciscans of Palos showed a stubborn loyalty to him, not only providing consolation—the mission of all of God's ministers—but declaring their willingness to fight for something they believed in. They had already decided, six years earlier, that Columbus's project was the work of providence and within the realm of human capability. They had gotten directly involved in an attempt to inspire the same convictions in the queen's mind. They had followed the progress of the discussions in Salamanca and elsewhere, when the judges were plunging the knives of doubt into the body of this defenseless believer as though he were a sacrificial lamb. They criticized the slowness of those meetings, as well as the confusion and the overly scrupulous, overly cautious hypocrisy of the judges. They probably were also irritated by the involvement of people from other religious offices and other orders; there is often more friction between likes than between contraries. In short, the Franciscans of Palos were not at all pleased and even less convinced by Talavera's verdict. And when Columbus arrived a defeated man at their monastery's doorstep, they did not limit themselves to comforting him; they told him that the battle is not over as long as you are still out in the field. They, the Franciscans of Palos, wanted to keep fighting and still had plenty of arrows left in their quivers.

They reexamined the question from top to bottom, together with Columbus. They pointed out the errors he had made in his calculations and carefully weighed the pros and cons of all the different points that had come out during the debate. They even consulted people from outside the monastery, such as the Palos physician García Hernández, who also knew some astronomy and was a great collector of seafaring tales. (Many years later, at an advanced age, Hernández gave a rather detailed account of these matters when he appeared as an eyewitness before a session of the trial initiated by Columbus's heirs several decades after his death.) Finally, and most importantly, they invited to their discussions a man who would become one of the main protagonists of Columbus's undertaking, for better or worse—the experienced seafarer Martín Alonzo Pinzón. In Palos and all along the coast, Pinzón was considered the best seaman in Andalusia. He enjoyed widespread fame, headed a family of excellent navigators and was a kind of dean of the seafaring arts. He was also quite wealthy, which certainly did not hurt. He owned a caravel of his own and a number of smaller vessels. He had sailed all over the Mediterranean and down the Atlantic coast to Guinea, and had ventured on the open sea as far as the Canary Islands. A year earlier he had visited with the cosmographers of the papal court, over which Innocent VIII presided at the time. He kept himself well informed regarding all new projects and developments in the field of navigation, and most likely was aware of Toscanelli's charts. Columbus had already met Pinzón. He didn't care much for the man's personality, which beamed with arrogance, but had great respect for his experience, practical knowledge and deep understanding of the sea.

For many days and nights these men discussed, amid the silence of La Rábida, how they might enter the cracks left open in the arguments of the judges of Salamanca. They decided there was still room for another attempt to overcome the resistance of the court advisers who had, with their doubts, created a barrier between Columbus and the two sovereigns, especially between Columbus and the queen. After his memorable encounter with Isabella at the Alcazar in the spring of 1486, the man destined to discover a new world for the glory of Spain had been unable to have any more direct communication with the queen. For almost six years now, the only people who had talked to the sovereigns about the matter were Columbus's judges, the very men who had shot down his project; this, then, was the crux of the problem. It was absolutely necessary that the queen, after six years, have another chance to listen to Columbus.

It is not all that unlikely that she actually wanted to see him. But there were many factors working against this: the pressures of the war, King Ferdinand's indifference to the kinds of things that concerned Columbus, the efforts of the judges to keep Columbus away from Isabella, the financial problems, which advisers shrewdly exaggerated in a period when the treasury was low. Thus even if she had had the will to do so, the circumstances made it impossible for her to make the first move. Someone had to persuade her.

Who? Certainly not Pinzón, who had no influence whatsoever at court, however great his power in Palos. One thing to bear in mind is that if the implementation of Columbus's project—which needed royal approval in any case—had been up to Pinzón, nothing would ever have happened. Pinzón had many virtues, but he was a rather rude, rebellious person incapable of any kind of negotiation that was not purely commercial or settled with swords. The man best suited to the task of reopening the door was Father Perez, who had had a great deal of experience in this sort of thing. He knew exactly how to proceed in the labyrinths of the court, enjoyed the privileges of his office and was privy to the secrets of the confessional. He knew Isabella and her manner of ruling. He took it on himself to reopen the Columbus case when it seemed that it already might be closed for good.

He sent a very restrained letter to the queen, which was brought to her in Seville by a seaman of the coast, Sebastian Rodríguez. No one knows, and in my opinion no one will ever know, what was in that letter. It is vain to speculate, as many have done, about secret confidences regarding Toscanelli's maps (him again!), or the story of the unknown helmsman who supposedly revealed to Columbus the route to the Indies and of whose existence Isabella was unaware only because Columbus had revealed none of this to his judges. I am much more inclined to believe that Perez's missive was of a rather intimate nature, and dealt more with feelings than with facts—a letter appealing to the queen's heart, which had to be shaken out of the troubles in which it had been wrapped up for so long. And since Isabella was in her heart instinctively predisposed to understanding Columbus and sympathizing with him, she answered the letter.

The reply arrived in Palos barely two weeks after Perez's letter had left for the royal palace of Seville, the old Moorish Alcazar next to the cathedral. The queen summoned Perez to the court; she wanted to consult with him. The door was open again.

There was a flurry of activity, of comings and goings, in the late autumn and early winter of 1491. Perez was no doubt quite eloquent in Seville. He was quite emphatic in his prediction that if Spain refused Columbus, another country—perhaps France, perhaps even Portugal—would eventually support him. This argument touched even King Ferdinand. The Spanish Crown was still living out a moment of triumph, and was more inclined to look toward expansion than toward conservation. In these new circumstances the prior of

La Rábida found more than a few allies among the throng of courtiers swarming around the throne. He had the ardent support of the Marquise de Moya, though her motives had little to do with politics, and probably a lot more to do with Columbus's fascination with her soft white, pleasant limbs. (She also, incidentally, was named Beatrice.) But he also managed to arouse the enthusiasm of her husband, Andrea de Cabrera, an important adviser to the court, who may or may not have been aware of the relations existing, or said to exist, between his wife and the navigator. Lobbying for the queen's support was Diego de Deza, the Dominican from Salamanca. But perhaps the most decisive actions were those of Luis de Santangel, a member of King Ferdinand's inner circle, treasurer of the house of Aragon and chief tax collector, as well as a prominent businessman in his own right with connections to Genoese and Florentine merchants established in Seville and Córdoba, who were already avidly seeking new dealings and investments in those areas just opened up by the conclusion of the war.

All in all, Santangel was a fairly obscure figure, but he was nonetheless blessed with shrewdness, enterprise and power—not to mention powers of persuasion that usually enabled him to get what he wanted. Santangel was a man who liked to take risks, if these risks opened the door to substantial gain. The queen, though she believed in Columbus, wondered where she would get the money to finance his expedition. But three caravels and a few dozen sailors were not, after all, that expensive. Santangel was quick to assure the queen that he—along with other associates in Seville, including the Genoese Ferdinando Pinello, a confidential secretary to the throne in financial matters and later a faithful friend of Columbus during the ocean voyages—was ready to lend her as much as she might need. Popular accounts tell us that Isabella, to get the loan from Santangel, offered her jewels as collateral. This fueled the legend of her as a brave, farsighted queen ready to deny herself to ensure future gains for Spain and also perhaps to indulge her partiality for matters of the intellect, which is in itself an act of love of sorts. In the Caribbean city of Santo Domingo, in front of the viceroy's palace built for Columbus (though he died before it was finished), there is a large statue of Isabella with jewel case in one hand and with the other hand pulling a necklace out of the case. This sculpture romanticizes the truth, however, since Isabella was never in a situation where she had to give up her necklaces, as did a number of celebrated ladies of ancient Rome. Santangel certainly sufficed—not only to guarantee beforehand the (relatively low) costs of the adventure, but also to underwrite it, beyond all political and scientific considerations. Santangel's gesture played a large part in tipping the scales from the negative to the affirmative.

It is believed that at this point a new council of experts was brought together in a great hurry, composed partially of some of the same members as before, partially of new judges less prejudiced by theological questions and generally more open-minded. The mood of the court seemed favorable, as did that of the businessmen, and the queen appeared to be totally won over by the cause. In all probability the cosmographers and geographers remained as doubtful as ever, but they were overwhelmed by the general enthusiasm and quickly removed all previous obstacles. This often happens, even nowadays, in long-drawn-out disputes. Once weariness builds up to a certain point or new enthusiasm materializes, convictions embraced steadfastly for years can make a sudden about-face in a matter of a few days. The dominant mood in Seville combined an impatient desire to focus on other concerns and a feeling of beneficence and generosity inspired by recent triumphs. Father Perez returned to Palos bearing a verbal message from Isabella to Columbus, to the effect that "he should rest assured in his hopes until he receives a letter from the queen."

The letter arrived shortly thereafter, granting Columbus an audience. Isabella wanted to see him in person, and sent him a purse of florins "so that he could dress himself decently, buy a horse and present himself to Her Highness." Columbus hurried to Seville, but the court in the meantime had moved to the military encampment at Santa Fé, a village of very few inhabitants a few kilometers from Granada, whose surrender was being negotiated with the last Moorish king in all of Spain, the young Boabdil.

When Columbus arrived in Santa Fé, crossing lands wasted by war on his way to the front, the encampment of tents was already turning into a full-fledged city of turrets and battlements, with a rectangular enclosure wall inside of which several thousand people—courtiers, officials, councillors, soldiers—had shelters and quarters. Confusion and excitement reigned amid a troubled military atmosphere. The stone walls framed the war scene in the green meadows beyond, with the bloodstone flanks of the Alhambra dominating the heights of Granada in the distance, and higher up the snows of the Sierra Nevada shining in the sun. All around the walls of Santa Fé was a large moat that could be crossed at the city's four gates, each at a cardinal point. Hence four exact quarters of the city corresponded to the four quarters of the wall; in the center a drill ground which the church and the royal palace, a one-story black and gray edifice, gave onto. This provisional city has remained unchanged to this day. Walking through it one has feeling of going backward through history, through the unchanged memory of the places themselves and the life that animated them. Columbus entered through those same gates, stopped in the drill ground and was led into the palace, where he saw Isabella again.

He was a changed man, different from the dreamer that the queen had met six years earlier in Córdoba. The trials had hardened him, and he now wore his pride like a suit of armor. His proposal had been accepted; now it was his turn to call the shots. His status had changed from that of bothersome suppliant to that of necessary, indispensable protagonist. They had called him here because they needed him.

The courtly preliminaries were brief, as were the queen's smile and the glance that the foreigner cast on her with his blue eyes. Then Columbus quickly set about laying down—better yet, dictating—his conditions. They were very exacting conditions, and his manner of presenting them somewhat arrogant. He wanted first of all a noble title, to help pull him out of the obscurity in which he lived as a foreigner without pedigree. He demanded the rank of admiral, just like the Grand Admiral of Castile, next to whom Columbus would become Admiral of the Ocean Sea. And along with this rank he wanted to be granted the powers of viceroy and governor general of all the lands that he might discover. The titles and power had to be hereditary, transmittable from father to son to son. In addition, he demanded a commission of ten percent on all traffic and commerce between the new domains and Spain, including the value of any gold, silver or gems found in the newly discovered lands.

Columbus's demands seemed absurd. His interlocutors listened in shock. The queen was taken aback; the king, when he learned of them, took a firm position against them. They tried to negotiate, to find other possible areas of agreement. Columbus would not budge. Neither the queen's smile nor the harshness of the king's advisers could make him give in. Moreover, he flew into a rage at any suggestion that he modify his claims. Isabella vacillated uselessly between the pride of the throne and the charm of the imagination. The military victory, in whose exalted atmosphere these talks were taking place, had enlarged all proportions including the sovereigns' own, and their desire for expansion. They were ready to make their march into Granada as liberators of the homeland and Christendom. And yet here was this foreigner dictating his terms to them. It was madness, inconceivable. The king and queen resisted. Columbus did not give in. The only solution left was to break off negotiations. Columbus got back on his horse, rode past the city's walls and left Santa Fé behind him. All he owned now was "the night and the day," as the Spanish say about someone who has lost everything.

But immediately those forces in the king and queen's entourage who wanted the project carried out went back to work. They included friars Perez and Deza, court councillors Quintanilla and Cabrera, businessmen like Santangel and Pinello, women such as the Marquise of Moya and the governess of one of the Canary Islands, Beatrice de Bobadilla, an intimate friend of the queen. Who could resist a united front of such forces as friendship, money and feminine charms?

The argument in favor of reconsideration was quite simple. Columbus's project had not itself been rejected since everyone was in agreement on it. What had been rejected were the excessive privileges that he had demanded in return, the exorbitance of his claims. Well, reasoned Columbus's friends, if in fact he succeeded in bringing the Indies to the Crown he would indeed have earned such privileges. If he did not succeed, he wouldn't get anything. What was the risk? His plan was bold, but not very costly. And the price to pay would be commensurate with his success, if in fact he succeeded. They had only to keep the document of their pledge a secret until he returned, proposed Santangel to the queen. It was all quite logical, once stripped of the pride with which Columbus had made it seem unacceptable. And so the queen once again gave in. She sent out an order to call him back.

Columbus's horse was no great steed. An *alguazil* (court beadle) on a very fast horse was sent out to find him. He caught up to him as he was crossing the Pinos bridge on the road to Córdoba. The *alguazil* enjoined him to present himself "at once" before the queen "as Her Highness is ready to conclude the affair."

Without hesitation, Columbus turned his horse around. He had won.

8

The Three Caravels

Columbus, back at court amid the smiles and reverences of friends and foes alike, did not waste a minute getting down to business. First of all, the contract confirming his new status and granting all the extraordinary privileges he had demanded had to be drawn up, and he wanted the document signed by the king and queen. This necessitated further negotiations, long consultations that took place outside the usual councils to the throne. The main points of contention, however, had already been settled, and so these discussions involved only formalities such as the type of document to be drawn up and the enumeration of the concessions granted. The queen took a personal interest in following the progress of the talks, which were carried out as work of the chancellery. She was represented by Juan de Cóloma, secretary to the king. The early drafts of the text were drawn up by Father Perez, who during this time leaned on his skill and experience as a man of the court.

The meetings were held in the small gray and white palace on Santa Fé plaza, a building now restored to look as it did then and adorned with an inscribed tablet commemorating the event. The work seemed easy enough. But bureaucracy has always had laws of its own. It took three months to settle matters. Columbus in the meantime stood by his royal hosts in festivities celebrating the conquest of Granada. He took part in the solemn procession that entered the city to the roll of drums, standards raised high, parade regimentals shining in the sunlight. But the king and queen of Spain did not settle in Granada. They entered the Alhambra, sat on the exquisitely fashioned ivory thrones and were paid homage by local notables. But they never went back there except for occasional formal duties that could be fulfilled during the daytime. At night they returned to Santa Fé, where they lived until the court moved to other cities in Spain.

Granada had been under Arab rule for seven centuries. The entire population had become Moslem generations ago, and hated the Christians as their
natural enemies. The feelings of the inhabitants had very deep, distant roots,
passed from father to son in a time almost beyond memory. Military conquest
was not enough to change their beliefs, and it was not yet time even to
consider converting them. They accepted their new king—and queen—with a
mixture of fear and suspicion. Ferdinand and Isabella were afraid of conspiracies and desperate, fanatical acts. They preferred to keep away from the site
of their triumph, contenting themselves with celebrating it with as much
visible pomp as possible. Then they left the field of battle to the inquisitors.
Granada, conquered without a shot being fired for Boabdil's surrender, had
not finished fighting its war. Indeed, it had just begun.

In Santa Fé, on the other hand, Columbus's war was over. On April 17,
1492, his contract with the sovereigns of Spain was signed and officially ratified. Under the words *"Yo el Rey"* and *"Yo la Reyna"* ("I the King" and "I
the Queen") elegantly penned at the foot of the document, Juan de Cóloma
affixed his own signature *"por mandado del Rey e de la Reyna"* (by order of
the king and queen). The document was in the form of a unilateral concession
promulgated by the sovereign authority, granting "those things requested by
Don Christopher Columbus as a manner of recompense for what he has
discovered."

In the five centuries that have passed since then, everything humanly
conceivable has been written regarding this document. The reader will notice
that it is in the form of a reply to Columbus's "requests"—a fully consenting
reply which masks, however, the fact that it had been bargained over. The
document states that the privileges granted are in reward for "what he has
discovered." The explicit intention here is to make the text of the agreement
valid only after Columbus's return from the voyage he was about to undertake, and only on the condition of success. This was the very same strategy
that had eliminated all opposition to the agreement. There was a good chance
that Columbus would bring much glory and wealth to Spain. What the
Crown promised him in return was very little in comparison, especially in
light of what eventually happened. For the moment, however, everything was
hypothetical, both credits and debits. In Santa Fé, Columbus received only a
few titles that cost nothing. The document referred to him already as "Don,"
a title of rank in which he put great store, much more than did those who
bestowed it on him.

But the important part was the rest of it. Many were taken quite by surprise by the outcome of the whole affair, which went against all the opinions, examinations and judgments of some of the most highly regarded figures in Spanish society, judgments so vehement in their denial that they should have been enough to destroy Columbus. And yet here he was being raised to the office of messenger of the Crown across the unknown reaches of the ocean, a charge so prestigious and so potentially profitable that all other coveted offices of the court paled in comparison. The great discoverer had, in a single bound, begun an entirely new chapter in his life: from a bothersome suppliant whose wishes had been refused for years and years, he had become the leader of an expedition headed for glory. Hope itself was a thing of the past. It was time for realization.

It was all in the Santa Fé document, by royal decree. The sovereigns had accepted all of his demands. Not even so much as a comma had been removed from what they had so indignantly rejected a few weeks earlier—now referred to as "requests" which they had agreed, with good grace, to grant. The text's final draft, which the Spanish archives have preserved to this day, is almost laconic in its brevity, fitting on little more than one page. The centuries have yellowed this valuable document, but the living sense of that day remains palpably intact in the clerk's careful, flawless handwriting, Juan de Cóloma's ornate signature, and above it, next to one another, the captions of power, *Yo el Rey* and *Yo la Reyna.*

The document contains only five paragraphs. The first confers upon "Don" Columbus the title of Admiral of the Ocean Sea for the whole of his natural life, a title to be passed on to his heirs "from one to the next" in perpetuity. The rank of admiral would endow Columbus with the same prerogatives as the Grand Admiral of Castile, Don Alfonso Enríquez. What a giant step for a foreigner who barely fifteen years earlier was struggling in Genoa between his father's debts and the small commercial commissions given him by merchants patronizing his family! But this was not the first time that Spain had appointed a foreigner admiral. The Bocanegras of Genoa, father and son, had both earned the title in the fourteenth century.

In the second paragraph, "it pleases Their Highnesses" to appoint Columbus as their viceroy and governor general "in all the terra firma and islands that he has discovered" in the above-mentioned Ocean Sea, with the authority to recommend for every office within his jurisdiction three trusted persons, from whom the sovereigns will choose one as their appointee.

The third paragraph concerns the fees to be accorded said admiral and viceroy. Just as Columbus had asked, however insolently, the Santa Fé document grants him a ten percent commission on all commerce, "whether pearls, precious stones, gold, silver, spices (products of the Orient, the same as those brought back by Marco Polo—clearly Ferdinand, Isabella and Columbus all had their sights set on the Indies!), and on any other kind of merchandise that might be bought and sold within the confines of the new admiralty.

The fourth paragraph specifies that in the case of any dispute on the part of any commercial parties regarding the duties exacted by the admiral, only he himself or someone designated to act in his stead at the site of the dispute will have authority to settle the controversy, "and no other judge."

The fifth paragraph deals with another of Columbus's requests initially rejected as unacceptable—the authorization to invest his own capital in any ship that does business with the new territories, up to a limit of one-eighth of the total expenditures, with a corresponding entitlement of one-eighth of all profits.

The paragraphs as a whole were called "capitulations," and as such they went down in history as the "capitulations of Santa Fé." Capitulation in this sense means transaction or agreement on privileges to be granted. It is a word used in diplomacy. But in this particular instance, when one considers the process and dispute leading up to it, the word's other meaning also seems quite apt.

Documents that are overly brief, such as these one-page capitulations, have both the merit of clarity and the drawback of omitting many things, things perhaps implicit but not stated. Which side should prevail, in the case of ambiguity? Many questions arose on this very matter, some of them raised by Columbus himself late in his life and later brought to court by his heirs after his death, over several generations. In the first paragraph of the capitulations the rank and privileges of Admiral of the Ocean Sea are made equal to those of Don Alfonso Enríquez, Grand Admiral of Castile. Don Alfonso, an uncle of the king, collected a tax of 30 percent—almost a third!—on all commerce between Castile and the islands, especially the Canary Islands, discovered some fifty years earlier. Much would be made of this one-third commission—and of Columbus's one-tenth commission on commerce and one-eighth return on ships—when Columbus later sat down to do his accounts. Was Columbus entitled to the same percentage? The Spanish Crown never recognized any such entitlement, nor did the courts to which his heirs appealed. In the end, his heirs were left with only the title of admiral, and no monetary entitlements.

Another disputed paragraph was the second one, which gave Columbus the authority to choose, and make answerable to him, all political, judiciary and fiscal officers in the territories in which he was viceroy and governor general. The Crown later stripped him of these powers, in order to reestablish the totality of its own power. Was it right to do so? Could the Spanish kings, now become the Catholic Kings, violate an agreement so solemnly decreed? Ferdinand and Isabella had not signed the document themselves, leaving to Juan de Cóloma the task of carrying out their will. But it was careless of them to leave such a point ambiguous, and it turned into a bone of contention that no one has since been able to settle in any kind of definitive manner.

Together with the capitulations, six additional documents were signed and turned over to Columbus. One of them contained further specifications regarding the titles conferred upon Columbus, his right to the designation of "Don," and the use of such privileges by his descendants. Another was a letter of recommendation to be presented to any foreign leaders with whom he might come into contact. A third was a kind of passport made out in the name of "Our noble captain Christopher Columbus," to be presented to the princes of the countries where he was expected to land, which would be, in both the sovereigns' and Columbus's estimations, Cipango or Cathay—Japan or China. The other three documents were ordinances of the Crown regarding the preparation of the fleet that was to make the ocean voyage.

Columbus was anxious to sail before the colder months set in. He left Santa Fé on May 12, taking leave of the sovereigns with an invocation of the Holy Trinity, a rather appropriate (if perhaps fortuitous) analogy to the triad of king, queen and navigator. It was unanimously decided that the port of departure would be Palos, a fated spot in Columbus's life, in good luck and bad. The choice was neither arbitrary nor simply sentimental. The tribunal of the Holy Inquisition was by now working tirelessly, and had recently had the Sovereigns sign an edict calling for the expulsion of the Jews, who were quite numerous in Spain at the time. Most were being sent to Africa and northern Italy in a complicated operation that was blocking the major ports of Castile, such as Seville and Cádiz. In Cádiz alone, more than eight thousand families were piled into every available kind of ship. The piers were mobbed with unending lines of wailing, suffering people.

Palos would in any case have suited Columbus just fine, given the friends he had there and the quality of the seamen who lived there, known to be expert, daring navigators. But the initial reception was anything but friendly. The sovereigns, with their customary obsession for thrift—which was in this instance a more or less unconscious way to avenge the concessions they had

had to make to Columbus and to smite the sense of pride that he derived from
them—resorted to a kind of subterfuge to bring together the fleet that Columbus needed, and it was the citizens of Palos who had to pay for it. They dug
up an old case of smuggling involving the importation of goods from Africa
or the islands by a number of Palos vessels without royal permission. There
were even accusations of piracy. The sovereigns passed sentence, saying: We
are compelled to punish the municipality of your city with a heavy fine; in
lieu of which you must give us, free of charge, "at your burden and cost," two
caravels fully equipped with everything necessary for a voyage of twelve
months. Columbus needed three caravels, and they had promised him three.
The first two they managed to confiscate, leaving only one that had to be paid
for.

    This order, signed by Ferdinand and Isabella, was solemnly read in the
parish Church of St. George on May 23 by the Palos notary, Francisco Fernández. This church still stands, next to the old castle ruins. It is made out of
piedra caliza, a yellow and brown limestone that lights up in the sunshine like
the cheeks of a fair young girl. If you enter the nave you can still see, in the
shadows of arches supported by strong pillars, the wrought-iron pulpit from
which the ordinance was read. Columbus was present for the reading. He
himself had handed the document to the mayor of Palos, who then turned it
over to the notary who read it from the pulpit.

    The church was swarming with commoners. As it is not a very large
building, many of them had to stand outside the doors, one of which faces a
mountain, the other a valley. This latter was and still is called *la puerta de
l'embarcadero,* the door to the pier. A little red dirt road runs from the door
down to the Río Tinto, to the loop that served as a port to sailing vessels. The
seamen of Palos crowded in this doorway as they listened to the ordinance.
And they certainly did not like what they heard. The royal decree demanded
that the caravels be fully rigged "within ten days of receipt of this order."

    The Crown's demands bordered on the absurd, and indeed they were not
met. Another mistake was the stipulation, also announced that day, that all
civil and penal proceedings would be suspended for anyone who signed up for
the expedition. The friars of La Rábida were dismayed by all of this. They felt
committed to the undertaking, had even staked their reputations on it, and
hence were incredulous when they heard that the crew would be made up of
criminals. Perhaps the sovereigns feared that in Palos there might not be any
seamen daring enough to confront the ocean's mysteries. Perhaps they expected to encounter a general reluctance to trust one's fate to a foreigner.

Whatever the reasons, the seamen of Palos, after hearing the ordinance read in the Church of St. George, scattered about to their various taverns ridiculing this Columbus, his friar patrons and their cortege of assassins and hoodlums.

Martín Alonso Pinzón was not in Palos that day. He returned some time later, and all waited anxiously to see what his reaction would be. Pinzón was a kind of rallying point for the people of Palos. Columbus became convinced that he could not play the game alone. The two men had already established a kind of understanding between them, but it was tinged with a certain mutual reticence. They held each other in high esteem, though they may not have liked each other. Pinzón saw Columbus as a parvenu come out of nowhere, short on experience but endowed with an extraordinary amount of energy, drive and new ideas. Columbus considered Pinzón a first-rate seaman and nothing more. He cared little for the man's insolent, suspicious, closed temperament. Columbus was afraid Pinzón might overshadow him. Pinzón envied Columbus's certainty of success. Their differences seemed irreconcilable. Friendship and candor might have been able to overcome them, but there was never any real friendship or candor between Columbus and Pinzón.

The only common ground on which they could meet was their mutual need for each other. They both believed in the project and wanted to carry it out. Pinzón, however, was of too low a social and educational level, and too lacking in imagination to overcome alone all the obstacles standing in the way of obtaining royal consent, without which it would have been pure madness to undertake the voyage. Columbus, for his part, could not do without Pinzón for entirely different reasons. First of all, Pinzón had it in his power to temper the hostility felt by the sailors of Palos against Columbus; Columbus certainly had no intention of taking to sea with a crew composed of men just released from prison. The expedition he was about to undertake called for very skilled men with a great deal of experience and know-how. If he could not have such a crew at his disposal, he would have to entertain a possibility that he had never accepted—failure. Columbus had never said anything about his past to either the sovereigns, the scholars who had questioned him, or even Pinzón. He said only that he had been sailing since his earliest years and that he knew all the seas known to man. He himself was of course well aware of having done most of this as a spectator rather than a navigator. He had indeed sailed on many ships as a passenger. But how much could he have learned about the seaman's trade from merely watching others practice it? Here Columbus was about to set out from Palos in command of three caravels and about a hundred men, admiral's flags flying high on the mainmasts, and yet he had never commanded a ship in his life! One may entertain presumptions and illusions about oneself only up to a certain point, but not beyond. Hence his need for Pinzón.

Columbus was a truly unusual man. He pursued his dream for years and years, from the days of his youth to the emergence of his first white hairs, which were fast beginning to cover his head. Dreams fade, elude our grasp. Columbus, however, was so tenacious in his pursuit of his that the object of his dream finally became confused with the dreamer himself. He had entered his own utopia, as though it were something that actually existed; and his utopia, in turn, had entered his heart. Imagination and reality, after having struggled for so long with one another, had become the same thing, indistinguishable from each other. This is how Columbus, for nearly twenty years an extravagant visionary, suddenly became a cautious realist when the moment came to grasp his dream. In so doing, however, he did not go against himself. He transformed himself naturally, like those animals that change color with variations in light or temperature.

Thus Columbus realized that a voyage as difficult and unpredictable as the one he was about to undertake called for a real navigator with a great deal of experience. He himself did not possess such qualifications, or at least he had never really had the chance to put them to the test. Pinzón did possess them, as did his loyal group of reliable, courageous sailors. Thus in the conversations between Columbus and Pinzón the two men worked out a rather sensible, realistic division of duties and responsibilities. To Columbus, master of the idea and explorer of dreams, fell the task of leading the expedition. No one else could span the reaches of his thought and imagination. Pinzón would see to the practical side of the undertaking, battling the sea and steering the vessels. Columbus viewed this division in the most condescending of fashions, like the relationship between lord and servant. He was not at all concerned about his rather spare knowledge of the trade, and certainly was not held back by any feelings of inferiority on the matter. On the contrary, his alliance with Pinzón freed him from the bother of having to deal with particulars, leaving him to follow the impulses of invention in the higher realm of the imagination.

And if they attained their goal, how would they share the glory? They would not; it would be Columbus's alone. Columbus's feelings were quite unambiguous: he had devoted his whole life to this dream and nothing else. Pinzón was but a necessary tool, little more than a hull or sail. Disputes and bitterness would later arise from all this. If you go to Palos today you will see, in the city's main square, a monument to America's discoverer: it is a statue portraying not Columbus but Martín Alonso Pinzón. Hence chauvinism further clouds the whole affair. But fame does not make mistakes: five centuries after the fact, the name of Christopher Columbus still resounds throughout the world. There is perhaps not a single name more famous than his, more universally known, not even those of the greatest poets and military commanders. How many people have heard of Pinzón? Time has buried him, swallowed him up. There is only the Palos monument to commemorate its illustrious native son, conferring virtues on him that exceed his actual merits.

The alliance was formed. From it, Pinzón hoped to make money and new business dealings to add to the wealth he already possessed. But he was also attracted by the adventure of confronting the risks that lay ahead, by the prospect of adding one more thrill to a life spent on the high seas. And he probably did not want to leave all the joys of the undertaking to a foreigner—since, after all, the excitement that inspires courage is above all a feeling of joy. These, then, were his most clearly manifest motivations. Deep down, however, he too may have had a dream of glory, as every man is entitled to have. A glory he was never to know.

As soon as word spread that Pinzón had joined Columbus, all the sailors of Palos became in favor of the voyage. Pinzón was a kind of guarantee to the men who knew him. They figured that with all his experience, he would keep an eye on that moody admiral on whom they would have to depend, come what may. This was an instinctive judgment on their part, and in any case a correct one. Columbus himself, in luring Pinzón to his side, had wanted to guarantee for himself the tutelage of experience. He never would have admitted it, and always kept it buried inside himself, but this was essentially why he sought the partnership in the first place.

Pinzón went around Palos, in all the taverns by the port, promising fortune and plenty to all who joined him. Across the ocean they would find houses with roofs of gold. None would ever again have to wallow in poverty. You will return rich and happy men, he told them, ridiculing those who had no intention of joining him as "miserable sardine-mongers." A certain Yáñez de Montilla, an old Palos sailor who lived well past this period and was still thriving at the time of the trials for Columbus's inheritance, made the following deposition in court: "Martín Alonso put much zeal into enlisting and encouraging crewmen, as though the discovery was to be for his and his children's sakes."

All this put an end to the possibility that the crew would be made up of jailbirds. Nevertheless, the very idea gave rise to the legend that Columbus set out to sea surrounded by a mob of criminals and incompetent sailors who wanted to turn back as soon as it became apparent that they would not reach land after the first few days of sailing. In actual fact, of the ninety men who took ship only four had cases pending with the law and had enlisted after hearing of the proclamation promising to suspend their sentences. The four had been condemned to death and had gone underground in the environs of Palos. One of them, a certain Bartolomé de Torres, sailor, had killed a man in a row in a port tavern. The other three were his friends and had helped him to escape. Pinzón knew all of them; they had sailed with him before. They behaved very well on the Columbus voyage. One of them, Juan de Moguer, later actually became a helmsman.

Of the ninety *tripulantes* (Spanish for "crew member" or "sailor" but very suggestive of toil and effort) we know the names of eighty-seven—almost the whole list of those who discovered America together with Columbus. The Spanish archives contain lists of public employees paid by the state treasury; since the wages of the sailors who took part in the expedition were paid by the Crown, the name of every sailor is faithfully recorded. Altogether, they cost 250,000 maravedis per month. The officers each received 2,000 per month, the sailors 1,000, and the *grumetes* (ship's boys and young servants) even less. A part of these sums was paid to the men in advance, while the rest was set aside for them to enjoy upon their return. On board there was of course nothing to buy or sell.

The crew was entirely Spanish with the exception of four individuals, five counting Columbus. Aside from the admiral, the other four foreigners were a mariner from Portugal, a Genoese by the name of Jacomo Rico, a Venetian and a Calabrian. As for the rest, the entire sailing force, not including a company of Basques on board Columbus's ship, was chosen one by one from the cream of the crop of young Andalusian sailors and from among friends of theirs who had sailed with them in the past and who came from such nearby ports as Cádiz and Seville. In other words, a great majority of the crew consisted of Pinzón's own men, enlisted by him and loyal to him, and in many cases coming from the same families, the most notable of which were the Niño and Pinzón families. The latter group, for example, had four representatives among the fleet's crews.

It may be a bit grandiose to call those three small sailing vessels—whose tonnage, taken altogether, measured little more than 200—a "fleet." But Columbus's three caravels—the *Santa Maria*, the *Pinta* and the *Niña*—were nevertheless three protagonists of the great voyage, and each, along with the famous names, had qualities, merits, defects and a history all its own. The two smaller ships, the *Pinta* and the *Niña*, had been furnished at the expense of the citizens of Palos, in compliance with the royal ordinance. The *Niña* had been built in the shipyards of Moguer, a few miles from Palos, and belonged to Juan Niño, who stayed on board and made the voyage with Columbus and the rest. The *Niña* was the lightest of the three ships, a real caravel in this sense—that is, a swift, very manageable ship suited for coastal traffic because of its shallow draft and, in Columbus's opinion, particularly good for the exploration of islands and coasts, which would be one of the missions of the fleet once it reached the end of its ocean voyage. In order to prepare so small a ship for the rigors of the high seas and the harshness of the Atlantic, the crew replaced the usual triangular sails—called lateen sails—with square ones, called *redondas* in Spanish. This operation involved the larger masts, the mainmast and the foremast. The mizzenmast retained its triangular sail while the bowsprit, at the end of the prow, was also given a square sail. The lateen sails were excellent at hugging the wind, but not so useful if the wind was blowing from behind, as Columbus expected it to do. The adjustment to square sails would make the going easier and safer amid the strong winds and large waves of the Atlantic.

The sails, however, were the only alterations made on these vessels, which were of a type that had remained by and large unchanged for at least two centuries. This type of vessel was still clearly medieval in structure, entirely empirical in nature, and built by craftsmen without the aid of studied, preconceived plans. Just as rudimentary were the navigational instruments, which served only to indicate one's course. In those days most sea voyages were made with the coast always in sight; if there were no other points of reference, one navigated with the always essential assistance of a compass, together with the perceptions and intuitions which came with experience and that special sense of the sea which had guided man for thousands of years. Columbus's fleet was indeed modest in size, but in terms of nautical quality it was downright second-rate. It was the men who made the voyage. Only their courage and the genius of the man leading them rendered it possible.

The *Niña*, for example, did not even change sails until it had reached the Canary Islands. And the only reason it did so was that it had already encountered some difficulties in sailing that first stretch of ocean, which was supposed to have been merely a prologue. The other requisitioned vessel, the *Pinta*, came from the river shipyards of Palos. It was a caravel of a clearly Pinzonian stamp, and carried officers, sailors and Pinzón family members on board. As a sailing ship it was excellent—perhaps not quite so fast as the *Niña*, but rather solid and well built. The homogeneity of its crew and the absolute authority with which Martín Alonso Pinzón commanded it made the *Pinta* an almost perfect ship, which could be trusted to sail smoothly through the unknown waters of the Atlantic.

Then there was the third caravel to go along with the two requisitioned ones. It was called the *Gallega,* since it had been built in Galicia and belonged to a Galician shipbuilder named Juan de la Cosa. It was in port in Palos at the time, waiting to be laden with cargo. Columbus came to an agreement with the owner—himself rather fond of sea adventures—and rented it from him with the queen's money. The *Gallega* was larger than the other two vessels. Its tonnage measured about one hundred; its hull was rather deep, and its bulwarks quite high. It was an Atlantic ship, more suited than the others to sailing on rough seas. Compared to the dimensions to which we are accustomed today, however, it was still little more than an oversized nutshell, roughly twenty-four meters in length and barely two or three meters longer than the Andalusian caravels.

As it was the largest ship in the fleet, Columbus made it the flagship and sailed on it. He also changed its name to the *Santa Maria*, in accordance with the devout custom of giving saintly attributes to vessels setting out to sea. *Santa Maria* became a famous name, perhaps the most famous ship's name in the world. But in fact, Columbus did not care much for the ship. The *Santa Maria* was squat and heavy, much less graceful in appearance than the *Niña* and the *Pinta*, not to mention less swift and manageable. Its draft was also greater than theirs, a drawback that was later to have serious consequences. Columbus's favorite of the ships was the *Niña*, which turned out to be the most durable of the three. The *Niña* was part of nearly all of Columbus's Atlantic crossings and continued to sail great distances even after the admiral's death.

I call all three of the ships caravels, though this is incorrect. I know this from having spoken with José Martínez-Hidalgo, director of the Naval Museum in Barcelona, considered the foremost historian of the seafaring arts during the centuries of Spanish conquest, which began in Columbus's era. Martínez-Hidalgo maintains—and there is every reason to believe him—that only the *Pinta* and the *Niña* were caravels, while the *Santa Maria* was a *nao,* a "ship." He wrote a book to back up this theory. I have learned many things from Martínez-Hidalgo, things I would not have known otherwise. But how can one speak of two caravels and a ship? I don't want to confuse the reader, and I'm hardly writing a treatise on navigation. Everyone has always thought of Columbus's three vessels as caravels. Columbus didn't discover America with two caravels and a ship; he did it with three caravels. Martínez-Hidalgo himself admits that the structural difference between the *Santa Maria* and the other two was minimal. I hope the illustrious scholar will forgive me my inaccuracy, but I shall continue to refer to all three vessels as caravels.

Martínez-Hidalgo, moreover, confessed to me that there are no extant documents or data of any sort that would permit a faithful reconstruction of Columbus's vessels. Nor are there any surviving paintings or drawings made from life which depict even one of the three "caravels." No one can really say exactly what they looked like. A number of replicas, however, have been constructed from circumstantial evidence, such as references in texts of the period and what is known of other caravels from the same period. In 1892, for the fourth centenary of America's discovery, a number of copies were reconstructed—one by Genoese scholars in Pegli, another for the Chicago exposition. All of them have details that are inaccurate or based on speculation. Martínez-Hidalgo himself reconstructed a *Santa Maria* about twenty years ago, but it was destroyed in a fire in the United States. He had another model made, which today is on display in Caracas.

One expert in these re-creations was a certain Julio Gallien, who also built a copy of the *Santa Maria* in 1927, for the Seville exposition. But these sorts of reconstructions seem hounded by bad luck. Gallien's model sank in the waters off Cartagena while being brought in to the docks for repairs. Gallien had a second copy made. It is still moored at the pier in Barcelona in front of the monument to Columbus.

It is indeed a large sailing vessel, with high bulwarks all painted black except for the floor timbers, which are red. With its bright contrast of colors, the *Santa Maria* of Barcelona looks like a beast imprisoned in a cage. It has only one upper deck, a rather narrow one, encumbered with ropes, masts, sails, deadeyes, water pumps, ballast kegs. At each end of the deck is a wooden structure, one at the prow, the other at the stern. The poop at the stern contained Columbus's cabin, a rather small and modestly furnished space with a canopy bed, a table, a chest containing navigational charts and documents, and a settle. On each of the room's three walls was a window.

Below this cabin was another small room for housing one or, at the most, two more officers.

The forecastle was even tinier. It served as a storeroom for sails, lines and other equipment, and perhaps as a protective space for the galley furnace during storms. There was no dormitory for the sailors. They would lie down to sleep in whatever space they could find, even in the open air if the weather was good. The place most fought over for sleeping was the hatchway, in the center of the ship. Since the deck was hog-backed—convex, that is—it was the only flat surface around, and therefore much desired.

Approximately forty men had to live, eat, work and sleep in those cramped spaces. The figure may seem a bit high, especially in light of modern-day crews or even the size of crew needed to man a sailing vessel in times before Columbus. It was the square sails that necessitated the greater number of hands. The spars had to be mounted onto the masts, and men had to climb up the masts to do this. Much more labor yet was needed for clewing up and disengaging the sails, which previously could be raised directly from the deck. The living conditions amid such crowding were, needless to say, quite harsh. Wooden ships were always letting in water, and the *Santa Maria* suffered not a little from this problem. The drainage pumps had to be used every day, yet in spite of this the bilge was always filling up with refuse water, which teemed with insects and sometimes emitted a terrible stench.

If we consider that the royal ordinance was delivered from the pulpit of St. George's Church in late May and the three caravels set sail on August 3— just over two months later, despite all the complications presented by the acquisition of the ships and the enlistment of the crew—the swiftness with which the expedition was prepared seems almost miraculous. After living so many years at a pace nearly exasperating in its slowness, Columbus was suddenly moving as fast as humanly possible. His innate energy had not run out during the wait. It was like a compressed coil, ready to spring any moment. He swept right past all obstacles and overcame, one by one, all the unforeseen last-minute problems. He was anxious to break free from anything that might hold him back. He didn't want to be caught unaware by a summer season too far advanced—nor, indeed, by the increasing weight of the years on his shoulders.

The last task was to procure a year's provisions—food, water and wine enough to last through a nonstop return voyage in the case of failure. Also purchased was "crude, cheap merchandise of the kind best suited for trade with primitive peoples"—for example, glass pearls, small mirrors, brooches, bells, colored hats. The African natives of the Gulf of Guinea had taken to such knickknacks with a great deal of enthusiasm. There was no reason to believe that Indians, Japanese and Chinese would behave any differently. The ships' holds were ballasted with balls of stone and lead which, if necessary, could also be used with the light artillery on board—iron bombards mounted on gun carriages on the deck and small cannons, called falconets, placed on the bulwarks to repel any unlikely assailants trying to board the ships. There was not a single man-at-arms among any of the crews; the only weapons the men possessed were a few crossbows and muskets. This was not a fleet equipped for combat and conquest, but for discovery and exploration.

By August 2 everything was ready. Thirty-nine men boarded the *Santa Maria*, twenty-seven the *Pinta* and thirty-four the *Niña*; these figures include officers, sailors, ship's boys and those persons with special duties on board the *Santa Maria*. All the men attended mass at the Church of St. George before departure. The caravels were anchored in a kind of lock in a branch of the Río Tinto which at the time turned toward the sea but today is underground. The church rises up just a short walk away from that point, on a slight incline in the terrain. This is the side of the church with the "door to the pier" through which Columbus's sailors entered to say their last prayers, and then exited to board their ships.

Few, no doubt, got much sleep that night, what with all the thoughts, fantasies and fears teeming in their heads—images of palaces with gold-tiled roofs, and of infinite, mysterious stretches of water, the Atlantic abyss that had to be crossed before they saw any riches. Each man's heart must have been racing, for any number of reasons, as always happens in life's moments of separation or change; and their beats must have been as great as those of a giant's heart, since they were about to take their leave of an entire epoch, which would no longer be the Middle Ages after their voyage, since they were on the verge of changing no less than the world itself.

9

The Day of the Halcyon

The ninety men about to set sail on the ocean were up on their feet and on the decks of their ships before sunrise. It had been a long, anxious August night, the sultry heat bearing down on the river, the ships and their crew. The darkness was beginning to fade in the corners of the sky, but there was not a breath of wind in the air. The first glow of the approaching dawn appeared as though nailed to the horizon. The sailors knew the meaning of this omen. It was the day of the halcyon. The day of the halcyon is the moment when the birds that we usually call sea gulls make their nests at sea out of algae foliage. The delicacy of this operation demands that air and sea be completely still.

The day's first light revealed a flat, steely-colored, opaque sea. Columbus was disturbed by this. His adventure was beginning without the wind's blessing, and on a Friday morning no less—not a good portent for navigators. Everyone stood around with heads bent back, gazing at the motionless sky, which seemed palpably heavy. The fierce heat was all one could feel, the torrid grip of the rising temperature. No one knew what next to expect. Perhaps the sun, in whose rays they would founder. But as soon as the dawn's first beams announced that the sun was about to appear, Columbus sprang into action. He had the moorings loosed; the repetition of commands from deck to deck and refrains that the sailors sang as they braced the rigging finally broke the silence. People had gathered along the riverbank, friends and relatives left behind, a group of women young and old. They shouted good-bye to the crews, also breaking the oppressive quiet of the day of the halcyon.

At exactly six o'clock, in a strong, steady voice, Columbus ordered the men to weigh anchor "in the name of Jesus." He had his admiral's banner hoisted on the *Santa Maria,* a flag bearing a dark-green cross against a white background. Above the arms of the cross were the initials F and Y, for

Ferdinand and Isabella. The banner, however, would not unfurl without the wind's help. The caravels advanced very slowly, sails empty and limp. They were forced to use their oars to go down the river, riding the current created by the receding tide.

Lazily, one after another, the three ships passed beneath the walls of the monastery. The friars were saying their offices, the prayers constituting the first of the canonical hours, recited at the beginning of the day. Columbus knelt down when they passed, and many joined him. Others removed whatever they were wearing on their heads, which in those days was usually the customary red-wool sailor's cap. By eight o'clock the ships had reached the Saltes Bar, which separates the mouth of the river from the open sea. They entered the so-called Canal of the Holy Father, passing between sand dunes scattered with pines. The outlet was rather tight, and must have seemed like Europe's last embrace to those about to leave it. Before long the ninety men found themselves alone on the ocean.

They immediately came upon a rather strong breeze, blowing contrary to the direction in which they were headed. The omens of the day of the halcyon had been wrong. The crew unfurled the sails, tightening the triangular ones and bracing the spars of the square ones—that is, turning them as much as possible, as the tack of the bowline demanded. The fleet sailed southward, trying to stay fairly close to the coast, in the direction of Cádiz and Gibraltar, in order to proceed as swiftly as possible. Toward evening, however, the wind suddenly changed direction, and the caravels, shifting direction to southwest to head straight for the Canary Islands, could now loose all their sails and move much faster. By now they were on the high seas, all land having vanished from sight. The favorable wind lifted everyone's spirits. Perhaps it would be a swift voyage, they thought, shorter than initially anticipated. Did Columbus dare entertain the same thoughts? In Cardinal d'Ailly's *Imago Mundi,* which Columbus took on board the *Santa Maria* with him, it is estimated that to cross the ocean between Europe and India it would take only a few days, *paucis diebus.* This was just the beginning. Columbus noted in his ship's log the distance covered: 60 miles. A modest advance toward the desired goal, which was much farther off than his hope would have it.

But already his life had changed. Columbus had left behind him not only dry land, but an entire period of uncertainty and waiting. He was in his own realm now, on the ocean he had dreamed so much about, his ship's prow pointing westward. Anyone who has ridden aboard a sailing craft knows how

the vessel's sounds, amid the silence of the sea, invigorate the spirit: the wood
creaking with the boat's rocking and the groans of the ropes pulled taut form
a kind of gentle refrain, together with the hissing wind inside the sails, the
waves breaking against the broadsides, and the shouts and echoes resounding
across the deck. It is a familiar yet mysterious universe, an unlikely blend of
motion and stasis in the boundless province of the sea, that strange, liquid
world that is changing and recomposing its forms at every moment, always
the same yet always different. Like life itself. If Columbus looked back on the
years that had dragged on between one court and the next, amid disputes and
refusals, how could he not have felt himself a man reborn, awakened from a
dream that had seemed endless? The world of trickery and deceit now lay
behind him. Before him beckoned the whispers of the unknown, the invention
of the future. Had providence marked out these roads?

Columbus was convinced of it. But if one hasn't the boldness to understand oneself, no outside assistance will ever suffice. This sort of courage is
different from the kind that overcomes fear in a man. Columbus's boldness
was of a much rarer sort, since he had discovered its roots within himself by
cutting himself off from everything that was not properly his own: affections,
ties, memories, the past—even the women he had loved and the city that had
spawned him. Only the future existed now. He himself was the future.

The first leg of the voyage, the passage to the Canary Islands, was like a
prologue to the unknown. The real adventure had yet to begin. To the Andalusian sailors the trip to the Canaries had by now become almost routine. The
islands had been a Spanish colony for more than half a century, and most of
the men had made the trip countless times. There was no mystery in those
seas, nor in their winds and expanses. Columbus, however, felt compelled to
choose this course. In Toscanelli's charts, as in his own, Cipango was situated
at the same latitude as the "Islands of the Blessed," as the Canaries had been
called since Pliny had first designated them as the Hesperides of myth. In
order to reach Cipango and the Asian coast, then, one only had to set off
from the Canaries and head straight across the ocean, due west. This was to
be the new route to the Indies.

The passage from Spain to the Canaries, however, was not without its
troublesome aspects, such as crosswinds and rough waters. It was the ocean,
after all. The Spanish seamen of the early 1400s had nicknamed this stretch of
ocean *el golfo de las yeguas,* the gulf of the mares, because their boats were
often laden with mares on their way to the Canaries for breeding—perhaps
overladen, since they often sank when storms swelled the waves. Columbus's

three caravels, however, stood the test well. The two smaller ones, the *Pinta* and the *Niña*, sailed along at faster speeds than their flagship. They were often forced to shorten sail just so as not to get too far ahead of the *Santa Maria*, which cruised at a slower speed. The ships had a system of signals designed to keep the fleet together. Sticking out from the stern of each caravel was an iron basin in which fires were made. At night, the flames could be seen from a good distance; during the day, with the proper ingredients, long plumes of smoke were created which were equally visible from a distance. Sometimes various different *fumos* or *fuegos* were made in succession, and their number indicated whether this meant to change course, to trim or to let out the sails, or to pull closer to the flagship to receive spoken instructions, shouted from one deck to the other. Aside from these, only one other kind of signal was prearranged—the shot of a cannon, which would signal the sighting of land, past the Canaries, on the other side of the ocean.

The three caravels, their white sails unfurled, must have looked like birds in flight across the expanse. The men steering the ships knew how to sail the ocean. Comparing their duties with those of today's navies, we could say that each ship had three officers: the captain, who had disciplinary authority over all men on board and their respective duties; the ship's master, a kind of second-in-command with direct control of the crew and responsibility for the sails and rigging; and the helmsman, a first mate whose duty it was to guide the navigation itself, to estimate the distance traveled, to chart the ship's course and to anticipate how much time would be needed. On the *Santa Maria*, where Columbus was captain as well as commander of the fleet, the ship's master was Juan de la Cosa and the helmsman Peralonso Niño, another member of the Niño family. On the *Pinta* the captain was Martín Alonso Pinzón, the ship's master Francisco Pinzón, and the helmsman Rafael Sarmiento. Another Pinzón, Vicente Yáñez, was the *Niña*'s captain, Juan Niño the ship's master and Sancho Ruiz the helmsman.

In addition to the mariners aboard the three ships there were a number of "civilians" with various different responsibilities, most of them on board the *Santa Maria*, making it the most crowded of the three caravels. Columbus had insisted on bringing an interpreter with him, convinced as he was of eventually reaching the land of the Great Khan. His name was Luis de Torres and he knew Hebrew and Aramaic, the two languages then considered the matrix of all tongues. Columbus also brought along his old friend from Córdoba, Diego de Harana, the cousin of Beatrice. He had had him appointed *alguazil de la armada,* chief police officer of the fleet. Harana's task was to punish those who transgressed the disciplinary code, and he had subordinates on the other two caravels. The notary and secretary of the fleet was Rodrigo de Escobedo, to whom fell the task of drawing up all official deeds, in the name of the Crown, for all newly discovered lands of which they took possession. Two other men of the court sailed together with him on the *Santa Maria*: inspector Rodrigo Sánchez, whose task was to keep an eye on expenditures and make sure that the Crown was receiving its proper—and presumably abundant—share in gold or precious stones; and a *repostero* or major-domo of the king, Pedro Gutiérrez. Actually, Gutiérrez had come along of his own accord and had no specific duties, inasmuch as Columbus already had at his disposal a steward and a page assigned to his personal service.

This *repostero* in fact was the only unnecessary passenger on board. He may have been a spy for Ferdinand, or for those courtiers who numbered among Columbus's enemies. Everyone else had a very precise responsibility: each ship had a surgeon, even though the fleet was bursting with health; an overseer assigned to watch over all sails and rigging and to make sure, for example, that rats did not eat the sails during stopovers at ports; a store-keeper in charge of victuals, the galley furnace and the training of ship's boys in the refrain that they had to recite during the changing of the guard.

The changing of the guard occurred every four hours, and was carried out by groups of roughly fifteen sailors at a time. Each group rotated in four-hour periods of duty and four-hour periods of rest, day and night. The first guard was mounted at seven in the morning and recited a Lord's Prayer, a Hail Mary and a Gloria to begin the day with God's blessing. The second was mounted at eleven o'clock, which was also the hour of the only hot meal served on board. Those about to go on duty were the first to eat, followed by those coming off duty. The basic foods were salted meat, cheese, barreled sardines and anchovies, ship's biscuit or hardtack stored in the dryest part of the ship, soups of chick-peas, lentils or beans, sometimes with a bit of rice. During the rest periods the sailors would fish with lines, and if they had good luck they would eat fresh fish for their hot meal, always a special treat. Of the men on duty, two would stand watch, one on the prow, the other in the crow's nest; the rest would maneuver the sails (when commanded to do so), keep the sheets and braces in order, and on some days tighten the ropes, which have a tendency to slacken. They also had to keep the decks always clean and see to all those things that keep a ship in good working order. The hardest shift was the last one of the night, from 3 A.M. until morning, the so-called "graveyard shift"—cold, silent and peopled with shadows.

At sea it is easy to lose one's sense of time. The day's rhythm was marked by these changes of the guard, whose regularity eventually became habit for all. The duration of each shift was measured with an hourglass containing half an hour's worth of sand. In the Spanish spoken by Columbus's sailors it was called an *ampolleta.* As soon as it emptied, a ship's boy would turn it over, and after eight turns the shift was changed. The men on board did not think of time in terms of hours, but in terms of *ampolletas.* Or else in terms of canonical time—terce, vespers, and compline, the hours of prayer that culminated in the *Salve Regina* sung by one and all at sunset, each in his own dissonant manner. They were hardly choirboys, these mariners, but they sang nonetheless, each according to his voice and conscience. (Columbus prayed alone in his *toldilla.* He was the only one allowed a direct dialogue with the Infinite.)

What sorts of instruments were used in the navigation? The only really essential one was the compass—which is actually the case even today, with the exception that nowadays we have countless electronic precision instruments to go along with the compass, whereas in Columbus's day they pretty much relied on that simple guide alone. Their compass was actually not much different from the kind currently in use, consisting of a disc-shaped compass card divided into 32 sections or rhumbs, the 32 points of the horizon, marked by triangles, lozenges or arrows. The only differences in today's compasses are their suspension and the better quality of their magnetic needles. Columbus's compass was inside a bowl and fixed to a pivot in such a manner as to be able to rotate with the ship's movements. The northward-pointing needle was magnetized with a piece of loadstone which the captain kept in his own care and treated as if it were the most priceless of treasures. The point signaled on the compass indicated the direction in which the ship was moving. Such has been the case for centuries.

Affixed to the *bitácora*—the binnacle—was a little hood which was placed over the compass to protect it from the wind and rain, and a small oil lamp to illuminate it at night. There was another compass on board, called the steering compass, next to the tiller for use by the helmsman. There were also many spare compasses and needles, at least twenty. The sailors could not "read" the compass, the names of the winds, the number of degrees or the signs of the cardinal points, since the compasses of the time never had any of this information written on them, for the simple reason that the sailors didn't know how to read. One distinguished the various directions from one another by the width, form and color of the various triangles, lozenges or arrows. The sailors knew these symbols by heart. Only the north was marked differently from the rest, using the fleur-de-lis as its unchanging symbol.

In order to determine the ship's location at a given moment, the captain had to know two other factors in addition to the direction indicated by the compass: time and speed. The *ampolleta,* the hourglass, measured time. Speed, on the other hand, was determined by the use of a little "boat" which the sailors called a *corredera,* and which corresponded more or less directly to the log chip and line. It was nothing more than a floating piece of wood furnished with a thin plate of lead, which was thrown out into the water attached to a line, a thin rope tied into knots at regular intervals. The number of knots that passed within a given period of time told the ship's rate of motion. This is why to this very day a ship's speed is measured in knots.

Columbus, as far as we know, did not use a *corredera.* He measured speed with his eyes, closely watching the velocity at which the waves breaking against the prow reached the stern. Or he would calculate it from the time it took for the foam raised in the ship's wake to disappear. He also tried to reckon the strength of the wind by studying the behavior of the waves. He had become accustomed to watching others do this over the years, on a wide variety of ships. The nautical instruments of the time were of precious little use. They were rather crude and rudimentary. The type of navigation practiced by Columbus was based on personal judgment. Nevertheless, the methods he employed constituted 99 percent of the art of navigation itself. Though it is true that Columbus had never commanded a ship before setting off into the unknown ocean, he had learned a great deal from observation and possessed a great store of experience and intuition.

In an excellent book devoted to a study of the seafaring talents demonstrated by Columbus, Jean Charcot wrote that "Columbus possessed a *sense of the sea,* that mysterious intelligence which in the glory days of sailing enabled captains lacking proper scientific knowledge to find, as it were by sense of smell, their course in the boundless expanses of the Seven Seas." Charcot was an old and learned seaman with a degree in medicine from the Sorbonne, but he spent his life exploring the ocean's polar routes in his famous *Pourquoi-Pas?,* a ship that went down in history. He died at sea in 1936, at the age of seventy. Charcot was one who knew whereof he spoke. Between his writings on Columbus and those of another illustrious expert on Columbus's navigations, the American Samuel Eliot Morison, there's not much one can add on this subject. Morison carefully reconstructed the course followed by Columbus in 1492, retracing it step by step and measuring it with modern-day instruments. His conclusion was that Columbus, who calculated the ship's speed by watching bubbles of foam across a vast distance of three thousand nautical miles—a jaunt of nearly 4,000 regular miles—was off by only about five percent in his estimation of the distance. (I have put four years into the preparation and writing of this book, four years which I have spent, so to speak, with Columbus. Yet I still cannot get used to the idea that merely by sniffing the air he could arrive at almost the exact same conclusions that we must depend on machines to give us. This has remained, for me, almost unbelievable.)

The method that Columbus used in mapping out a ship's course is called "navigation by reckoning." Another method is "celestial navigation," also called "astronavigation." The latter consists in determining the ship's position by observing the positions of the heavenly bodies. Astronavigation was already in existence in Columbus's day. Indeed, it was an ancient method: Ulysses navigated by observing the stars, and both Homer and Virgil sang of the miracles of sea and sky. But the routes were familiar, all of them contained within that fishbowl of water called the Mediterranean. Columbus was confronting far vaster solitudes and expanses. To head into the unknown under the guidance of the stars would have demanded precision instruments and a broad knowledge of the heavens. Columbus possessed neither. Looking to the sky would not suffice to get him across the ocean. Columbus made his journey with his eyes fixed more on the sea than on the sky.

Nevertheless, he liked to pretend he was an expert on astronavigation. He had "taken in" a good bit of the sun on his voyage to Guinea, and often spent time observing the altitude of the North Star, which enables one to determine a ship's latitude. When deeply engrossed in these calculations, he could sense the admiration of those watching him. Astronomy is a total mystery to the uninitiated. To them, to be able to survey the stars is like being endowed with visionary powers. Columbus liked this aura of enigma; it was just another part of his fantasy.

He had of course acquired some knowledge of astronomy and astronomical geography. He had made use of this knowledge, without much success, during the disputes at Salamanca. Although his understanding was, to be sure, only partial and even sometimes confused, it is true on the other hand that reliable precision instruments for observing the heavenly bodies did not exist in his day, or had not at least been introduced into practice. And without precision instruments the science of astronomy may be fascinating indeed, but it does not lead very far.

Columbus navigated with a quadrant, and on his first ocean voyage perhaps an astrolabe as well. The astrolabe is really nothing more than an improved quadrant capable of providing more particularized, but at the same time more complex information. What kind of information? By means of two little holes bored through a strip of wood, the quadrant enabled one to align the star under observation—usually the North Star—onto a vertical plane with respect to the water's surface. When the star appeared in the frame of the two holes, one could read an estimate of its altitude, indicated on the quadrant's graduated ring by a plumb line. But how difficult it must have been to keep the relationship between ship and star always balanced and consistent! The ship's pitching and rolling was always moving the target star out of view. Sometimes it was very difficult to find it again, and then to reestablish the correct positions on the level of the two small holes, aimed at a vast stretch of sky from the rolling deck of a sailing vessel. (We shall not discuss the astrolabe. It was too complicated an instrument for Columbus, and it seems indeed that he did not know how to use it. We have no indication of its being among the equipment used for his other voyages after the discovery of America. Those who have sung the astrolabe's praises, saying that Columbus made it to America thanks to it, did not know Columbus the man. The discovery of America was the fruit of imagination, not of technics. It is for this very reason that Columbus is a major figure in history.)

The truth of the matter is that astronomy in the late Middle Ages was studied only by men of science. Their studies had made considerable progress in the last few decades of the fifteenth century, but these advances remained confined to the realm of theory. Seamen, even the best of them, did not apply astronomical methods in navigation. And Columbus for his part did not use them to guide him across the ocean. He used astronomy only in certain calculations of observation, some of which turned out to be quite valuable and even innovative. He did not, however, make use of the quadrant and the stars until after his discovery of America. Let us not forget that he was a cartographer. After arriving in America he wanted to determine with as much accuracy as possible the geography of the new coastlines and the positions of the islands, and then trace this information onto the maps that he was making. At this point the quadrant became very useful to him. The instrument's precision increases when it is used in a harbor in calm seas, or better yet, on land. In sum, it is safe to conclude that to cross the ocean Columbus navigated for the most part by reckoning, and resorted very little to astronavigation. Astronomy was of much more use to him as a geographical tool that aided him in tracing the outlines and giving real contours to the places he had discovered.

All of this becomes very clear in the ship's log that Columbus wrote very methodically and carefully on his voyage, starting the day of departure from Palos. Though he probably kept similar logs on his later voyages, this is the only one that has survived, and we are fortunate that it is the log of the first crossing. I believe it safe to call it the most fascinating nautical journal ever written. Columbus lived in an era of great voyages—those of Dias, Magellan, da Gama and Cabot, among others. But none of these memorable voyages was described with as much precision and richness of detail as his; or, especially, with as much freshness of voice, that breath of poetry which stirred in Columbus's restless spirit.

Columbus's ship's log was not handed down to posterity in its original form. Upon returning from his first voyage he turned his notebooks over to the king and queen so that they in turn could pass them on to experts for study, all the while keeping their contents secret, as though it were a matter of state. Indeed, all knowledge and information pertaining to the new discoveries was regarded as such. The sovereigns promised to return to Columbus his ship's log after having copies transcribed. It is not too clear what happened next—whether or how the texts got confused and who got what texts. It would appear that Isabella sent one of the copies to Columbus and kept the original. It also seems fairly certain that Columbus's eldest son Diego, who as a young boy was put up together with his father by the friars at La Rábida, took his copy of the log to Santo Domingo where he resided as governor, not to mention viceroy, by hereditary right. (The viceroy's palace in Santo Domingo is still standing. In the surrounding gardens is the statue of Isabella mentioned earlier.) Las Casas, who wrote the first biography of Columbus, consulted Diego's copy of the log when he was in Santo Domingo as a missionary. Las Casas was a very meticulous, precise researcher, but a very slow one as well. He copied some passages from the diary verbatim; others he referred to indirectly. He did not, in any case, leave out anything of great importance, and since the copy of the log in Diego's possession was eventually lost and no others are known still to exist, Las Casas's book is the only source that enables us to piece it back together. It is, nevertheless, a summary revised twenty years later. If it still shows flashes of brilliance and has preserved some of the vivid sense of the things described, the credit must go entirely to Columbus. Imagine what the original text must have been like, and what a rich patrimony of information we should have at our disposal if the other logs written on the subsequent voyages, with their mixed fortunes, had also survived!

From Columbus's log we know that the three caravels took only six days to reach the Canaries from Palos; usually the voyage took eight to ten days. This means that the sailing went exceptionally well for the three ships, that favorable winds swept them swiftly through waters which are often intemperate and rough. The ships were unaccustomed to the Atlantic's swell, winds and waves. The journey, as we have said, was swift and fortunate. But fortune's wheel suddenly began to turn shortly before arrival. On August 7, with the Canary Islands already in view—the coastlines breaking the line of the horizon and, above them, the tall peaks rimmed with clouds—the *Pinta*'s rudder came off its hinges. Pinzón signaled with smoke that he was in difficulty, and Columbus at once pulled his ship alongside and boarded the crippled caravel. In his log he states that Pinzón suspected sabotage. Pinzón had noticed some strange gatherings of people at the very moment of the fleet's departure from Palos and suspected that the caravel's owner himself, Cristóbal Quintero, may not have wanted his vessel to sail beyond the Canaries, for fear of losing it. Quintero had had himself signed up with the crew as a sailor. A small arrangement with one of his men would have been enough to bring about a breakdown serious enough to take the *Pinta* out of the picture.

Pinzón was by nature inclined to distrust others. He was determined to fix the rudder, and he succeeded. Columbus praised him for this in his log, calling him "a brave man of very shrewd intelligence." Their agreement was apparently working rather well. The very next day, however, a day of high winds and rough seas, the incident repeated itself. Emergency repairs in the middle of the Atlantic do not hold out well. This time the *Pinta*'s rudder was almost completely torn off. The vessel started sagging to leeward and began to ship water. There was no way to assist it. The other two ships continued on their course, which was nearing the end of its first stage, with the understanding that they would all meet back up at the port of Las Palmas in the Grand Canary Island, where there was a shipyard properly equipped to forge iron and to repair any kind of damage.

But the *Santa Maria* and the *Niña*, which reached the waters of the main island on August 8, had their own run-in with ill luck when head winds began to push them out to sea. The *Pinta* was by now out of sight, and Columbus had actually decided to look for another caravel to reform the fleet. Apparently there was one on its way to Gomera, a smaller island not far from the Grand Canary. It was another Galician ship like the *Santa Maria*, of lesser tonnage but of proven durability, having been built for ocean voyages to the Atlantic archipelagoes known to exist at the time. For this reason Columbus set sail for Gomera, which he reached on August 12, a Sunday. But this was not the only reason: Gomera is the greenest and most fertile of the Canary Islands, and he hoped to replenish his provisions of water, wood and victuals. Moreover, Gomera was governed by a woman he knew, Beatrice de Bobadilla, an intimate friend of the Marquise de Moya and frequent visitor to Isabella's court. Columbus had made her acquaintance in Santa Fé at the most decisive moment in his life, and had sensed that this new Beatrice supported him. Beatrice de Bobadilla was young, a widow and governor of the island. She attracted the admiration of everyone, starting with King Ferdinand who had focused politely amorous attentions on her. She also by coincidence had ties to a circle of important Genoese merchants headed by Francisco Riberol, who was originally from Rivarolo in Val Polcévera, just a bit upstream from Genoa. In sum, it seems safe to say that Columbus's stop in Gomera was not an arbitrary decision.

He stayed on there for many days, prey to the gnawing anxiety that autumn was approaching, itching finally to cross this ocean that washed the shores at his feet, and wanting to act on his intuition that the winds at that moment were favorable to his mission. But the Galician ship had not yet arrived, nor had the lady-governor with the lovely black hair. The *Pinta*, moreover, had still not yet reached Las Palmas, and this delay distressed Columbus a great deal. After a seemingly auspicious beginning, the voyage now unexpectedly appeared in danger of running aground.

Days and nights passed as Columbus waited anxiously in the castle of San Sebastián, where Beatrice de Bobadilla made her home. Only a small ruin of it still stands, the only wing of the building that has withstood the centuries. It is known as the *Torre del Conde*. In his log, Columbus recounts that he met "many honorable gentlemen of Spain" at the castle, frequenters of Beatrice's court (which was always open), themselves awaiting her return. A number of these guests came from the island of Hierro (then called Ferro), the westernmost of the Canaries, the one farthest out in the open sea. Knowing what goals Columbus had before him, they were quick to tell him how on certain days when the sky was brighter than usual, the contours of a blue island would emerge on the horizon in the remote distance. It would appear and disappear, like the flashes of a signal. Clearly these were fictions, illusions. Nevertheless, they whetted Columbus's anxious desire to leave.

He lasted a week in Gomera. He had in the meantime sent a number of his men to Las Palmas with instructions for Pinzón. Not one had returned with a reply. Finally he decided to go and see for himself. When he arrived in the port of Las Palmas and did not see the *Pinta* at the piers, he was furious and desperate. He may have suspected treachery of some sort, since eleven days had passed since he took leave of the *Pinta*, which at the time was in sight of the islands.

The *Pinta* arrived the very next day, August 24. It had gone adrift for twelve whole days, with the crew all the while going through exhausting maneuvers to set it back on course, which it continually kept losing. The transition from delay to haste was a frantic one. Columbus and Pinzón practically took the shipyard by storm, and in less than a week the rudder's pintles were rebuilt, put back in place, tested and set aright with great precision. The planking that had given way was repaired. Smiths, carpenters and caulkers were immediately put to work. When it was all over the *Pinta* seemed good as new, and Columbus gave up the idea of replacing it with another ship. He also spoke with the *Niña*'s owner, Juan Niño, and persuaded him to change the ship's sails from triangular to square, so that all three caravels could from that point on take on the ocean with the same kind of rigging. By the first of September all the new arrangements had been completed. The work had been done rapidly, but then some twenty days had already passed since their arrival in the Canaries.

They had to return to Gomera for new provisions. The three caravels arrived there on September 2. Beatrice de Bobadilla had finally returned, and her company cheered Columbus up a bit. She received him very warmly. Judging from his encounters with the various women in his life, Columbus must have been a fascinating man. Everyone always took an immediate liking to him, and women were inclined by instinct to accept him with open arms— certainly more inclined than he was in their regard, or more than he initially intended to be. But each of them did it in a different way: Doña Moniz with her youthful freshness; Beatrice of Córdoba with naïveté and trust; the Marquise de Moya with fiery passion; and Isabella—dare we say?—with a queenly reserve which perhaps masked a few flutters of the heart. And Beatrice of Gomera? Much has been made of her relationship to Columbus, the subject of whispers even at the time and fertile ground for invention in the centuries that followed. There may have been something between them. It is possible that the lady governor and the explorer did more than exchange polite smiles. On his second voyage, Columbus returned to Gomera and saw Beatrice de Bobadilla again. Perhaps it wasn't until this second visit that they finally dropped all inhibitions. Beatrice was an energetic, impetuous woman. She always knew what she wanted. Columbus was no womanizer, but neither was he much accustomed to saying no. I can judge no more than the reader in these matters. One may speculate as one likes: there are no documents, only the real lives of these men and women, whose blood coursed through their veins as ours does through our own.

One thing, at least, we do know: Beatrice de Bobadilla did everything in her power to guarantee excellent reinforcements at the best possible price. The caravels were stuffed with meats, flour, cheeses. The sailors went around the island collecting wood and water. Gomera had thickly wooded terrain and a freshwater river running through the island. The day before departure everyone went to confess their sins and hear the Mass in the Church of the Assumption, which sits atop the esplanade of the port amid cobblestone streets and low white houses. The little square in front of the church still has a few shade trees which provide refuge from the hot, humid climate. The Tropic of Cancer passes not far from the Canary Islands.

A full moon was expected for the night of September 6. Columbus, however, did not wait for the moon to rise. He was informed that a few Portuguese caravels had been spotted passing by to the north of the island, perhaps to spy, perhaps to wait somewhere in ambush. They probably had been assigned the task of determining whether or not Columbus and his fleet were headed toward African coasts, which the Portuguese considered an area of ocean that belonged to them alone. The admiral turned over and over in his mind the memory of his uneven relations with King John, who had initially taken an interest in his project then rejected it, and to whom he had later written again when it seemed that all hope was lost. John had responded by inviting him back to Portugal, an invitation to which Columbus had never replied. Columbus had sought aid from Portugal, and here he was in the service of Castile. Did King John perhaps want revenge?

Such questions as these troubled Columbus's thoughts. There was only one way to dispel them, and that was to leave as soon as possible. At the first hint of sunlight on the morning of September 6, 1492, the fleet weighed anchor and unfurled the sails. The command to the pilots and coxswains was simple and precise: due west. This meant straight ahead, into the ocean, all the way to the end. The immortal voyage was beginning.

10

⚴

The Immortal Voyage

The journey started out at a slow, almost cautious pace. The ships did not go right out and confront the waters; rather, they tested them first, like someone who has just set foot on unknown ground and takes his first steps with circumspection. There seemed nothing terribly unusual about the surrounding landscape of water and sky, except perhaps for the thrill of sailing along an edge of the globe never before explored. It was like looking out from a balcony onto a view that had never been witnessed before.

This is how the first day passed, slowly and lazily, with the distant shapes of the Canaries still in view. The ships barely moved on the windless sea. It wasn't until the end of the day, when the sun began to set on the horizon, that the first wonder of the long voyage presented itself. A great blanket of purple stretched across the ocean, the rays of the sunset beaming straight into the sailors' eyes as their prow pointed due west.

The wonder was not in the fact that the sun was setting, but that it was setting with such splendid effect, with a purple fire that brightened the sky with unexpected shades of color. Many of Columbus's sailors had, like him, sailed in the past to regions near the equator along the African coast. But there the spaces were not so great, nor the sky so deep as they were here, where all was so totally surrounded by water as to seem immersed in it. Above all, the direction was different. In Africa, one sailed away from the sunset, whereas these sailors were decidedly going toward it, as though their ships were heading straight into the sun. It would be the same for many long days and nights—how many, only God knew. As there were no boundaries before them, they might have thought that the splendid light that had accompanied them the first night would accompany them forever. As the sails plunged into that flaming glare, the entire fleet, from crow's nests to bulwarks, took on the color of the tropical sunset. No doubt it conjured the color of gold in the sailors' minds, touching the hopes that had driven many of them to risk their lives by confronting the unknown.

The unknown. For the moment it showed itself to be a rather calm, almost friendly realm. The sea was as smooth as a young girl's cheek, the winds so mild and insubstantial that by the second day of sailing the fleet was heaved to. The lull continued until the morning of September 9, which was a Sunday. A northeasterly breeze, strong enough to get the caravels moving from their current position from which the Canaries were still in view, began to blow as soon as the sun rose. Before midday the last trace of the island of Hierro, the westernmost of the archipelago, disappeared behind the horizon. Fernando Columbus, in narrating his father's exploits, described the scene as follows: "As Hierro disappeared, so did the rest of the world." Many hearts sank at that moment. Some of the younger mates, many still boys, went pale in the face. They were now in the ocean's void. There seemed to be nothing left behind them, and nothing before them except the purple blanket of the sunset. All the rest was water, sea, ocean. And a few light clouds in the sky— the sign, still unknown, of trade winds.

Let us talk for a moment about these mysterious, magnificent winds. It was they that carried Columbus's ships across the Atlantic. At the time, one traveled the seas only on the strength of the air flapping inside the sails, and a lot depended on the force and direction of this invisible push. Hence the importance of discussing here the winds that Columbus encountered and used to his advantage. Most historians and chroniclers have bent over backward in praise of the trade winds that favored Columbus in his Atlantic crossing. To read some of them, one almost gets the impression that it was the trade winds themselves, and not Columbus, that discovered America. Other writers speak of them as though *they* were the first to discover them; as for the rest, it's an endless procession of exaltation, encomium and eulogy for those fascinating winds.

All this is off the mark. I for one do not believe that Columbus was unaware of the existence of the trade winds. These much-lauded winds have one great virtue: they always blow in the same direction, never changing, every day of every month of every year. This invariability is unique among winds. The ancients, whose nautical knowledge was limited to the Mediterranean, were completely ignorant of the existence of constant winds. The Mediterranean's siroccos, southwesterlies, *garbinos,* northeasterlies, north winds and mistrals are all variable winds. They appear, disappear, and sometimes merge with each other. Not the trade winds. The trade winds are forever blowing in the same direction.

Even their locations are specific and unchanging, which is quite extraordinary for something that is nothing more than a barely perceptible movement of air. The trade winds' running track girds the globe at the tropical latitudes, shifting slightly to higher or lower parallels with changes in season. As for their direction, they blow only from east to west—the very direction Columbus had chosen to take—and within the very strip of ocean in which Columbus had chosen to sail. It was as though a hand had appeared out of nowhere to push him and help him along, a sure and guiding hand.

Did Columbus know about the trade winds? Where the sea is concerned, one knows for certain only what one has experienced. Nobody at that point in time had ever known any invisible hand to push him along for thousands of miles—not even the Viking fishermen when they made their hypothetical (though likely) crossings, or any other Nordic sea voyagers, since at those latitudes there are no trade winds. And even if some other mariner had at some point wandered by chance onto their path, because of a storm or something else, it could not have made history since no one had ever returned to tell of the experience.

Whatever Columbus might have known about the trade winds he learned firsthand, during his long sojourn in Madeira or during his voyage to Guinea, both being places on the Atlantic within the tropical region where the trade winds blow. But the breezes he experienced would have to have been mere hints of the winds themselves, light puffs at the edge of the trade-wind corridor, of whose existence he knew no more than that, like a man who looks down into a valley and sees as far as he can see, but no farther. Columbus had noticed that in Madeira, and especially in Guinea, the wind was always blowing from the east and slightly east-northeast, and never from anywhere else. Clearly such wind would be propitious for sailing westward, toward the sunset. We know that in Columbus's mind, that was where the Indies lay. Noticing that the wind never seemed to stray from that course, how could he not have striven to learn more about it, to try and determine how much help it could be to him, if this would facilitate the undertaking that he was already determined to carry out?

In my opinion, this is most likely what happened. Columbus made great efforts to understand the true nature of the trade winds. His premonition of how unusually useful they might be must have seemed providential to him. He made investigations, talked to people and, above all, made his own observations based on intuition. Columbus's intuition was his single most effective weapon, the key to his triumph; it was a kind of secret weapon which others did not possess, a form of inspiration fueled by genius.

This is to say that in fact Columbus did not really know much about or understand the trade winds; he had no idea of their range and did not know that they blew continuously. But he had breathed their air and felt them to be within his grasp. It is quite likely that Columbus would have made it across the Atlantic even without their help. Discovering them simply made his voyage much more feasible. It also bolstered his confidence, the principal element of hope. Throughout the entire voyage he never once was overcome by doubt or despondency, despite the fact that he and his fleet were advancing into the unknown, toward unknown destinations. The trade winds served to strengthen his resolve. They followed him faithfully all the way to the end, and he for his part faithfully entrusted his fate to them. He had made many errors in his calculations of the world's geography, but in his prescience of the wind patterns he had not been mistaken. Today, half a millennium later, the only natural route from the Canaries to the Caribbean, which for centuries after Columbus was followed by all sailing vessels and is still followed by knowledgeable sailing sportsmen of our own day, is the very same one that we are retracing here. Columbus is famous for having discovered America; he also discovered the best route for getting there. This may not be as celebrated an achievement as the discovery of a new world, but it was every bit as difficult and lasting in value.

I hope the reader does not think that I have imagined or invented any of the things contained in my description of the voyage. Not only because what is presented here has been drawn from the ship's log written by Columbus himself and from a number of testimonies given by his contemporaries, but also because I myself followed this same route almost step for step, crossing the ocean in a boat powered by wind alone, several years ago when I was first planning to write this book and trying to immerse myself entirely in Columbus's mind, in the spirit of his undertaking, and in what he might have felt and seen when he found himself in the ocean's endless expanse on a little wooden shell with a few yards' worth of canvas and the wind's helping hand —the very same sailing equipment at my own disposal. Like him, I followed the course of the sun—it seemed so near at sunset, so near I could almost touch it!—cruising to the rhythm of the wind in the sails, a rhythm unaltered by the centuries, the same as that followed by Ulysses and Aeneas in one of the oldest methods of travel after walking, running and riding on horseback.

Getting back to our narration of Columbus's voyage, would it be too much to say that a few days after the departure from Gomera he didn't merely encounter the trade winds, but actually "saw" them? I too "saw" them. It may seem strange to say that a wind, an invisible thing, can be "seen." And yet it's true of the trade winds. They are always accompanied by a procession of clouds large and small and all in a line like soldiers. If winds do not have this train of clouds they cannot be trade winds. Whenever the trade winds finally do appear, these gray, amusing vapors will without fail materialize in the tropical sky astern, behind the boat as though following a prey they are determined to catch. Together with them, also astern, the wind blows straight into the sails, the good trade wind blowing westward, toward America. (The main difference between Columbus's voyage and mine was of course that I knew where I was headed, whereas he had no idea. This, indeed, is what sets him miles apart from all others. It is the key to his immortality.)

It was a constant, certain wind. In his log, Columbus wrote, "We are sailing as though between a river's banks." Since the clouds move faster than a sailing vessel, before long the procession catches up to the boat, flies briefly above it and then passes it by. But soon, behind the first group, another one rises up from the horizon, pressing from all sides until the sky is filled with a procession in motion. As the clouds advance, they begin to swirl into circular and semicircular shapes, looking like so many crowns and garlands made up of cat's-tails and tufts spread across the sky but always remaining whole, floating on the wind with tidy patterns that never overlap.

The more one looks at these clouds, the more they resemble the little clouds with which painters surround the halos of Madonnas and angels in miracle paintings. How many such paintings must Columbus have seen in the monasteries and churches of Córdoba, Seville and Salamanca! Now it was as though he were living inside one, inside a nimbus, inside a miracle. His small fleet was crowned as it were by those clouds, and rode the waves on the strength of their winds. On the surface this voyage seemed like any other. Yet those spectacles never before seen—the purple blanket and the procession of the trade winds—already made it clear that they were entering a new realm, where something was coming to them from the limits of the universe. Doesn't the spiral of trade winds move eternally from east to west? Is this not like the vortex of the atom itself, the force that has kept the world alive since the beginning of creation? Such thoughts as these filled my head as I gazed out into the expanse of ocean, following Columbus's course, pursued by the same winds as he, bathed in the light of the same dazzling, unreachable sunset.

Columbus had, in a certain sense, penetrated the world's inner order, the movement of life itself. From this point forward, there was no way he could fail.

That was indeed how it was, and even with few mishaps, especially for a voyage which, in a sense, was taking place in the future. Some have written that Columbus's Atlantic crossing was in fact more like a sea voyage—though so long as to seem endless—than a daring struggle with the vast, wild ocean. It's true that Atlantic routes around the Tropic of Cancer, with their favorable trade winds and very low incidence of storms, are generally very calm, even routes. I myself, who am quite a novice in matters of sailing, was quite surprised by the relative ease and smoothness of this voyage, considered perilous by most. But although one may not encounter any problems with the condition of the waters and winds, there is still the anguish of solitude and distance to contend with, an anxiety that works its way inside you and fills you with fear and awe for the endless space around you. Though I knew exactly where our ship was headed and how long it would take to get there, I still felt this sense of bewilderment. What must it have been like for Columbus, who had no such comforting knowledge? What sorts of feelings of uncertainty must the sailors have felt as the days went by?

Columbus was enough aware of their feelings that when he wrote in his log the number of miles traveled every twenty-four hours, starting from the very first day of sailing, he entered figures which were increasingly less than the actual distance covered. This he did "so that his men would not get frightened or discouraged if the voyage became too long." It was a subtle deception, of little effect aside from manifesting Columbus's own apprehensions regarding the courage of his crews, his suspicion that the voyage might not in fact be so short as at first thought, and his determination to proceed at all costs. On this latter question he had no doubts whatsoever. After leaving the Canaries behind him Columbus headed directly west, along the 28th parallel, and never changed course. This was the course that he maintained would get him to Cipango, in three or four weeks' time.

After the fleet entered the spiral of trade winds on Sunday September 9, the sailing proceeded smoothly for another ten days or so. Along with the winds, the season also favored them, with its warm, mild air. "It was like April in Andalusia," wrote Columbus in the log. "The beautiful mornings were a source of great pleasure for all, and lacked nothing to make them more enchanting, except perhaps a song of nightingales." After waiting so many years and finding his hopes still intact and triumph on the horizon, Columbus could finally allow himself some joy and enthusiasm! Everything confirmed that he had been right in his choice—not the calculations on the charts and maps, which are always inaccurate reflections of reality, but everything around him: the ocean's brackish scent and deep-blue color, the whistling of the wind, the friendly clouds above and gentle waves below.

The farther they advanced into the solitary expanse, the more the watery desert seemed to grow populated. The ocean was alive; it had a life unknown and indifferent to them. Two or three days after leaving the Canaries, the first birds were sighted. They seemed to have come from the west, flying in the opposite direction from Columbus's course, as though coming from the places that he wanted to reach. There were herons, the birds of the sun; albatross with huge gray wings, sea eagles, also known as frigates; and sea swallows and wheatears that shot through the air like arrows, guided by their fine, slender tails.

All this movement aroused the men's curiosity. They stood looking out from the bulwarks, discussing every new bird that appeared. The birds might be a sign of land nearby, said some. Herons, for example, never go out to sea more than thirty or so miles from shore. During the second week of sailing the sight of birds became more frequent. A few petrels with light plumage even appeared in the sky. It was believed that the ships were coming near to some island, one of those mythical Atlantic islands that people had been talking about for centuries. Maybe those birds were coming from Antilia, which in the primitive geographical maps of the Middle Ages had been placed to the north of the course followed by Columbus. The winds, however, continued to blow westward, and the birds grew fewer.

Aside from birds, the sailors were now beginning to see fish as well in the warm ocean waters. The ocean's color was becoming steadily brighter, its sharp blue turning to violet in the distance—an almost magical transformation. The fish, which had to withstand the pressures of the depths, were large and tapered in form, with elongated, compressed bodies. They were almost all of one same genus, which the Spanish called *indorado* or *dorado,* for the golden reflections given off by the fish's belly when it leaps out of the water, a bit in the manner of a dolphin. The sailors managed to catch a few of these fish, no mean feat considering the extraordinary vigor with which they usually manage to break free of any hook or line that might momentarily stop their movements. Their meat is in fact quite exquisite. I myself had a chance to taste it during my crossing, after having encountered the same birds and fish in roughly the same places as Columbus.

It was the same with the floating clusters of sargasso weed. Columbus notes in his log that they were first spotted on September 16, the second Sunday of the voyage. It was named "Sargasso Sunday" for this reason. The log describes them as "great banks of very green grass that looks as though it was just recently cut from the earth. We all figured that we must be near an island." The first thing to enter everyone's mind was the hope that the voyage was nearing its end. But the days went by and the sea of grass continued to flow past, growing all the while. By now it covered the entire horizon with its ubiquitous floating algae, ranging in color from straw yellow to meadow green. It was a very strange, amazing stretch of ocean. The soldiers feared that the layers of grass, algae, or whatever it might be were so thick that they might obstruct the passage of the ships. The sargassos were so dense, they said, that the prows risked getting tangled up in them. Columbus, who had learned from some old Palos sailors about the phenomenon and knew that the ships could proceed without incident since "grass does not hamper navigation," had a difficult time explaining to the crew that the plants presented no danger, only a marvelous spectacle of nature. As they watched the sargassos parade past the ship, they could see that they were living organisms. The freshness of their wet but firm branches, the brightness of their colors, the seeming confidence of their movement gives anyone who sees them the impression of looking at something with a life of its own, something to be reckoned with. From time to time Columbus's sailors would discover small animals nested amid those plants, crabs and the like. They gazed down at the water caught between curiosity, anticipation of new events, and a fear of inauspicious omens. Deep down, the crew's morale and common faith in the undertaking had begun to totter with the appearance of the sargassos, which constituted an indecipherable augury casting little hope on the future of the voyage, now entering its third solitary week.

Another crisis developed at about the same time, brought on by the magnetic declination of the compass. It was an unheard-of phenomenon to all. In his log, Columbus described it as follows: "At the start of the night the compass needles had moved toward northwest, and by morning they had shifted even farther in that direction." (Columbus even invented a verb to describe exactly what was happening: *las agujas noruesteaban*—the needles were "northwesting," tending toward northwest.) They had shifted a good half rhumb. This meant that if the helm was directed due west, as had been ordered once the fleet left the Canaries, the needle was deviating to north. Columbus noticed this shift and at first reproached his sailors for what seemed to him a poor job of steering. Then he realized that the directional shifts were due not to human error but to some sort of movement in the heavens. Columbus was a very sharp observer of natural phenomena. He immediately noticed the magnetic needle's variation, and correctly interpreted it as a magnetic inclination toward some other point away from the North Star. His son Fernando explains: "From this my father realized that the needle was not pointing directly toward the North Star, but toward some other fixed but invisible point."

Nowadays everyone knows that magnetic declination occurs because the geographical north does not coincide with the magnetic north, and that a magnetized needle should not be considered either infallible or invariable. Columbus discovered this under the crystal-clear skies of those days on the ocean, when he could regularly observe the position of the North Star. If he had not done so, his course would have been irremediably altered, and the fleet might have gotten lost in the empty expanses of the Atlantic, farther to the north. The sailors followed the progress of this unexpected development with apprehension. It added yet another element of mystery and uncertainty to the voyage. Time was passing inexorably. The men had been at sea for many days and nights by now; it seemed ages ago that they had seen the last island disappear on the horizon. In Las Casas's faithful narration of the voyage, this was the point at which the discontent of the crew first entered the scene: "They began to grumble about the voyage and about the man who had got them into this fix."

After encountering the fortunate assistance of the trade winds during the first leg of the journey, the three caravels entered a period of long lulls. The speed of the ships diminished to a slow crawl. In the north, the sky filled with a thick haze and large groups of birds appeared, heading west. Once again the men were tempted to hope for land nearby. I have calculated that at this point Columbus had completed slightly more than one third of the journey; I wonder what would have happened if the sailors had had any idea of how much ocean they still had to cross. They were men accustomed to seeing land every day, at the end of their usual commercial runs. None of them had ever been at sea for so long a time. The farthest they had sailed was to places like the Azores and the Cape Verde Islands, trips of five hundred or so nautical miles, which seemed like the limit of human capability. Here they had already covered twice as much distance, and there was still more than that left. They had encountered, at several different points, reassuring indications that land might be nearby, but it never appeared; after each disappointment the men despaired a little more, fearing that they would never be able to turn back, having gone too far already.

The sea remained smooth, the winds weak and irregular. The fleet made a few maneuvers in an attempt to look for stronger breezes. It shifted to northwest by one rhumb, then by another half rhumb. But still the ships barely moved. When the other caravels pulled near to the *Santa Maria* to confer with Columbus he heard harsh, stinging words in the air, even curses, which went right to his heart. Sailors are often an insolent lot, quick to cross the bounds of respect. Columbus was a foreigner to boot, and never so foreign as when things went badly.

The ocean continued to slide indifferently by, beneath the angry eyes of the crew members. At one point a whale appeared near the ships, floated awhile alongside them, then took its leave as though entirely uninterested in their exploits. Now and then new patches of algae appeared. Two pelicans alighted next to the *Niña,* and the sailors at another point caught with their hands a bird that resembled a sea gull, "but looked to them like a river bird, not a sea bird."

On the day of the twenty-second a head wind rose up, with the ships still steering a westward course slightly inclined to the north. But the obstacle was a welcome one. "This head wind was utterly indispensable to me," one reads in the log, "because my sailors by now must have been quite worked up against me, thinking that there were no winds capable of bringing our ships back to Spain." The strong wind blew from the southwest and lasted for several days. In order to advance at all, the ships were forced to maintain their northerly tack. The water currents were also very strong and pulled the ships off course. There was a cloudburst, but then the waters grew calm. Actually the wind died down and the water, on the contrary, began to swell, dense and heavy, arching up like a mountain ridge in motion. It was an extraordinary spectacle, this ocean that turned into a mountain, sand dune, or the croup of a giant horse. It rose and fell all the way to the horizon without raising even a single breaker or bubble of foam, with none of those white and leaden curls that fill the sea during a storm. Just these heavy, monstrous waves, which as they moved forward pulled their slopes and valleys intact behind them, inside and out. They approached as placid as camels and as big as hills, plummeting slowly and inexorably from the tops of their crests to the depths of their cavities. They were the tail end, the echoes, of storms that had raged somewhere far away, perhaps hundreds of miles to the north. Navigators of the Atlantic know them well. They call them "long waves." They can grow to one hundred feet in height and one hundred feet in width. Sailing ships are made more for riding the waves than for cleaving them. Columbus's caravels climbed the ocean's heights and then plunged into its hollows. That swollen, windless sea, at first a source of terror, soon became an object of wonder. For Columbus it was a miraculous occurrence, a sign of God's favor. He wrote in his log: "A miracle of this sort has not come to pass since the Egyptians took to pursuing Moses and the Jews he had freed from slavery." Moses and himself in a single breath: Columbus clearly felt an aura of miracle all around him. The waters had opened under the will of God, and had carried him a little closer to the goal for which he had been chosen. America's future discoverer had never felt so strong as he did at this moment, though right in the middle of a difficult predicament.

Indeed, they had been already twenty days at sea, and there was nothing in sight to quell the fears and whispers which grew in proportion to the distance traveled. Columbus had resumed the direct, westward course. He sensed the others' resistance, but continued to make reassurances and promises. It is rather difficult to reconstruct those moments, to know exactly what was passing through the minds of those embittered, frightened and in any case angry men. Columbus and Pinzón still had their agreement to divide responsibilities, whereby the Palos navigator was to take care of the technical aspects of the voyage, which included, to a certain degree, the mood and behavior of the crews. Pinzón had demonstrated his great influence when still in Palos, when his intervention changed the local mariners' attitude toward the voyage from one of sarcasm to one of support. After having scorned it as folly, many ended signing on for it. It is quite possible that during the voyage Pinzón and his men, faced with the dangerous prospect that the rampant discontent might turn into an out-and-out mutiny, acted as a dam against the flood, insisting on the mission with which the fleet had been entrusted, on the shame they would have to live with if they returned home hands empty and defeated—appealing to their sense of pride, their strength of character. He who sets himself a task must carry out that task, proving his manliness by doing it well and seeing it through to the end. Such might have been Pinzón's approach, given the circumstances.

At about this time Columbus had a meeting with Pinzón "regarding a map that he had sent to him." Pinzón came aboard the *Santa Maria* and went below deck, where the two men talked about some islands which, according to the map, should have been somewhere in the vicinity. They were in agreement on the likelihood of this hypothesis. They concluded that if they had not yet come across these islands it was because of the ocean currents and head winds that had carried them northward. Columbus had let Pinzón see the map, and Pinzón had sent it back to him with a nautical rope. (Naturally, just what this mysterious map really was has been the subject of debate for centuries. It may have been a copy of Toscanelli's map, somehow purloined from Lisbon or perhaps even sent by Toscanelli himself to Columbus, as was formerly held to have been the case by many. This is Las Casas's interpretation. Las Casas in fact claims to have seen Toscanelli's map with his own eyes and to have kept it with him for a period of time. But even admitting that this may be true, how could a map drawn up for purposes more theoretical than nautical, a map certainly not suitable to be followed when charting a course at sea, have been of any use at all to Columbus's navigation? The map's information is quite general and for the most part hypothetical. We also know that it contained gross errors which, if believed and followed, would have taken Columbus so far off course that he almost surely would have met with disaster. Toscanelli's map had indeed served a specific function when all was still at the planning and theoretical stages, and it had helped to strengthen the intuitive convictions that Columbus was maturing in his own mind, encouraging him to persevere. But in the middle of the ocean, what meaning could those strokes of fantasy have possibly had, when the important thing was to act, to make decisions, to imagine things in concrete terms and to overcome the dangers of time and distance?)

Whether it was inspiration or something else, the day after their meeting, Columbus and Pinzón began talking about land within sight. Pinzón was the first to point out to everyone the indistinct contours of something to the southwest "that clearly resembled an island." Columbus made the same judgment, and the two of them agreed that it was probably about thirty miles away. Many sailors fell to their knees. *"Gloria in excelsis Deo"* rang out from the decks. The men climbed up masts and shrouds, gazing until nightfall in the direction of the coveted island. Columbus even had the ships change direction by one rhumb to the south, leaving the westward course for a short stretch. The outline of land had shifted a bit to the south, and Columbus wanted to go toward it. But by morning their hopes had vanished. The horizon was deserted. "What we had believed to be land was nothing but sky."

The general letdown was fierce. The small gatherings of sailors on the decks grew larger and more frequent, their discussions more spirited. Discontent was growing, and with it the desire to turn back. There was no room left for the Pinzóns' appeals to bravery and glory; indeed, it is not unlikely that with the tide of bitterness rising, they too took a position of hostility toward Columbus, considered by most to be unpracticed in matters of seafaring and incapable of taking command in a crisis so serious and puzzling as this. I base such speculations on what I know to be true about the persons involved. I am certain, however, that no one will ever really settle these questions with any certainty. Not even those living at the time these events took place were able to shed any light on this aspect of the voyage, and the testimony that came out in the years immediately afterward, during the trials over Columbus's estate, served more to cloud than to clarify the whole emotional side of the solitary expedition. Facts can be easily presented and described, but feelings are elusive. In his log, Columbus makes only a vague reference to the crew's weariness. As for Pinzón, he died just a few days after returning from the voyage, and he said nothing. The biographers closer in time to the events they describe—Las Casas and Fernando Columbus—seem too concerned with leaving behind their moral judgment not to become, in the end, partisan observers. In my opinion, the best source on this matter remains the first official account of the discovery of the Indies, written by Fernandez Oviedo in 1533, some forty years after the crossing. Oviedo makes us look at the facts with a more rational eye, pointing out that protests and disgruntlements were inevitable in those circumstances, as was the taking of sides according to similarities of origin, friendships and interests. There was clearly a Pinzón clan that tried to take control of the situation and force Columbus to make decisions that conformed to the way they felt. And there was, on Columbus's part, a natural, stubborn resistance to letting them get the better of him. But all, at one point or another, felt torn between hope and fear. Each went through his own personal drama of uncertainty. This should be borne in mind, as should the facts that there were no mutinies (as Oviedo points out) and that exaggerations of what actually happened during the historic voyage were common in later versions of the story.

The voyage in the meantime moved forward, but slowly, the ocean having returned to a state of dead calm. It had already been several days since the trade winds disappeared, and their procession of light clouds apparently vanished from the horizon. The ships had been, as it were, groping their way along for some time now, their course having been shifted by their earlier tack in the face of head winds and by the strong currents. The voyage had clearly entered a phase of uncertainty. Columbus's obsession with keeping the helm pointed due west started raising not a few doubts. Perhaps the fleet was going too far, too far forward. There were fears that they might have passed groups of islands, either to leeward or to windward. Some even suspected that they had passed Cipango and were heading straight for the Asian continent, toward Marco Polo's Cathay. Both Columbus and Pinzón by now sensed the imminent proximity of land. But in what direction?

The period of lull left the crews idle. There was little to be done with the sails and rigging. It was a dangerous situation, since the idling men on the decks were getting lost in discussions and criticisms. The protests were rising in pitch. By now a month had passed since departure. No one had ever been so long at sea without even knowing where he was going or how many more days—or weeks, or months—the voyage would last. The ships dragged along in the middle of the ocean as though on a lake, slowly, maddeningly. How many miles had they come? Hundreds and hundreds and more: thousands. Thousands of miles from Spain, from home. Why persist in this delusion? "There is no courage against God," Paul Claudel has his sailors say in his play about Columbus. "We are lost in the Void. Why do you want us to die?" they shout despairingly at their admiral—who, according to the considerably less dramatic account of Pietro Martire (a witness of Columbus's return from his eventful voyage), tried to pacify his men *blandis verbis, ampla spe:* with the sweetest words and the broadest hopes. But this did not suffice in Martire's account, where a few hotheads suggest heaving the admiral overboard so they can head back home without any further obstacles. No doubt they said such things—"Let's toss him into the sea; we can say he fell in while gazing at the stars!"—but apparently sailors were accustomed to overstepping all limits in words. This does not at all mean, however, that they had any intention of doing what they said. It was customary, for example, for sailors to slip in a few little personal curses when saying evening prayers. Nevertheless, they all believed firmly in God.

The fifth of October arrived, a Friday. The wind had finally picked up, and the little trade clouds had reappeared triumphantly in the sky. A large flock of petrels flew over the ships. About thirty of them alighted on the masts and shrouds. It was like an invasion, and a sign of land nearby. With the great commotion of fluttering wings the captains of the ships sprang into action. Pinzón, studying the birds' flight, proposed that they sheer to southwest. On Saturday October 6 a conference of captains was held on board the *Santa Maria.* (The log says nothing about this, and even Las Casas's and Fernando's accounts are spare on details. But in the course of Columbus's inheritance trials—the famous *pleitos*—a number of old sailors of the *Niña* and *Pinta* still living testified on the events of those days. Their depositions have become part of Columbian lore.)

The conference was rather animated. No words were minced. It was clear where the parties stood with regard to the essential question: the crews wanted to turn back, the Pinzóns were undecided, and Columbus alone wanted to keep going, regardless. His position is alluded to in the log, in a note that clearly refers back to these days of uncertainty: "The admiral added that it was useless to complain, since he had made up his mind to sail to the Indies and intended to continue the voyage until, God willing, he should reach them."

In all likelihood no real decisions were taken. The middle path was chosen, no party being ready yet to fight to the finish for continuing or returning. In Gomera, the length of the voyage had been estimated at about 750 leagues, a bit more than 2,000 nautical miles. By this point they had already come that far, if not farther. Columbus, however, tried to demonstrate with his purposely underestimated reckonings that they had not yet covered the distance estimated beforehand. Be that as it may, they resolved to proceed for another three or four days and to study closely the flights of birds, the foam of the waves, and the wind patterns for positive signs of land; then they would decide. Was it just a delaying tactic? Columbus didn't even give it a thought. To anyone who asked whether they would turn back if those three or four days of sailing proved fruitless he would respond, "If we do not find land you are permitted to cut off my head; that way you can sail home in peace." This is another quotation from the *pleitos.* Perhaps it is just legend, or at least a product of the debates between those who gave Columbus the credit for insisting on continuing the voyage and those who would give it to Pinzón. *("Adelante! Adelante!"* Pinzón supposedly shouted, according to one of the witnesses. "Onward! Onward! What? We've just barely left and you're already thinking about turning back?")

The fleet pushed onward. The tail wind blew so vigorously that the ships reached cruising speeds of up to ten knots, a prodigious feat. At sunrise on October 7, the fifth Sunday of the voyage, the *Niña,* which was sailing faster than the other two, hoisted the flag on the mainmast and fired a shot from the bombard, signaling that land had been sighted. Joy spread from ship to ship. But once again no land was to be found, and the day passed with no further events. The resulting disappointment was only slightly lessened by the sounds of "great multitudes of birds" flying over the ships during the night. Birds, especially when in large groups of the marine variety, were considered infallible harbingers of land, more reliable as guides than maps designed by men. Seabirds had played a major role in all the Portuguese discoveries of islands in the Atlantic—the Azores, Madeira, the Cape Verde archipelago. By studying their direction, their number and the vigor of their flight, the Portuguese mariners were able to find the right course. In the history of the great ocean voyages of the late fifteenth and early sixteenth centuries, seabirds were invaluable messengers. The flight of petrels was watched very closely. Pinzón suggested a shift in course of one rhumb to southwest, since the general impression was that land was imminent, and any clues that might help to find it should be followed. The latitude of the crossing, which had already descended to the 26th parallel after the lulls encountered midway, now dropped another two degrees to the 24th parallel.

The eighth of October marked the thirty-third day of sailing. Those who had counted them might have been thinking of the number of years Christ spent on this earth, adding new fuel to their grumblings. But that night more flocks of birds, flying west with the wind, were heard passing overhead. The ninth and tenth days of October passed, the wind still blowing strongly. The landscape of sea and sky remained unchanged, the sun setting every evening with the same purple blanket; it was as though they had been sailing on a motionless horizon, within a barrier of solitude, for four whole weeks. And yet, the air seemed filled with something new, an inexplicable anticipation, an almost certain sense that everything was about to change. It wasn't just the flights of petrels and sea eagles that aroused this feeling. The premonition came from darker, more hidden places—from the combination of despair and excitement in the hearts of the men. The discovery that they now felt to be imminent seemed the fruit not so much of celestial observation as of pure willpower, as though the land that lay ahead were being created out of nothing, by force of feelings alone.

On Thursday October 11 the days of extension granted to Columbus were up. But nobody raised any objections to continuing, as all by now were prey to the excitement of discovery, as though it were a rendezvous that they could no longer afford to miss. The trade winds blew that day with the force of a gale, and the three caravels, under its powerful thrust, took on the roughest sea that they had had to face in the entire voyage. A west-southwest course was maintained. The ships cruised at 12 knots. Signs of land began to multiply: a reed passed by the *Santa Maria*, then a cane, a stick that appeared to have been carved by human hands, and a small branch that looked as though recently torn from a shrub, with a small flower "similar to the dog-rose of Castile" at its tip. Night fell. A setting quarter-moon lightened the sky. The wind had swept away all clouds, leaving the horizon perfectly clear.

All remained awake. The captains paced up and down the quarterdecks of their caravels. The watchmen stood alert on the forecastle decks, and the topmen peered into the night from the crow's nests. It was important to be the first to sight land. For some poor sailor it would mean a total transformation of his life: the Crown had promised a lifetime pension of ten thousand maravedis yearly to the man who sighted new land before anyone else, a considerable sum for someone who could count on it for the rest of his life.

The caravels, spurred on by this mirage as well, raced with each other in the wind that carried them forward. Pinzón's ship, the *Pinta*, had moved to the front of the fleet. Columbus sailed along not far behind, trying to take in the whole scene, not only everything within his field of vision, but everything that the others might be able to see as well. At about ten o'clock that night Columbus, standing on the forecastle deck in an attempt to see as far ahead into the sea as possible, thought he saw a light. He did not dare announce this discovery out loud; he also doubted that it could really be land, with the sea so rough and foamy and the moon's reflection dancing on the waves like so many little torches in the darkness. He quietly called to his side Pedro Gutiér-rez, the king's majordomo or *repostero* who had come aboard almost furtively. He told him what he thought he had seen, and asked him to have a look himself. Gutiérrez looked, and then confirmed that there was indeed a light. But Rodrigo Sánchez, the royal inspector, when asked his opinion said instead that he could see no light in the direction indicated. Columbus remained silent, concentrating. In the log he writes that after having spoken of it the first time he saw the light again, intermittently: "It was like a little wax candle whose flame went up and down, something which very few would have thought to be evidence of land."

It has been estimated that the fleet at that moment was about thirty miles from the shoreline which it was approaching unknowingly. From a distance of thirty miles one cannot see the light of a candle, torch, or any other kind of small fire. Las Casas speculated that the light might have come from torches carried by fishermen out at sea, but it wasn't the right time of the night for fishing, and one does not go fishing thirty miles out at sea in gale conditions. Nor could it have been a group of people walking on land, trying to light their way in the darkness. (Las Casas says that the native population used torches "perhaps when going by night to perform their natural functions.")

In all likelihood Columbus saw nothing. He couldn't possibly have seen anything from that distance. He too had let himself be carried away by the intense desire to see something, which dominated everyone's thoughts and kept the fleet in a state of great tension. It wasn't until around 2 A.M.—2 A.M. of Friday October 12, a fateful day—that a sailor on the *Pinta* shouted the long-awaited words: "Land ho! Land ho!" Pinzón checked with his own eyes and confirmed the sailor's finding. The agreed-upon signals were sent, the bombard fired. The crews were in a state of commotion, singing, praying, crying for joy. The sailor who had sighted the land, Rodrigo de Triana, was embraced by his companions. They congratulated him on his success, on the lifetime pension that he had won for himself. Some perhaps even envied him. But Rodrigo de Triana never got a single maravedi for his discovery. Columbus challenged his claim to having been the first, asserting that he had anticipated him by several hours in seeing signs of land. It was a rather cruel abuse of power on Columbus's part, since the sovereigns naturally believed Columbus's version, and the ten thousand maravedis per year went to him. As we already know, the person who reaped this benefit was Beatrice de Harana, the mistress Columbus had left in Córdoba. Was he repaying her out of gratitude, nostalgia or remorse? Why did he do it? Not for Beatrice's sake, since there certainly were other ways to repay her. He probably did it out of principle, out of his rigid sense of authority: only he, commander and leader of the entire venture, should be considered the discoverer of the land they had reached. The sighting made by the sailor of the *Pinta* was a fortuitous occurrence, not deserving of notice. For history, and for that future glory in which Columbus believed so firmly, the man to have first seen land on the other side of the ocean could only be he, who had planned the voyage that was already becoming—that very night—immortal. (Rodrigo de Triana, outraged by the indignity, came to a bad end. Some say he hanged himself from a ship's mast, others say he converted to Islam and perished in battle alongside the Moors.)

The men on the caravels were eager to reach land, which by now was barely six miles away, judging from its appearance in the moonlight: a white strip of beach and the black silhouette of a promontory. Columbus wisely decided to wait until dawn: the sea was too agitated, and landing maneuvers might prove difficult with the strong winds; moreover, rocks might suddenly appear out of nowhere. Julien de la Gravière, a skilled navigator, wrote: "The rocks of the Lucayas are treacherous. If Columbus had not been a good sailor, he would never have made it back." The ships lay to, sails furled. The men bided their time, held back by the wind, awake and waiting. As Samuel

Eliot Morison, another man of the sea, put it: "It was the night most fraught with coming events that has ever been lived, on any ship and on any sea."

America lay waiting before that handful of men who, without knowing it, had already become part of posterity.

11

The Good Savage

As it was already well into the month of October, the first gleams of dawn began to lighten the island just after five A.M. The land had been sighted at two A.M., "the most landlike land of all the land that any sailor has ever seen." The three hours spent waiting for the night to end seemed interminable. But it wasn't just the darkness of one night between sunset and sunrise that was coming to an end, it was the night of a hundred thousand years, during which millions of people had lived in ignorance of the fact that there were millions of other people living on the other side of the globe, and that an enormous continent lay between two equally unknown oceans. Unconsciously, the two peoples had been awaiting each other. The Europeans, led by Columbus, had succeeded in discovering America. But what about those on the other side of the ocean, the peoples of the so-called New World, who had lived for millennia content in their solitude, undisturbed, with no impatience for change?

There they were that morning, unaware of anything, waking up just as they had done every morning since time immemorial. The whole island was waking up, silent and indifferent. There was nothing solemn or dramatic about the manner in which their isolation, which had lasted since the primeval night, came to an end once and for all. From their boats the Spaniards saw a sandy white beach washed gently by the waves in the morning light. It was deserted. Behind the beach were many brightly colored trees that seemed as though painted against the blue sky. Carried on the morning breeze, the murmur of the sea and a rustling of land and forest reached the ships. Spellbound by the moment, nobody spoke.

For a while no sign of human life could be seen. The natives were hiding behind the trees, astonished and uncertain. They didn't know whether those huge monsters on the sea were fish, birds or ghosts. In Lope de Vega's play he has them exclaim, "There are three houses on the water!" In the meantime the caravels were coming closer to shore, but slowly, for fear of shallows. A great chirruping of birds filled the air. The sailors saw heaps of shells on the beach, a few gigantic palm trees with monkeys on their branches, and a procession of pelicans walking along the shore. Finally the inhabitants emerged. They went down to the beach, full of curiosity but without fear. They were pointing out the ships to each other, gesturing toward those bizarre apparitions. The meeting had taken place. History was already changed.

Unfortunately, it was impossible for the Spaniards to disembark. The sea was rough and windy, and the entire island appeared to be surrounded by dangerous reefs at water level. Columbus decided to look for a safe landing place, and began to circle the island in a westward direction, to leeward. It was not much of an island—more like a large rock just a few dozen square miles in area. Heading northward back up the shore, at about midday of the same day the ships found a small bay with calm waters, an area sheltered from the breakers and extending for several hundred meters. It was here that Columbus dropped anchor, in water five fathoms deep. Three launches were lowered into the water, one from each caravel, and then rowed to shore. The meeting of old and new worlds took place on the shore of that bay, where Columbus disembarked under a bright sun. (The place has preserved a name whose origin remains unknown: it is called Fernández Bay.)

At Columbus's side were the other two captains, Martín Alonso Pinzón and his younger brother Vicente Yáñez, commander of the *Niña*. Joining them were the officials and functionaries of the fleet, including the notary Rodrigo de Escobedo, whose duty it was to draft all deeds. Columbus was wearing his most sumptuous clothes, and in his right hand he grasped the royal standard and held it high in the air. They all gave thanks to the Lord, kneeling down and kissing the earth. Columbus solemnly proclaimed that they would give the island the name of the holy Savior, San Salvador. And he declared it the property of the king and queen his sovereigns. Escobedo wrote down every word. Those present signed the deed as witnesses. The natives made their way in silence to the spot where this colorful group of men had gathered, men of whose existence they had had no idea just one hour earlier. To them it seemed the men were performing some sort of magical rite, some unfamiliar act of sorcery.

Las Casas gives an eloquent description of the now famous first encounter between Indians and Spaniards: "The Indians, of whom there was a large number, gazed dumbstruck at the Christians, looking with wonder at their beards, their clothes and the whiteness of their skin. They directed their attentions towards the men with beards, but especially toward the admiral, who they realized was the most important of the group, either from his imposing physical presence or from his scarlet clothing. They touched the men's beards with their fingers and carefully examined the paleness of their hands and faces. Seeing that they were innocent, the admiral and his men did not resist their actions."

This scene, no doubt more idyllic here than it really was in fact, has been represented countless times over the centuries in popular images celebrating the event. In most of these it is the fantastical side of the experience, rather than its reality, that has been emphasized. The Spaniards are usually depicted wearing large hats with ostrich plumes and suits of shining armor—"tortoise shells," in the natives' opinion—, battle standards flying in the wind. In the foreground stands Columbus, standard-bearer and servant of the faith—like St. Christopher, the man who "carried Christ"—wearing the inspired expression of someone carrying out a design of providence. He has long, fair hair, much like Christ himself. Perhaps this is why he is also usually depicted with a beard, which he never wore. Next to the armor-clad Spaniards, the un-clothed natives strike a humble contrast: two utterly different worlds, which perhaps should never have met.

These sorts of images and descriptions, though naïve in appearance, are actually consciously devised to convey a desired effect to the general population. They present the very message that the authorities wanted to convey just after the discovery. America, as such, has not yet entered the picture. Perhaps there is no need to repeat it, but at the time of Columbus's voyage and for many years after it, nobody imagined that a new continent had been discovered. Nobody—least of all Columbus, perhaps the most stubborn one of all, the most unwilling to see his error, whose prisoner he remained until death—thought of America as an unknown land that had been discovered. Columbus and everyone else was convinced that he had landed in Asia according to plan —a plan in itself quite adventurous and fantastical. Everyone talked about Cipango, Cathay and the Indies. The men who had run out to see the miraculous ships were called Indians, a name that has stuck with them ever since. In those popular images representing the landing at San Salvador, America does not exist, either as theme or as subject. And since our account of events has been following them as they happen, it would be anachronistic to speak of

America, of the idea of America, at this point in our story, since this notion did not exist at the time.

What sort of messages, then, do these images put forward for the general population? I can make out at least two. The first is that Columbus's great achievement was carried out in Christ's name and was directly inspired by Him. This is the meaning behind the standards with the Cross, the men holding their hands up to the sky, and the "Christification" of Columbus. He had opened the door to the conversion of a vast sector of the world which before his arrival knew nothing of Christ's word. Columbus was a soldier of the faith. *This* was ostensibly the significance of his endeavor, and this same interpretation would soon be used to justify all of its consequences. During his life and especially after his death, Columbus's fortunes were rather mixed. But this sense of him as a redeemer of souls, as a symbolic "thirteenth apostle" freeing men from the bonds of sin, has remained to cast a favorable light on his image. After having been obscured for several hundreds of years, Columbus's fame as a universal figure has reemerged dominant in history precisely because of his image as redeemer. One cannot easily forget, much less hide, the fact that out of the one billion or so Christians scattered around the world, more than half live in the Americas, and Columbus's arrival in the New World was the single most decisive factor in bringing this about.

Then there is the second, one might say laic response to the image created by the first descriptions of the arrival. This is the fascinating notion of the "good savage" so cherished by European cultures in their early post-medieval periods, a notion that reached its apotheosis during the Enlightenment. These surprising "Indians," who "bore no arms, nor knew of them"; who "had no iron" and "went around as naked as the day their mothers bore them"; who were "quite poor and lacking in everything, yet with no instinct for greed"; who "willingly gave everything they had," did they not perhaps belong to the dawn of humanity? The legendary Golden Age had always been thought to be the creation of poets. But when they landed in San Salvador, the Europeans really did see "their ancestors in their natural state."

Just after the expedition's return to Spain, Pietro Martire, a chronicler by trade, hastened to write to his friends in Italy and France that "those people knew nothing of money's pernicious use." He had seen in Barcelona the few Indians that Columbus had brought back with him to show to the king and queen. He described them as follows: "They are content to live according to nature, and are spared the perpetual worry of knowing what lies ahead." This meant: They are not like us, but as we once were, before we were corrupted. Throughout their history, Christians had always been tormented by the belief that man, by nature, was good, and that civilization and progress had led him to express violence, hate and cruelty. Antonio Pigafetta, who accompanied Magellan, though speaking of other primitive peoples saw the savages as "people who love peace, idleness and tranquillity."

The myth of the good savage grew deep roots in European soil. For the intellectuals of the 1500s, Columbus's voyage had recovered an age of man buried for millennia. It was as though Columbus had actually encountered people living in the Golden Age. A number of illusions arose from all this— such as the idea that by taking as models the indigenous communities as they were before the fateful arrival of the caravels, one could build an ideal society. But people dreamed up even more outlandish things than this, such as the "fountain of youth" that supposedly flowed under those distant skies, amid fecund plants in an environment where life was still pure and unsullied. It was the promise of eternal happiness, the Faustian dream a few generations before its time. In 1512 Ponce de Leon led an expedition, ordered by King Ferdinand himself, in search of the secret of eternal youth. So much for discovering America! Like those who today formulate theories for going backward toward stars already dead for thousands of years but still shining because light can only travel so fast, Europe in the early 1500s wanted to recapture the past. Columbus's modernity had broken the chains of the Middle Ages, but the revolution he brought about was so profound that it dissolved all confines of time, even those separating past from present.

The good savage, moreover, served a purpose. "I think," wrote Columbus in the log, "that Christendom will do good business with these Indians, especially Spain, whose subjects they must all become." He judged that "with fifty armed men these people could be brought under control and made to do whatever one might wish." He was of the opinion that they would make "good servants," and could easily be made Christian, "since it appears that they have no religion." Thus was the groundwork laid for the future. Columbus was not at that moment thinking of slavery. But, alas, it was not far away. In that small bay where the two worlds met, the Spaniards' swords aroused the curiosity of many natives. They wanted to look at them, touch them. They were "sharper than fishbone." One of the natives grabbed a blade and hurt himself, bloodying his whole hand. Lope de Vega has the Indians' chief, Dulcanquellin, exclaim, "These men are more than simple people!"

In the evening the men who had disembarked returned to the ships. The following morning, Columbus had the sails hoisted anew and set off to explore the rest of the island. They went north for another short stretch along the shore, but saw nothing of much interest. Columbus did not want to waste any time. At midday he gave the order to quit the waters of San Salvador and to bring the ships about so they could head south, where the natives had indicated to him that there were more islands, many more. They had named him more than a hundred.

All in all, the landing at San Salvador had been something of a disappointment. Columbus had reached a dusty, semidesert island with no precious goods, the only gold being a few small pendants in the nostrils of the vainer natives, clearly not produced on the island. Columbus wanted instead to find "the place where gold is born," an indication that gold played a major role in the dream on which he had built his hopes. That he felt guided by divine providence is beyond doubt. But could not gold, sign of wealth and power, have also been part of the celestial design whose protagonist he felt himself to be? He did in fact define his quest for gold in these very terms, as an ineluctable destiny: "God would show me the place where gold is born."

A far cry from such a place, San Salvador left only memories of idle nudity, an odor of burnt wood such as one finds in all poverty-stricken sites, and the stench of rotten leaves, a smell of damp vegetation that extends across the tropics like a staleness always hanging in the air. The immortal voyage's arrival had been an unlucky one. In that wondrous stretch of ocean where Columbus had landed there are thousands of islands, a veritable galaxy, a labyrinth of islands. Columbus's fleet had by chance ended up in the most godforsaken corner of that galaxy, the outermost rock of a fringe archipelago that used to be called the Lucayas and is now known as the Bahamas. No one would even remember San Salvador today if Columbus had not disembarked there. It even lost the name Columbus gave it when it was renamed Watling Island for an English buccaneer, John Watling, who made it his impregnable headquarters. Today it is called San Salvador. But the original Indian name was probably the most beautiful: Guanahani. Many Caribbean islands have since become famous, either through historical events or tourism. San Salvador, however, enjoyed only that brief moment of glory, three October days five hundred years ago.

Yet despite the disappointment of this first discovery, Columbus, with his brilliant stubbornness, firmly believed that San Salvador "must" be part of the Indies, since it was located where the Indies were supposed to be. But the unreality of Columbus's voyage did not end with San Salvador. In his cosmography, which was fantastic and personal and all his own, Cipango and

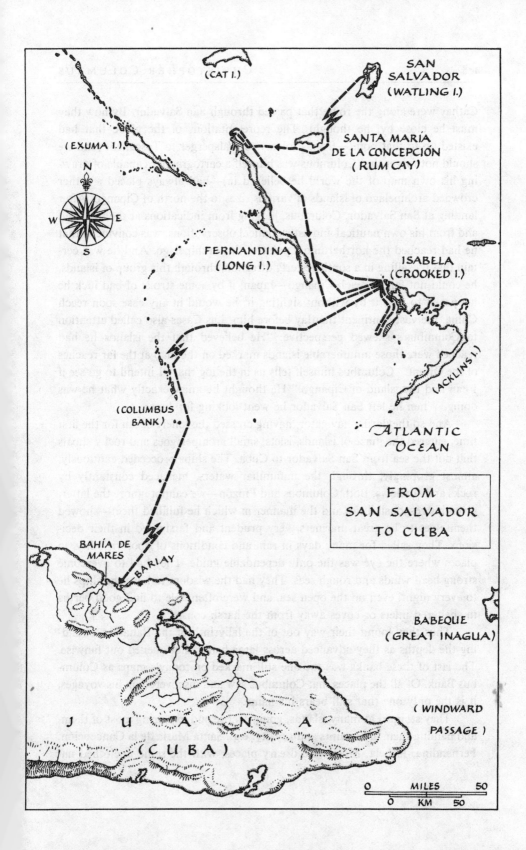

(CAT I.)

SAN
SALVADOR
(WATLING I.)

(EXUMA I.)

SANTA MARÍA
DE LA CONCEPCIÓN
(RUM CAY)

N

W   E

S

FERNANDINA
(LONG I.)

ISABELA
(CROOKED I.)

(ACKLINS I.)

(COLUMBUS
BANK)

ATLANTIC
OCEAN

FROM
SAN SALVADOR
TO CUBA

BAHÍA DE
MARES

BARIAY

BABEQUE
(GREAT INAGUA)

(WINDWARD
PASSAGE)

J U A N A

(CUBA)

0   MILES   50
0   KM   50

Cathay were along the route that passed through San Salvador. By now they must be close by, he thought. The representations of the globe that had existed up to that point—from Ptolemy to Walsperger to Toscanelli (and we should not forget that Columbus was himself a cartographer capable of drawing his own map of the world he believed in)—had always placed a rather crowded archipelago of islands of various sizes to the north of Cipango. After landing at San Salvador, Columbus, judging from indications at the site itself and from his own nautical and astronomical observations, was convinced that he had reached the northernmost point of this archipelago. And he was certain that by sailing in a southwesterly direction, through this group of islands, he could not fail to reach Cipango—Japan; if by some stroke of bad luck he happened to pass it by without sighting it, he would in any case soon reach China, the vast continent that lay before him. Las Casas also called attention to Columbus's skewed perspective: "He believed that the islands he had reached were those innumerable islands marked on the map at the far reaches of the Orient." Columbus himself tells us in the log that "I intend to go see if I can find the island of Cipango." He thought he knew exactly what he was doing. When he left San Salvador he went looking for Japan.

And so the daring navigator, having crossed the lonely ocean for the first time, entered the maze of islands, islets, small archipelagoes and rocky shoals that dot the sea from San Salvador to Cuba. The ships proceeded cautiously, almost gropingly, through the unfamiliar waters, menaced constantly by rocks and shallows. Both Columbus and Pinzón—we cannot ignore the latter, given his responsibilities and the manner in which he fulfilled them—showed themselves to be great mariners, very prudent and farsighted in their decisions. They sailed for many days in rain and conditions of poor visibility, in places where the eye was the only dependable guide. They had to overcome strong head winds and rough seas. They had the wisdom to have the ships lie to every night, even on the open sea, and were often able to find good berths in sheltered inlets or coves away from the harsh coasts.

Thus they found their way out of the labyrinth of the Bahamas, sounding the depths as they advanced across large banks that opened out fanwise. The last of these banks was the one still marked on today's maps as Columbus Bank. Of all the places that Columbus saw and discovered on his voyages, it is the only one that still bears his name.

They stopped at many islands, going ashore and exploring most of them, and naming them after saints and royalty: e.g., Santa María de la Concepción, Fernandina, Isabela. Most were dreary places, with the same unclothed natives offering as barter such things as skeins of cotton, javelin tips and cassava bread, an unleavened bread made of manioc roots, which the Spanish found inedible. In exchange the natives received little pearls and mirrors. And they were bombarded with questions about gold. No one had any, but the "men from the sky," as the Spanish were now called in those seas, might find some on the next island. Every time, the natives gestured toward the south, as though there really was gold there. The six Indians from San Salvador, brought along as guides and interpreters, confirmed these indications. The Spanish mariners found all the natives courteous, docile and respectful. The good savage was living up to his name.

When Columbus and his men went ashore they visited the natives' huts, which were made of tree branches and had roofs of palm leaves. There they made some exchanges, more for food than for anything else: fruit, edible grasses, and fresh water—of which the fleet's supply was running low, since not one of the islands they had visited had a freshwater river. The natives drank rainwater instead, which they collected in wells. There was also a lack of meat, there being no sheep or goats on these islands, only birds. The Spaniards would come back disappointed from their visits to the villages. Their only source of pleasure was seeing if the young women here were the same as everywhere else.

They discovered hammocks, "beds similar to cotton nets, and made like suspenders." The weave of crossed threads reminded them of "the sieves made in Seville out of esparto grass. One sleeps very well on them, especially as it never gets cold here." They took a few hammocks with them and used them on board the ships. The American Navy used hammocks until shortly before the Second World War; the Italian Navy didn't stop using them until after the war.

Columbus, a very sharp observer, kept notes of everything in his log. Finding little else to get excited about, he praised the climate and vegetation, always with a bit of exaggeration, to make the discovery of these few novelties seem more worthwhile, even in his own mind. "I never grow tired of looking at this splendid vegetation, so vastly different from our own. I believe that it contains many plants and shrubs that would be highly valued in Spain as sources of dye, medicine and spice. But I don't know how to recognize them, which vexes me greatly." He had brought along an expert in Hebrew and Aramaic who was of no use whatsoever to him; a botanist would have been a much better idea. That way, while waiting to find gold he might at least have found some *merces subtiles.* His men did, nevertheless, manage to gather some cinnamon, a bit of aloe and some aromatic resins.

After about ten days of sailing from one island to the next, the natives began talking about a much larger island where there were sailors, ships, a king and, finally, gold. The island was called Colba, or Cuba. Next to it was another large island, which the natives called Bohio and which today comprises Haiti and the Dominican Republic. From their description, Columbus imagined that this Colba, or Cuba, was Japan, and Bohio just another island that Marco Polo had missed. He expressed this belief in the log: "I maintain that Colba is the island of Cipango, since on the globes and planispheres I have seen it is situated in this region, to the southwest. I sailed in that direction."

Following this hunch, Columbus reached Cuba on October 28, 1492, another Sunday. The landing, whose exact location is the subject of much picayune debate, was made in the eastern part of the island, perhaps in the Bay of Bariay, located in that part of the island now called, appropriately, Oriente (the Eastern) Province. Columbus's fleet came from the north, pushed by trade winds. After sighting the shore, with its high mountains in the background, Columbus headed toward "a beautiful river which presented no danger of reefs or other obstacles." He entered the river's mouth and dropped anchor. Had he reached Japan?

A launch was immediately lowered into the water to take Columbus and his escort ashore. As they landed, Columbus was the first to disembark. He ran up the deserted beach. The sad reality of the place soon became apparent. The few fishermen's huts along the shore were shabby and empty. The fishermen had run away. They had left fishhooks and bone harpoons inside their hovels and crude nets of palm fibers out in the sun. But there was no sign of humans still in the vicinity. There was only "a dog that did not bark." Columbus had imagined that he would see balconies of ivory and alabaster, houses roofed with gold, dignitaries dressed in silk and carried around by their servants in palanquins. He expected temple bells to ring and trumpets to sound, since this was how he imagined Japan. Had he come to the wrong place again?

Columbus was soon convinced of his error and without hesitation embraced a contrary hypothesis. His geography was an imagined, invented geography. He was pursuing a dream. When reality did not conform to it, the error lay not with the dream but with reality. A century after Columbus, another great hero of the imagination named Don Quixote behaved in much the same manner. Don Quixote, however, was a literary creation, whereas Columbus belonged to the world of men. Both were motivated by deep, mysterious convictions, and by a very personal way of construing reality. They were guided not by logic but by fancy, by the mirage of their illusion. Didn't everyone say that Columbus was a bit mad? They said the same of Don Quixote. Both became universal figures. They were new, unusual men in a changing world, champions of impossible chimerae. Their actions overstepped the limits of reality, which they saw as limits only in the minds of other men. Columbus and Don Quixote, each in his own way, extended these limits, expanded the minds of other men. They gave others a glimpse of new freedoms attainable only through a rejection of common sense, the authority of knowledge and the conventional strictures within which life flows by everyone's tacit consent. Columbus prefigures Don Quixote in time.

When Quixote appears on the scene, the mentality of his contemporaries is already beginning to change from the effects of Columbus's endeavor, which was an act of rebellion against what was considered to be reality, logic and the foundations of science. Don Quixote arrives in time to confirm that illusions are no less real than certitudes. His absurdity is vital. It is no accident that these two timeless experiences—that of the navigator and that of the knight-errant—arise from the same Spanish matrix, at a time when the society is triumphantly throwing off the yoke of centuries and embarking on an unstoppable expansion toward an alluring new world. Don Quixote rode across this burning terrain, but Columbus invented it. The realm of victory for both was the imagination.

Following a geography that existed only for him, Columbus, after arriving in Cuba, became quickly convinced that he had landed on a continent, not an island, and that this land was China, not Japan. Japan, naturally, had become in his mind the other large island nearby, Bohio (Haiti). The first indications that the land beneath his feet might not be Japan came from what he saw in his explorations of the place, which did not correspond to his image of Japan. But the decisive confirmation of this suspicion came three or four days after landing, when one night in the bay at Mares with a full moon overhead, he carefully took his bearings from the North Star. He had reached the bay on November 1, there discovering the largest mouth of any river seen thus far on the voyage. This fact fed his suspicion that Cuba was not an island, but the outer extension of a continent, since the river seemed by all appearances too large for an island. He named the river Río de Mares. Today the place is called Puerto Gibara, one of the better landing places on the Cuban coast.

Under the November 1 entry in the log one finds the following comments: "I am certain that what was indicated to me to be an island is in fact the continent, and that I am somewhere near Zayto or Quinsay [the names given by Marco Polo to two large cities in China]" . . . "We must be a few hundred leagues, more or less, from one place or the other. I made this judgment from observing the sea, which is coming in differently from before; and yesterday, when sailing west, I found that it was cold." He had heard some natives say the word *Cubanacan. Nacan,* in the island dialect, meant center or city. Columbus, however, immediately thought of the Khan, the Great Khan whom he was impatient to meet. It is incredible how he kept giving credence, almost blindly, to his "interpreters." He followed their advice, even though they kept moving the location of the gold from one island to the next. He also tried to determine his position from what they said. Everything was imaginary, improbable, unclear. But how else could he overcome these uncertainties if not by clinging stubbornly to the conviction that they coincided with what he had constructed in his imagination?

The reading of the North Star that Columbus made on the night of November 2 produced results which to us seem shocking in their inaccuracy. Columbus, at that moment, was at about 21° latitude north of the equator. And yet the figure he came up with in this reading was 42°, the latitude of Boston! Columbus must have been aware that the measurement was erroneous. He had always said and believed that Guanahani—San Salvador, the first island at which they landed—was at the same parallel as the Canary Islands. The course followed during the crossing had never strayed much from this line, after the fleet had pushed off from Gomera and the "due west" command had been given. After San Salvador, all the fleet's movements had been southward. Clearly Columbus could not have believed the data obtained from his reading. He probably thought that something was wrong with the quadrant, and this is how a number of historians have interpreted the episode. They mention Columbus's lack of skill and experience in using the instrument. Las Casas defends his great contemporary as much as possible. He blames the error on copyists and their ignorance of latitudes and longitudes. For the latter are also relevant here. Columbus calculated that he had come slightly more than 3,500 nautical miles in a westerly direction. He was very, very far from Asia's actual location. We know, however, that he had underestimated the size of the globe and overestimated the extent of the Asian conti-

nent. Having set off on his journey with these errors firmly lodged in his mind
—his invented geography—he could easily have come to believe that he had
reached China. And he acted as though this was indeed the case.

Upon learning that there was a "great city" with a "great king"—images
communicated to him by the natives through emphatic gestures—not far
inland from the point where they found themselves, he decided to send a
delegation to visit the place and the person, who might be the Emperor of
China himself. He named an "ambassador" right on the spot, giving the
charge to the interpreter Luis de Torres, who had had nothing to do up to
that point. He gave him Ferdinand and Isabella's letters of recommendation,
which were written in Latin. And with him he sent along Rodrigo de Xeres,
who had once made a visit to a black king in Guinea. The two delegates set
off with an armed escort. Their only instructions were to come back, no
matter what, within six days' time.

They returned the night of November 5 with very discouraging news.
They had gone through a valley and seen many plants and birds. Soon reaching the "city," however, they had found only a rather wretched and primitive
village of about five hundred huts. (Modern Columbian explorers who have
scoured the topography of the time believe that this village corresponds to the
city of Holguín.) De Torres, as ambassador to the king, was carried on the
natives' shoulders up to the hut of the chief, the *cacique* of the region. Formal
greetings were exchanged. Several dozen natives were allowed to touch the
"men from the sky" with their hands. They touched, knelt to the ground and
kissed the hands and feet of the Spanish men. Gold was discussed vaguely.
There was no gold in the village. Gold did not come from this land. De
Torres and Don Rodrigo decided to turn back. The expedition had been a
failure.

(They did, however, come upon a source of great wealth without knowing it. Las Casas tells us that on their way back "the two Christians met many
people along the path, men and women carrying torches of herbs whose
smoke they drank, though it is impossible to see what sort of pleasure or
profit they could have derived from it." They called these "torches" *tobacos*.
They would breathe in the smoke two or three times, then pass the burning
herb to a companion. Within a century all of Europe had learned to do the
same. And Las Casas notwithstanding, they indeed derived pleasure from it,
not to mention the profits reaped by those who procured the herb, perhaps
the New World's greatest gift to the old.)

Columbus once again came away disappointed. But he did not want to give up. He began carefully to explore the northern coast of that eastern extremity of the island of Cuba. He tried to move the fleet eastward, but the trade winds were blowing strongly from that very direction, preventing them from going anywhere and forcing the fleet to remain another few days at the river's mouth. The men used this extra time to scout the waterway in launches and parties on foot. One of these expeditions was made by Martín Alonso Pinzón, who was beginning to feel quite disturbed by the way things were going. He accused Columbus of being "reckless and heedless." He said they were taking too many risks by sailing so aimlessly over rocky shoals, and had no way of knowing if they were even heading in the right direction. Pinzón returned from his expedition up the river with specimens of resin quite similar to Chios mastic, as well as samples of wild cotton and a number of spices, one of which was cinnamon. More importantly, the natives had told him something very interesting regarding the question of gold. When they finally realized what it was that the Spaniards were so doggedly seeking, the natives had pointed their fingers eastward, gesturing toward other islands and repeating a name with a magical sound: Babeque. The island of Babeque. There, according to the natives—still communicating through gesture alone, of course—the people gathered gold on the beach at night, using large hammers to pound it into rods. It was a legend of theirs, and it became a legend for the Spanish as well. Pinzón related all of this to Columbus, who gave the order for the caravels to sail for Babeque, which was assumed to be to the north of Cuba's easternmost point (and which was perhaps the island today called the Great Inagua, located in the channel of water between Cuba and Haiti).

But despite repeated attempts and zigzag courses through rough waters and torrential rains, Babeque, which the men on several occasions thought they had sighted on the horizon, always vanished like a mirage. The skies were very misty, giving an eerie quality of unreality to the physical space, as though it belonged to the realm of dream. During one of those greed-inspired sallies out into the open sea, the *Pinta* itself disappeared, and Pinzón with it. Was this a desired, premeditated separation? Or was it just a confusion of routes or perhaps of signals not correctly understood, or not seen at all?

Posterity has wavered between both hypotheses, one of which finds Pinzón guilty, the other innocent. During the final days of November, while looking for Babeque, the fleet made a long excursion into the open sea, several dozen miles from the Cuban coast. The course had to be repeatedly rerouted eastward, and these changes of direction had to be repeatedly communicated

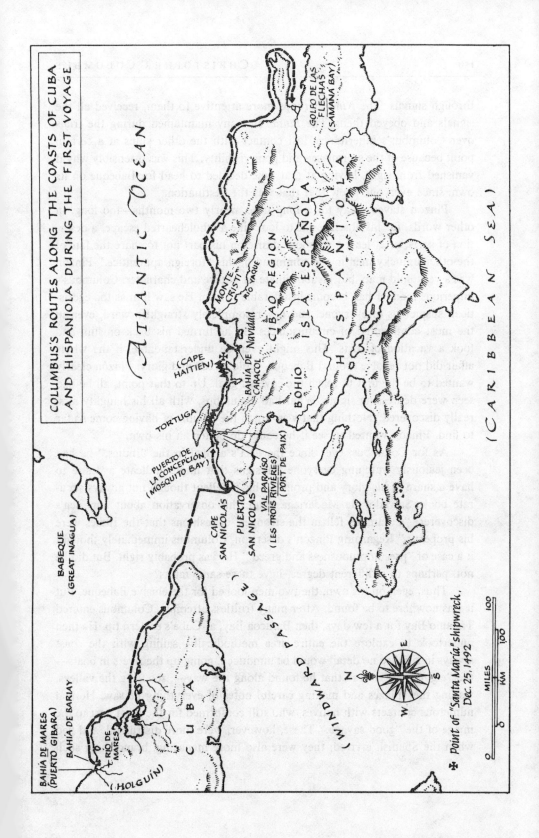

COLUMBUS'S ROUTES ALONG THE COASTS OF CUBA
AND HISPANIOLA DURING THE FIRST VOYAGE

ATLANTIC OCEAN

GOLFO DE LAS
FLECHAS
(SAMANÁ BAY)

ISLA ESPAÑOLA
HISPANIOLA

CIBAO REGION

MONTE
CRISTI

RÍO YAQUE

BOHÍO

BAHÍA DE Navidad

BAHÍA DE
CARACOL

(CAPE
HAITIEN)

TORTUGA

PUERTO DE
LA CONCEPCIÓN
(MOSQUITO BAY)

VAL PARAÍSO
(PORT DE PAIX)

LES TROIS RIVIÈRES
(PORT DE PAIX)

PUERTO
SAN NICOLÁS

CAPE
SAN NICOLÁS

(CARIBBEAN SEA)

BABEQUE
(GREAT INAGUA)

CUBA

BAHÍA DE MARES
(PUERTO GIBARA)

BAHÍA DE BARIAY

RÍO DE MARES

(HOLGUÍN)

WINDWARD PASSAGE

N
W   E
S

MILES
0   100
KM
0   100

✠ Point of "Santa María" shipwreck.
Dec. 25, 1492

through signals. The *Niña,* perhaps more attentive to them, received all the signals and obeyed them. The *Pinta,* as many maintained during the trials over Columbus's inheritance, lost contact with the other ships at a certain point because of the stormy sea and poor visibility. This was ostensibly why it vanished from sight, having at that time decided to head for Babeque on its own, since everyone knew that that was the destination.

Pinzón stayed away for a long time, nearly two months—too long, in other words, for his absence not to look like a wholehearted escape, a desertion of sorts, or at least a stubborn desire on his part not to share the fate of the other unlucky men in the command of this "foreign apprentice." Pinzón was a very bold man, but insubordinate by nature and character. Columbus's imperious manner had become insufferable to him. He saw him as too egotistical, suspicious of everyone, and never completely straightforward, even in the most confidential of circumstances. So he turned his back on him and took a vacation of sorts. This might even be understandable, if the whole affair did not revolve around Babeque—gold, greed and glory. Pinzón clearly wanted to be the first to reach the coveted goal. Up to that point, all he had seen were depressing sights. What had Columbus, with all his haughty airs, really discovered? Nothing that was worth the trouble of having come so far to find. Pinzón wanted to see if he could do better on his own.

As for Columbus, ever since the fleet's arrival in the "Indies," he had been jealously watching everyone for signs that might indicate a desire to have a share of his glory and profit. In his excellent though not always accurate book, Salvador de Madariaga made this observation about America's discoverer: "Columbus felt in the strongest of fashions that the Indies were his property." Regarding Pinzón's desertion, Columbus immediately thought it a case of "presumptuousness and greed." He was probably right. But did he not, perhaps to a different degree, have these same faults?

Thus, each on his own, the two men looked for the elusive Babeque. But it was nowhere to be found. After many fruitless attempts, Columbus entered Tánamo Bay for a few days, then Baracoa Bay, at Cuba's eastern tip. He then undertook to explore the entire area methodically, sailing with the coast always in sight so no detail would be unnoticed, going up the rivers in boats— the "eight great rivers" that he found along the way—, scouring the valleys, visiting the villages and making careful notes of everything he saw. He had numerous contacts with natives, who still conformed for the most part to the image of the "good savage." These, however, were more distrustful, and fled when the Spanish arrived; they were also more menacing, brandishing such weapons as javelins and spears. They lived surrounded by islands that were not always friendly. They had experienced violence and the need to defend themselves. They were especially afraid of a tribe of plunderers called the Canibs or Caribs, who attacked from the sea and fed on human flesh. Everyone was terrified of them. The terms "cannibal," for man-eater, and "Caribbean," for the sea surrounding these islands, both derive from variants of this name.

But of gold the Spaniards found not even a gram. And nothing that even vaguely resembled the China described by Marco Polo. Columbus was certain he was there; he merely convinced himself that he was in a region very far from the urban centers, an area at the outer limits of the continent where there was no commerce or life, like so many other outlying areas around wealthy and important places. He did not, however, have the necessary means to go farther inland, so he decided to abandon this project, which would have proved fruitless. He would return to Cuba another time, in the future. For now it was better to leave. And so he directed his ships—the *Santa Maria* and the *Niña,* as the *Pinta* was still missing—toward the land that could not fail to be Japan: the large island of Bohio (Haiti). It was not far. A branch of sea about fifty miles wide, now known as the Windward Passage, was all that separated it from Cuba. Columbus crossed it at dawn on the fifth of December. A trade wind blowing from the northeast rose up that morning, and the two caravels had to sail close to the wind on a port tack. It took them the entire day of the fifth and part of the sixth to cross the channel. Once across, the mariners found themselves before a new island, at the entrance to a port "as large as the bay of Cádiz." As December 6 was St. Nicholas' Day, Columbus christened the new haven in his name: Puerto San Nicolás, a name it has kept to this day, while all of the other places he had named up to this point today bear different names. Cuba he had named Juana, in honor of Don Juan, heir to the throne of Castile and Aragon. Though the voyage may have been destined never to fade from human memory, the names Columbus gave to his discoveries were not long for this world. As the saying goes: *Nomina temporis pulvis,* names are but the dust of time.

12

Christmas Disaster: The Santa Maria Sinks

The arrival at San Nicolás (now Môle Saint Nicolas) Haiti's westernmost point, marked the beginning of a new chapter of Columbus's voyage of discovery. It also marked the beginning of a new chapter of Columbus's life, in which the still unknown island was to play a central role, in good luck and bad. Columbus's America was for the most part Haiti. There he founded the first cities, discovered the first gold, sowed the first seeds. Haiti became his third country, after Genoa and Spain. And despite the misfortunes that the island had in store for him, it was to remain the only form of success he enjoyed from the undertaking to which he had devoted his whole life.

When he arrived there for the first time, the evening of the landing at San Nicolás, on December 6, 1492, nothing of what he had seen or encountered since disembarking at San Salvador had given him much cause for enthusiasm. He had crossed the ocean, dispelling one of the last great mysteries of world geography. Yet he still had no certain proof of having reached the Indies or the outer limits of the Asian continent. He had seen only naked savages and villages of miserable huts: no brocades, no gold. How could he convince the sovereigns that the splendid Cuban coast along which he had sailed for five weeks was actually part of greater Cathay? Among the attractive prospects of this mysterious part of the globe were the mild climate, the luxuriant valleys, the generally pleasurable surroundings, "good, healthful waters quite unlike the pestiferous rivers of Guinea; so far, not one of my men has suffered from so much as a headache." There was, finally, the prospect of converting to Christianity thousands of savages, which would perhaps constitute, in the eyes of the Catholic sovereigns, the most positive of the opportunities that had thus far emerged. But it all amounted to very little. If Columbus were to return to Spain with only this, his ocean voyage would be seen as little more than a total failure, given all the hopes and expectations it had raised. He didn't even have any stories of monsters to tell, of men with tails or dogs' heads, the kind of exotic mutants that had inspired delectable shudders of horror in those who had read the travel stories of Sir John Mandeville or the chronicles of Marco Polo, which were more authentic but not without their digressions into fantasy. Monsters were in fashion, being a kind of extension of old medieval mysteries into the wider horizons of the current age. But what sort of phantoms could Columbus dream up on top of what he had already seen?

San Nicolás was a magnificent natural port, its deep waters well sheltered from the open sea. The ships could be moored so close to shore that it was possible to disembark directly onto the grass from gangplanks extended from the ships onto dry land. Columbus, however, decided it best not to stop there, and by the next morning, December 7, the ships were sailing past the promontory to the north of the port on their way toward the island's northern coast. Pushed along by land breezes blowing in the right direction, the caravels headed east, always remaining in view of the shore.

Pinzón's prolonged absence had put Columbus in a state of great agitation. He feared Pinzón might find gold before he did, and then race back to Spain to steal his glory. The *Pinta* was faster and lighter than the *Santa Maria*, and Pinzón a seaman of great experience and willpower. This was why Columbus was in such a hurry. And being firmly convinced that the right way to explore the new island was by circling it in an eastward direction, he wanted to make use of the land breezes blowing in that direction, since just a short distance off shore, strong trade winds were blowing in the opposite direction. The land breeze rose up in the evening and did not last long past morning. Columbus thus had to take advantage of the nighttime hours, or at least the dawn and early morning hours, if he was to make progress in that direction. It was perhaps a necessary course of action, but also an imprudent one. The conditions in which he was sailing were not of the most favorable sort. On the contrary. Hugging the coast in this manner—from distances of a mile, a half mile, and sometimes even less—meant running the risk of striking rocky shoals. And sailing at night, even by the light of the moon, which Columbus was trying to use to his advantage, only increased the danger.

On the day of the seventh, just after midday, the caravels were once again forced to drop anchor, in a bay surrounded by hills. It was the eve of the day of the Immaculate Conception. Columbus, moved more by faith than by imagination, named the port Puerto de la Concepción. As soon as the men went ashore, however, they were attacked by swarms of insects so thick and annoying that they decided to call the bay by the more prosaic name of Bahía de los Mosquitos. It still bears this name today.

The sky remained dark and threatened rain, and blustering easterlies continued to swirl in the air. It was impossible to head any farther east. Although it was not the best of berths, Columbus was forced to stop at Mosquitos. The stay dragged on for several days. The sailors battled their boredom by going fishing. They caught a gray mullet, the first fish that resembled "those of Castile." They also caught a few soles and other kinds of fish found in Spanish waters. Even the trees along the shore seemed familiar. They resembled the oaks, holm oaks and cane apples found in the Palos countryside. The weather had become rather cold: "It was almost like winter, or like October in the hinterland of Andalusia." The natives had fled to the hills, "where they made fires, in the manner of warring people sending signals from afar." As for the vegetation and landscape, it became more apparent each day that the island was "large and splendid." The Indians that Columbus had brought with him as guides indicated to him that beyond the island lay a continent "without end," which they kept calling "the land of the Caribs," their terrible, man-eating enemies. Columbus became convinced that this continent must be Asia, the Indies, and that the Caribs must be Chinese pirates who terrorized the islands with their raids.

On the morning of Sunday December 9 Columbus went ashore to plant a large cross at the top of the Mosquitos promontory. From that height he saw, extending farther inland, "beautiful plains, which reminded me of those in Spain, though these are much lovelier." Struck by the vista before him, Columbus "gave this land the name of Hispaniola," the little Spain across the ocean. He took official possession of it, in the name of King Ferdinand and Queen Isabella.

The island's natives, with whom the Spaniards came into contact in the days that followed, were of much more pleasing physical appearance than those of Cuba, being tall, slender and well-proportioned, the men as well as the women. The Spaniards noticed two very young women in particular, "with skin so light they might have been from Spain." The inhabitants of Hispaniola also seemed blessed with better products of the soil and had more developed customs, though they too went around "as naked as the day they were born." As for gold, still nothing, except for a few ornaments worn by "the most noble of the women." The Spaniards asked in gestures where the metal came from. The natives' response, as usual, was vague; the gold was always somewhere else. Babeque was mentioned again, and Columbus's Indian guides assured him that Babeque lay to the north of a small island that he had already glimpsed in front of the bay of the Mosquitos, an island in the shape of a turtle. Columbus had christened it on the spot with the Spanish word for turtle, Tortuga.

It wasn't until December 14, after a whole week of waiting in the Bay of Mosquitos, that the ships could attempt to set sail in the direction of Tortuga. The caravels got as far as the shores of the island, which looked like a large plateau. But when they tried to sail beyond it, in the direction that they had been told would take them to Babeque, they came up against a strong head wind. They were forced to turn around and go back to Mosquitos. They tried again the following day, but the trade winds pushed them into the channel between Tortuga and Hispaniola (Haiti). The sea was very agitated, and they had to hurry to find a landing place on the other side of the canal, facing Tortuga, a few miles past their previous berth.

They found themselves at the mouth of a rather forceful river, whose strong current made it impossible to go upstream in the launches. But the valley before them was strikingly beautiful, opening up into lush, colorful plains full of trees and plants of all kinds. Las Casas describes it as "so beautiful as to seem almost unbelievable." Columbus, abandoning his saintly nomenclature, dubbed it Paradise Valley (Val Paraíso). In the seventeenth century, the French founded a city there and called it Port-de-Paix, the name it still bears today.

Paradise Valley gave the Spanish a magnificent reception. The natives flooded the beach en masse, led by a young cacique barely more than twenty years old. They were quite fascinated by the ships, but at the same time remained very composed. In exchange for a few harness bells and tinted pearls, they gave of their own accord the few grams of very fine gold that several of them were wearing on their noses or ears. They were very beautiful, "the most beautiful creatures we have encountered thus far, with complexions almost white enough to mistake them for real Spaniards."

December 18, the day Spain had made Annunciation Day, a day of prophecy, used to be celebrated in Spain with the announcement of all manner of extraordinary events to come. Columbus sailed the very seas of prophecy. He probably thought, with great pride, that he himself was a prophet caught up in the search for the extraordinary events that he had predicted.

On that day he decided to give a great celebration on board the ships, inviting the local dignitaries to come. The *Santa Maria* and *Niña* were bedecked with festive trimmings, banners flying from the shrouds, spars and masts, heraldic bearings hung from the bulwarks. The bombards fired salvos of greeting. The blasts echoed a long time in the valley, sounding as loud and unnatural as a funeral tribute.

The young cacique, with his retinue, appeared on the beach lying on a kind of palanquin held aloft by four tribesmen. Columbus treated the occasion as though it were a solemn affair of state. But the young cacique did no less. Recounting the event for the king and queen in his log, Columbus wrote: "It would have pleased Your Highnesses to see the dignity of that savage, and the respect shown him by his people, even though they all went about in the nude." The natives were offered the food and drink of Castile. The cacique tasted only a little bit, just out of politeness. When the celebration was over and the young chief was stepping ashore with solemn gait and kingly bearing, Columbus gave him the full naval salute, the bombards firing the prescribed volleys. The cacique was appreciative. But he didn't even turn around.

How depressing it is to read the comments in the log that follow this description of sober elegance! "Your Highnesses should know that this island, and all the others, belong to you as much as Castile does. To rule here, one need only get settled and assert authority over the natives, who will carry out whatever they are ordered to do. I, with my crew—barely a handful of men— could conquer all these islands with no resistance whatsoever. The Indians always run away; they have no arms, nor the warring spirit. They are naked and defenseless, hence ready to be given orders and put to work."

From the very first, Columbus never once considered that the relationship between Spaniards and Indians could be anything but a master-slave relationship. One might have thought that Christian principles had defeated slavery once and for all. Christ's example admonished men to shun greed and cruelty. Nevertheless, Annunciation Day itself was not enough to prevent Columbus from foreseeing a future of oppression, and from finding this a pleasing thought. Thus began a spiral of violence that would last for centuries and fill some of the blackest pages of human history. Las Casas, a man of faith, a Dominican as well as Columbus's devoted friend and defender of his glory, could not keep himself from exclaiming: "Columbus ought never to have uttered those words, since from them arose the abuse inflicted by him and his successors on the Indians."

The principal source of corruption was gold—the anxious, frantic search for gold—and Columbus was its principle agent. Even during his peaceful sojourn in Val Paraíso, he never stopped asking, and having others ask, about gold. From one of the cacique's old counselors he learned that within a radius of one hundred miles there were many islands that produced gold from the earth. He even mentioned "an island made entirely of gold." As we know today, the nearest gold was actually in Costa Rica—beyond the islands, on the continent in places quite far from where Columbus was looking for it. The old man may have vaguely known that there were gold mines in countries whose people had come into contact with Haiti when making the rounds of the islands. Columbus remained convinced that the land of gold lay somewhere to the east. And so on December 19 he stubbornly set sail again in that direction. He advanced farther into the Tortuga channel, wanting to pass all the way through it. From where he began it was only about fifteen miles to the end. But once again the ships sailed into a stiff wind, advancing with great difficulty and only by tacking very close to the wind. The sky was studded with stars, and the sea near shore looked rather calm. Columbus dared to try to exploit the land breezes. He stayed very close to shore, sailing even at night. On December 21, the feast of St. Thomas the Apostle, he sighted a sheltered cove and brought the ships ashore, plumbing all the while the rocky shallows that formed a ring around the bay. The following day he tried to go back out to sea, but the winds forced him at once to beat a retreat. The area was under the rule of another cacique, named Guacanagarí. From his village a dozen or so miles away he sent Columbus messengers bearing gifts. One of these gifts was a gold mask "with ears, tongue and nose made of pure gold." Columbus was overjoyed. "May God in his mercy help me to find this gold—that is, the mine from which it is extracted—for here there are many who claim to know of it." Ten years earlier Columbus had visited a gold mine in Guinea, at La Mina. The image of all that wealth springing forth naturally from the earth's womb had never faded from his memory.

In his discussions with the natives, Columbus heard the word Cibao pronounced. Cibao was the name of the central region of Hispaniola, and it still goes by that name today. But the Admiral mistakenly thought that the name corresponded to Cipango. His desire for this to be true was so strong that he wrote: "I have learned that in Cibao there is a great deal of gold." Christmastime was near, a time to rest one's drives and passions. But gold was also near. Columbus's attraction to it was irresistible, like that of a bee to honey. He felt he had finally reached Cipango. The fabulous palaces with roofs of gold were there, within reach. And so Columbus, unwisely, set off again.

He left the safe haven of St. Thomas on December 23, advancing farther east. Everything that attracted him—gold, the land called Cibao, the powerful cacique Guacanagarí—lay in that direction, and from what he had been given to believe, they were just a short distance from St. Thomas, a stretch of sea that could be sailed in as little as one day. All the things he coveted converged at that single point. He would celebrate the Nativity with the noble Guacanagarí, who had sent him the gold mask as a gift. Guacanagarí was, in a manner of speaking, a lord of Cibao. Columbus beamed with anticipation. He was about to spend a festive Christmas in Japan.

Since this is a very important point in the story of Columbus's voyage, I would like the reader to know exactly where Columbus was at that moment, where he was headed and how he was navigating. I think my description of these things will be aided by the fact that I myself scoured that same stretch of coast slowly enough to study all its details, conducting my exploration from land and keeping my eyes always fixed on the sea on which Columbus was sailing.

It is in fact true that St. Thomas is not many miles from the havens of Cibao. But there are many obstacles that must be overcome along the way. The first is the high promontory that Columbus named Punta Santa, which today bears the name of Cape Haiti. It is the most extended projection of Haiti's northern coast and has very high, mountainous spurs, some of them close to 10,000 feet in altitude. When Columbus saw this enormous, impenetrable wall, it reminded him of Pico de Tenerife, which he had seen in the Canary Islands. Even today, except for a small, populated valley of great attraction to tourists, Cape Haiti is still a mountain wilderness covered with nearly impenetrable forests and brush. The mountain rises up alone, but is part of the range that runs from St. Thomas all the way to the havens of Cibao. This group of mountains must have had a very stormy geological history. The side facing the ocean is harsh and tortuous. Looking as if nature's ravages—earthquakes, seaquakes, landslips—had carved it up in past ages, practically chewed it to pieces, many isolated masses and reefs jut out of the sea, continuing the mountain spur. They look like so many rocks flung into the sea, scattered everywhere. Some of them are quite big, often reaching heights of close to one thousand feet.

Thus the second obstacle: a sea strewn with rocks and reefs across a large area. Columbus had to get around the promontory, sailing first northward then southward, using maneuvers made difficult by the wind direction; then he had to avoid with extreme caution the myriad of rocky masses that jutted out from the water and no doubt branched out into other rocks kept barely concealed by the waves.

A third danger he created himself: that is, it resulted from a conscious decision he had taken. Having combated for days the strong head winds blowing from east to west—the same trade winds whose favor he had enjoyed during the ocean crossing, when his course had coincided with their path—he had no illusions about being able to avoid them if he continued in that direction. With Christmas just one day away, he was afraid their resistance was slowing him down, and he wanted to reach Cibao and Guacanagarí before Christmas. What did he do? He decided to sail only by force of the land breezes, which were blowing more or less gently in the right direction; in other words, he decided to keep as close to shore as possible, sailing almost exclusively by night, before the favorable breeze died down.

Thus he left St. Thomas shortly before the early morning hours of Christmas Eve. He had some difficulty rounding Cape Haiti, which loomed vast and dark and forced the ships to make numerous tacks in order to stay close to the coast on both sides of it. They had to alternate between sailing close-hauled and slackening the bowline, which required a great deal of physical labor on top of the excitement that all were beginning to feel, what with Christmas and gold on the horizon. By nightfall the two ships had passed the headland and could resume their course along the coast, whose white sands and tall trees could be seen leaning seaward in the distance.

On the other side of Cape Haiti, however, the wind dropped almost entirely. The ships kept moving, more by inertia than by anything else, carried more by the current than by the breeze. The sea had become flat as a table, "as calm as water in a dish," according to Columbus. There was a bit of moon in the sky, a moon in the first quarter low on the horizon and on the verge of setting. The light that it reflected off the waves was dim and of no help in navigation. The two caravels, with the *Niña* leading the way "at a distance of about half a league," moved very slowly, but did not really advance. They lay practically still, sails slack.

At eleven o'clock that night, the ship's boy flipped over the hourglass, and the change of shift got under way. The men were very tired, not having slept for more than twenty-four hours because of all the preparations they had had to make for the departure from St. Thomas and the continuous maneuvers required when rounding Cape Haiti. All those who were off duty lay down on the deck and along the bulwarks. Columbus himself walked around a bit on the quarterdeck, exchanged a few words with Juan de la Cosa, who was in charge of the men on duty, and then retired to his cabin. Kneeling down beside his bed, he was probably thinking of Bethlehem and of the great event that was about to be reenacted in the memories of millions of people. He soon fell into a deep sleep.

As soon as they saw him disappear into his cabin, the ship's boys, watchmen and even the men on duty looked for a spot on the deck where they might shut their eyes for a few minutes. It was a strange night, sluggish and lifeless. It gave the men a feeling of abandon much like a sense of safety, which is always a dangerous illusion at sea. Even Juan de la Cosa, ship's master of the *Santa Maria* and second in command, succumbed to the temptation. He made sure the *Niña* was still in front of the ship, showed the helmsman a bright star on which to steady the course, and after commanding him to call for him if the weather or wind should change, he too went below to his bunk to catch some sleep.

The torpor that had overwhelmed most of the crew seemed invincible, and even the helmsman began to nod. Fearing that he might not be able to keep his eyes open at the helm, with a kick he woke up the ship's boy assigned to the hourglass, who lay curled up next to him. Then he entrusted the boy "for a moment" with the tiller, which was large, heavy and hard to maneuver. Columbus had strictly forbidden this, under any circumstances. Thus of the forty men aboard the flagship (not counting the Indian prisoners), not one was still awake by midnight, except for the young ship's boy grappling with the tiller.

And right around midnight, at the very start of Christmas Day, the irreparable occurred—and the unforeseeable—on a very calm sea, barely two or three hundred meters from the shore. I have seen the spot, and have studied at great length the sea where the incident occurred. Just slightly off shore there is a kind of rocky platform not far below the surface, with toothlike projections that come up almost to water level. The local fishermen know them well. They recounted to me how the hooks of their lines often get entangled in the spikes of undersea rock and will no longer come free. Some say that it is the ghosts of men buried in the depths, "some of them sailors from Europe," who in so doing are avenging themselves. In the Creole dialect of Haiti they call these phantoms *aloa*. They are very afraid of them—a fear that neither Columbus, Juan de la Cosa, nor the sleeping helmsman felt.

The poor ship's boy watched the star that he had been told to watch. The

Santa Maria was barely moving, carried forward almost imperceptibly by the current toward the deadly reef. The log describes the moment of impact in the briefest and most telling of fashions: "The boy felt the rudder drag, heard the sound, and started to scream." The admiral was the first to spring to the quarterdeck, together with Juan de la Cosa, who had bolted out of his bed. In a flash the deck was swarming with sailors, the night's silence shattered by shouts and curses. And by orders, of course. Columbus realized at once that the *Santa Maria*'s prow had run aground, though not seriously. The vessel, however, drew more at the stern than at the prow, and in order to get it floating again they had to back it up. Columbus ordered the men to drop the anchor back before where the shoal began, and then to pull on the rope with the capstan so that the boat could move backward and extricate itself—a maneuver known in nautical jargon as "warping." The anchor and the rope, however, had to be taken to the desired spot with the ship's launch, which was lowered into the water at once. Juan de la Cosa jumped into the launch, but no sooner was he aboard than, instead of carrying out the maneuver, he headed as fast as his oars would take him toward the *Niña*, which was still moving forward.

This episode, like so many others, has been interpreted in many ways. Columbus accused de la Cosa of base cowardice and treachery. There had always been a certain ill will between de la Cosa and the admiral. De la Cosa, the ship's master of the *Santa Maria*, was Basque, and made his base in Galicia. A feeling of mutual animosity existed between the Basques and the Castilians on board the *Santa Maria*. De la Cosa was even accused of having used the occasion to bring about Columbus's ruin. Yet the ship belonged to him, and he had no interest in losing it. He justified his actions by saying that as there appeared to be no sign of imminent danger, he left to get help from the *Niña*'s crew. Other reasons for de la Cosa's behavior probably include a sense of dismay over feeling responsible for the disaster, and a fear of punishment. I don't think anyone could ever really explain the reasons for a flight of this sort, the desertion of a frightened, horrified man. But shipwreck was now, in all likelihood, inevitable. And because of the circumstances in which it occurred, the fame that the ship enjoyed in later times, and the man in charge of the ship, it still ranks as one of the most famous shipwrecks in history.

Nearly beside himself with rage, Columbus barked commands in a desperate attempt to save the ship. He ordered the mainmast cut to lighten the vessel's weight and had the ballast jettisoned, along with all other nonessential cargo. But the water was already getting the better of the *Santa Maria*. A wave of undertow breaking against the shallows sufficed to push the vessel farther down on top of the shoal, whose rocks had punctured it and now breached its sides. The stern swung around, and the ship turned crosswise in relation to the sea. Every subsequent wave lifted it up momentarily, only to bring it crashing down again on the shoal's sharp blades. Large, frightening holes quickly opened up in the planking; the boards were all coming apart, the water entering the boat in torrents. At a certain point "the caravel could no longer breathe" and it settled on the bottom, slightly bent, half submerged in the sea. It was mortally wounded . . . and beyond help.

Columbus realized the uselessness of trying to wrench the *Santa Maria* away from its fate. He didn't even wait for day to break. That same night, he and the rest of the crew got into the launches and made their way to the *Niña*, where they all crowded the decks as they watched the flagship in its death throes. At dawn they got immediately to work recovering the ship's provisions, cargo and rigging, until the vessel was little more than an empty scrap of wood impaled on the sea. The shore was so near that the salvage was carried out without much difficulty. Columbus himself went in a launch to the site of the accident. It was his first Christmas on this side of the ocean. Gazing on his lost ship, America's discoverer let the tears stream down his face.

In those moments of anguish the assistance of the cacique Guacanagarí proved invaluable to Columbus. His village was only a few miles from the site of the shipwreck, in a bay that looked a bit like a labyrinth, and which Columbus later named Caracol Bay because of its snail shape. With one of the two launches, Diego de Harana and Pedro Gutiérrez went to ask the cacique for help. Guacanagarí expressed a sincere regret, and ordered at once that the strongest men take all the canoes and head for the site of the disaster to lend a hand in unloading the ship. They worked so energetically that the job was completed before evening. The cacique and his brothers personally stood watch to see that nothing discharged was stolen. "Not even so much as a piece of string was missing," writes Columbus. This sharing of feelings and purpose between "men of the sky" and "savages" was a comforting page in the young history of the New World. Solidarity in misfortune is a natural human response. Columbus commented on the Indians' actions with an allusion to the gospel: "They love their neighbor as themselves."

At Caracol, the cacique Guacanagarí lodged the Spaniards in his houses. Two of the houses were reserved for storing the recovered cargo. The tension of the ordeal began to fade. At first timidly and then somewhat insistently, the Indians began to barter for some of the necklaces, bells and other trifles that had aroused their curiosity during the transport of goods from the ship to shore. They noticed that the Spaniards wanted gold more than anything else. And for the price of a few falcon bells, red berets and little mirrors, they brought many pieces of gold. This surprising abundance of the precious metal lifted Columbus's spirits a bit. Noticing his relief, the cacique hastened to let him know that not far from Caracol, to the east, there was gold in great quantity. It came right out of the ground, he indicated, "in such abundance that the people considered it of little value."

How many times had Columbus been told that there was gold nearby? Each time he had believed it, and each time, just before reaching it, he had been sent elsewhere. Nearby, but elsewhere. This time, too, he believed. He had never seen so much gold, nor in pieces so large, as in the village of Caracol. Guacanagarí, the cacique, had shown him great friendship and honesty. Why would he lie, in such warm circumstances as these? Columbus's intuition worked very swiftly, and his imagination quickly turned his intuition into concrete thoughts and reflections, no longer distinguishing between what was real and what was imagined. This process occurred especially in the face of obstacles, as a kind of antidote to disappointment, a sudden transformation of discouragement into hope. The *Santa Maria* had sunk, and on Christmas night no less. This could only be a message sent from on high. God's will had manifested itself. The shipwreck would compel Columbus to leave a number of his men ashore, whom the *Niña* would not be able to carry across the ocean on the return voyage. These men were destined to stay in this place and eventually to discover the gold mine described by Guacanagarí. Columbus had heard the cacique also mention repeatedly the name of the region where they were: Cibao. There could no longer be any doubt that this was Cipango, Japan. This was precisely why Guacanagarí's gold was a surer thing than all the earlier promises, nearer and more accessible than gold had been at any previous point in the voyage. God had willed the shipwreck of the *Santa Maria* so that a colony would be founded in Cibao, and gold discovered. This is almost certainly how Columbus reasoned at the time. His thoughts are transparent in the log entries for those particular days. At one point he goes so far as to say to his sovereigns: "When I return here from Castile I shall find such riches extracted from this land that the king and queen, within three years' time, will be able to prepare and carry out the reconquest of the Holy Sepulcher in Jerusalem."

This confidence is astonishing, coming barely forty-eight hours after the disaster, from a man left with only one ship out of the three with which he had set out. But who can stop the imagination? Columbus did not waste a single day putting his new plan into action. He selected thirty-nine men from the crews of the two caravels to stay behind and await his return. Their task in the meantime would be to discover "the exact location of the mine from which the gold is extracted." Then, with the timber of the *Santa Maria* dismantled piece by piece from the deck, the keel, the masts, the quarterdeck, the forecastle, the prow, the stern and anything else that might serve as building material, he ordered the men to build "as good a tower and fort as possible, and a wide moat." He had underground cellars dug out and filled with more than a year's supply of wine, bread, grain for sowing, and other things necessary for a long stay. The site where the little fort was erected was almost directly facing the fatal rocks, though a bit farther down the strand in the direction of Caracol, on a wide beach of fine white sand. Today this beach is covered with mangrove swamps, and a thickly wooded area lies behind it. No trace remains of what was the first European colony in America. No one even bothers anymore to try to find it. As the people of the island say, here every abandoned place is quickly engulfed by the tropical forest. Five centuries is surely more than enough time. All that has remained is the name that Columbus gave to the place: Bahía de la Navidad, Christmas Bay. Not far from here is a small village of fishermen called Limonade. They moor their fishing craft at Navidad, along the shore.

The men who were to stay behind were put under the command of Diego de Harana, Columbus's friend from Córdoba. Many of them had chosen to stay of their own accord, such as Pedro Gutiérrez, the King's adventurous majordomo; the surgeons of the two caravels, who were needed to cure the fevers and other new illnesses emerging from the swampy land; the *Niña*'s carpenter, who would oversee all constructions; and even de Escobedo, the interpreter, who up to now had been without purpose but would be even more so if he returned to Spain. Many others begged Columbus to let them stay; they wanted to be the first to get their hands on the gold, since they were all of the opinion that before long all of Castile would be racing to Cibao. Columbus left the garrison one of the two launches, so they could use it to explore the coast in their search for the mine. He also left them the *Santa Maria*'s bombards and falconets, which he had them fire for several rounds so that the natives would realize that these men were not a group of castaways abandoned on the shore, but the subjects of a great sovereign power.

Everything was proceeding smoothly toward Columbus's imminent departure when unexpectedly, on December 27, a number of Indians came to the fort with news that "another house on the water" had been seen berthed at the mouth of a river to the east, a two days' sail from there. It could only be the *Pinta,* since there clearly were no other such "houses" in those waters. Columbus immediately sent a messenger in a canoe to the place indicated. He carried a letter inviting Pinzón to come back, promising that there would be no reprisals. Columbus realized that he could not undertake to explore the island with only one ship. Another grounding or mishap of any kind would endanger their chances of returning to Spain at all. He needed Pinzón.

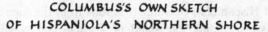

COLUMBUS'S OWN SKETCH
OF HISPANIOLA'S NORTHERN SHORE

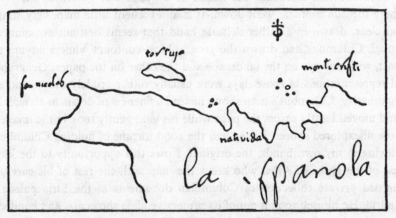

There never was a reply to the letter, however, because the messenger was unable to find the *Pinta.* Two days later another Indian said he had seen it, in the same general area as before. Columbus decided to take the *Niña* in that direction. According to what he had been told, the *Pinta* was in the heart of Cibao. Had Pinzón found gold? Was he preparing to sail back to Spain with news of the discovery and the newfound riches?

Columbus got everything ready for departure, and gave a large farewell party for the men staying behind and for Guacanagarí, who had shown him such kindness. The cacique "showed great sadness, like a friend taking leave of a friend." The admiral put in a good word to him for Harana, Escobedo and Gutiérrez, whom he was leaving behind as his lieutenants, telling the cacique to consider them his "brothers." Water, wood and victuals were loaded onto the ship. And thus on January 4, 1493, the new year already begun, he set sail eastward in search of the *Pinta*.

The going was not easy. The winds were contrary and mixed. "The admiral had never before experienced such winds," wrote Las Casas. The sea was studded with rock formations, shoals and small islands that sprang up everywhere. The *Niña* kept as far off shore as possible, and dropped anchor on January 5 in a bay that was subsequently named Monte Cristi. Many new promontories, havens and small island groups were discovered along the way. Columbus always carefully sketched everything he saw. His collection of maps and simple topographical sketches was quite rich and varied. Unfortunately, of all this work only one illustration has survived, an outline of that very stretch of Hispaniola's coastline that runs from the cape of San Nicolás to Monte Cristi, including the island of Tortuga and Navidad, the point where the *Santa Maria* went down. It is an excellent little map, very simple and clear, drawn in a rather delicate hand that seems hesitant at points, as though Columbus had drawn the geographical contours while studying the coast, with one eye on the landscape and the other on the paper. Geographical representations in those days were usually rather crudely drawn and approximative. Columbus's map shows instead a fineness of detail, as though his hand moved lightly across the page while his gaze gently took in the image of those unexplored shores. I have had the good fortune of holding Columbus's drawing in my own hands, the original. I owe this opportunity to the kindness of the Duke of Alba, who keeps the map with the rest of his carefully guarded private collection of Columbian documents at the Liria palace in Madrid. He himself took it out of its protective glass showcase, and handed it to me that I might have a closer look at it. My hands trembled when I took it. The paper was yellowed, spotted here and there with age. But the drawing was still alive, its lines fresh and eloquent. It was almost like having Columbus himself before me. There are so many uncertainties and conflicts in his image as a man. Yet that document conveyed to me, in an overwhelming fashion, one of the unquestionable virtues that he did indeed possess: his sense of poetry, his love of life and nature. It was as though I could feel and hear him breathing.

Encountering difficulty with winds and shallows in those same seas that we see on the map, Columbus sent a sailor up to the crow's nest to have a look around. The sailor saw the *Pinta* riding a stiff stern wind and racing toward them. In a moment the *Pinta* sighted the *Niña* as well, and the two ships exchanged signals. As there were no berths nearby, they decided to turn around and sail back to Monte Cristi. They got there by evening, and upon arrival, Pinzón immediately boarded the *Niña* to speak to Columbus. It was a cool, guarded encounter, but without incident. Columbus listened in silence to Pinzón's self-justifications and excuses: he had not wanted to abandon the fleet, but had gotten lost in the fog. He had just learned what had happened to the *Santa Maria* and was on his way to bring help when they crossed paths. Columbus did not believe him, but he dissembled his resentment. It amounted to a kind of pardon. Columbus always showed a lack of firmness when faced with problems in human relationships. In material conflicts, such as making practical decisions or choosing a course of action, he could even be too quick and impetuous. But in personal conflicts he never dared attack. He would weigh all the possible consequences very carefully, and the result always came out in favor of prudence. In this particular instance, he knew that he needed Pinzón and his company. How could he sail back to Spain with only one ship? Pinzón, moreover, now that he was back, formed a majority with the sailors of the *Niña,* many of whom were from Palos or Moguer, places where Pinzón was considered something of a guardian angel. The *Niña*'s commander was his own brother. Columbus witnessed the embrace the two brothers exchanged upon seeing each other, and heard the shouts of joy that greeted Martín Alonso Pinzón and the other sailors of the *Pinta*. If he had given vent to his anger, he would have found himself isolated, cast aside. It was wiser to play the card of forgiveness, which appeared noble and generous.

Pinzón told him he had reached the island of Babeque, the Great Inagua, but hadn't found a speck of gold. He had, on the other hand, come upon great quantities of it along the coast of Hispaniola. The *Pinta* had sailed eastward along the coast until it reached a small bay not far from Monte Cristi, where it stopped for many days. Pinzón did not say how much gold he had found, nor what he had done with it. He said somewhat vaguely that farther inland, along a large river, there was supposed to be a large deposit of the precious metal. Pinzón's son, Martín Pérez, recounted many years later what his father had told him. The territory where Pinzón had landed was part of Cibao and governed by a very powerful cacique named Caonabó. Pinzón made some very profitable exchanges with him. "For a little strip of ribbon," said Martín Pérez, who sailed on the *Pinta* after his father's death, "the Indians gave away gold pieces the size of two fingers, and sometimes as large as a hand."

On January 10, the two newly reunited caravels berthed in the small bay described by Pinzón. Pinzón, in a spirit of emulation tinged with a bit of vainglory, had named the river flowing into the cove after himself, Río de Martín Alonso. Columbus wasted no time annulling this name and renaming it Río de Gracias, to underscore the fact that he had pardoned Pinzón. Pinzón is said to have responded in bitterness, "I deserve as much, for having raised you to your present rank." Their dealings with each other remained in any case tense and mutually suspicious. Columbus did not want to make any further investigations into matters concerning gold in the presence of his adversary. He knew now that it was there, that there was a mine just a few miles from the coast, and that Navidad was not far from it. The settlers from the *Santa Maria* would find it easily. He did not mention any of this to Pinzón.

By now almost all of the island's northern shore had been sailed and explored. (In terms of current geography, the two caravels were now in what is known today as the Dominican Republic, which shares with Haiti the island that Columbus named Hispaniola.) The sailors were showing signs of weariness and an anxiousness to return home to Spain. Some of the ill humor of the voyage across started to reappear, brought on by the impatient desire to see family and friends, all of whom were totally unaware of what had transpired in the last four months. But both the *Pinta* and the *Niña* were beginning to take in water: apparently the caulking job done in Palos before departure had been performed too hastily. Given the length and presumed difficulty of the return voyage that lay ahead, it was better to have the ships in top working order before setting off.

The men looked for a beach where they could pull the ships ashore and repair and recaulk the keels. They found a suitable site at Cape Samaná, which had a very wide, well-sheltered entrance and a large sandy beach. Everything seemed to be going quite well when suddenly a rather unfriendly-looking group of natives appeared on the beach. The Spaniards had not seen any Indians like them before. They had colored their faces black with charred wood and wore their hair "as long as the women of Castile," their heads crowned with strange, many-colored headdresses made of the feathers of parrots and other birds. Worse yet, they were armed with bows and arrows, implements of war of which none of the other tribes thus far encountered had shown any knowledge. The Spaniards thought they were looking at the dreaded Caribs that they had heard so much about. When the natives began to advance, brandishing their arms and dragging large ropes with which they apparently wanted to tie up the Spaniards, the latter responded by drawing their swords and counterattacking, injuring two Indians in the process, one of them in the buttocks. The warriors, who were in a group of fifty, quickly took to their heels, leaving bows and arrows behind on the beach.

It was not really much of a battle, but a bit of blood was in fact spilled. It was the first clash between Europeans and Americans, and by no means the last. The Indians at Samaná were *cigayos,* another bellicose tribe. They continued to prowl about the area until January 16, when, with a good westerly wind blowing, Columbus ordered the ships to set sail for Europe. They named the inlet the Bay of Arrows. It was a foretaste of what lay in store for Europe on the new continent.

13

⋙

Glory in Springtime:
Columbus Returns
Triumphant

Sailing from the Antilles to Europe is an easy thing nowadays. Most of all, the route is a sure one. Thousands of ships have taken it for centuries. But when Columbus set off for Spain from the Bay of Arrows, no man, no sailing vessel had ever done so before. It was an entirely uncharted course.

All that Columbus knew was that he could not retrace the course of the outward journey, because the trade winds that had carried him west would be meeting him head-on. He would have had to sail close to the wind all the way back. His caravels had square sails, which were not "weatherly," as were triangular sails. This made all movements rather binding. While the trade winds had brought him straight to those islands as surely as a railroad track, this track certainly would not take him back to Spain. He had to look northward for winds more favorable to the return voyage, beyond the trade-wind corridor, which he would have to cross diagonally. He did not know where the trade winds ended, just as nobody knew anything, or knew very little, about the ocean before Columbus conquered it. He had tamed it successfully on the journey out. Now he had to tame it sailing against the sun. It would not be so easy this time.

Europe, his destination, lay to the east, but as he had to tack to hug the wind, he was forced to bear north. He hoped that he might reach a zone of favorable winds with one long tack, without having to go through too many disorienting maneuvers. And so he planned the following course: he would intersect the course taken coming over, keep sailing toward more northern latitudes, and finally veer in the direction of Iberian shores. This was the "long tack" that he wanted to take. Thus he ordered the caravels to set a course for east-northeast; east, because Spain lay to the east, but one rhumb to north in order to reach higher latitudes.

The sea has never been a place where preestablished intentions can be strictly followed. Its conditions are variable, and do not always conform to one's plans. Thus one must often make one's plans conform to it, and this is what Columbus had to do on his return voyage. He found he was unable to steer an east-northeast course as he had set out to do. His sails did not hug the winds sufficiently well to allow him to do so. He tried everything in his power to stay as much as possible on his initially chosen course, but ended up sailing in various directions between east and north, on a starboard tack; and sometimes on a port tack when the wind pushed the ships southward. Thus, rather than sailing on a single tack as he had originally hoped, Columbus was forced to make many short ones in a variety of directions. All in all, the maneuvers took him more north than east. When the ships had climbed as far north as the latitude of the Bermudas, they encountered westerly winds blowing astern, toward Spain. This route, which Columbus inaugurated unintentionally, later became the customary lane for ocean voyages from the central areas of North America to Europe. (For the reader's information: Columbus set off from Hispaniola at a latitude of about 20 degrees; the Bermudas are at a latitude of around 30 degrees; the Spanish coast that he wanted to reach is at a latitude of slightly less than 40 degrees.)

The first part of the voyage did not present many problems. The ships moved relatively swiftly. Though they had to haul the wind, the waves breaking against their prows were not so large as to impede their progress. The first few days the air was still balmy and tranquil, "and the sea, thank God, still calm." But as the two ships drew farther away from the tropics, the air grew cooler and cooler until the pleasant springlike weather vanished altogether. They soon began to encounter the same phenomena they had seen on the outward voyage: days on end of floating sargassos and flights of petrels and other birds such as gannets, which are similar to cormorants. They were all flying in a southeasterly direction, which led Columbus to believe that there must be islands in that direction. The itinerary of his second voyage was determined in part by these observations.

It has been estimated that the two ships crossed the path of their initial voyage around January 22 or 23, thus entering a more northern area of the Atlantic entirely unfamiliar to them. The sailors caught various kinds of fish, a dolphin, many dorados, and even a large shark. These catches enriched their food supply, which had dwindled to the bare essentials: bread, wine, yams and a bit of dried fish. On January 31, Columbus reached the latitude of the Bermudas, at a point presumably about five or six hundred miles to the east of them, in the middle of the ocean. There he found westerly winds favoring his course. The *Pinta* and *Niña* managed to cover more than one hundred miles per day. The ocean remained calm. On board, there reigned a feeling of contentment, of having accomplished something of great importance, and a sense that the homecoming was rapidly approaching.

As they sailed along in the middle of the Atlantic, it was difficult to judge exactly where they were. On February 6 there was an animated discussion on board the *Niña* regarding the ship's location at that moment. These kinds of disputes often occurred on sailing vessels in those days. Reckonings could only be very approximate, based as they were on experience, intuition, and a rough estimate of the distance covered—and on direct observation of the surrounding sky and sea. The *Niña*'s commander, Vicente Yáñez Pinzón, estimated that they were south of the Azores and west of Madeira. Bartolomé Roldán, an amateur astronomer who had devoted himself to studying navigation during the voyage, reckoned that the ship was already east of Madeira, hence much closer to Spain. Peralonso Niño situated it north of Madeira and west of the Azores. All three were off by hundreds of miles. Columbus more accurately figured that they were about seventy-five miles south of the Azores. He was off by only a couple of dozen miles. Several days later the men presented their reckonings again: in Columbus's opinion, the ships were approaching Flores, the first island of the Azores along the route between the United States and Europe. Admiral Samuel Eliot Morison, who conducted the most complete and thorough study of Columbus's voyage, considered his reckoning to be almost exact. But this we can infer for ourselves today. In February of 1493 Columbus was proceeding blindly for the most part, not really knowing where he was, how far European shores might be, or if the course he was taking would even get him to where he wanted to go. Madeira and the Azores might have served as points of reference, but they were specks of land in the middle of the vast ocean. It was far more probable that the men would not even see them and would sail past them at a good distance than that they would see them appear on the horizon, which by now had been empty for nearly a month.

One night Columbus had the quadrant brought to him on deck, so that he might try once and for all to determine the ships' position. He had used it before with less than desirable results but had blamed the instrument, saying that it did not function well and gave erroneous readings. He had hung it from a nail in his cabin and resolved to have it checked once back in Europe. This night, the problem was compounded by rough seas that made an accurate reading impossible. It was better to observe the North Star unaided. Columbus noted in the log: "The North Star seemed as high as it appears at Cape St. Vincent in Portugal." Cape St. Vincent is situated at 37 degrees latitude north; Columbus at that moment must have been at about 34 or 35 degrees latitude. Says Morison: "Not a bad result for an observation made with the naked eye." The colder currents coming down from the north, as well as the changing weather conditions, also provided Columbus with increasingly reliable evidence. Transcribing from the log, Las Casas writes: "The sky was very changed and rainy, and it was quite cold. This led the admiral to believe that he was at the latitude of the Azores."

The winter of 1493 was indeed an exceptionally cold and stormy one. The Gulf of Genoa froze over, and at Lisbon ships were trapped in the port for months because of head winds blocking the exit and dissuading sailors from setting out to sea. The two caravels, at this point in our narration, had just entered one of the most turbulent parts of the Atlantic—that stretch of ocean where large masses of cold air come down from the Arctic and clash with warm and humid air rising up from the tropics. The greater the difference in their respective temperatures, the greater the violence and force of the colliding clouds. The winter in which Columbus made his return crossing, the skies over the Atlantic were in one of these dramatic, volatile states. The collision of the two air fronts was a very violent one, and had a fearful effect on water conditions. As the two ships approached the Azores, it is safe to assume that they crossed the meeting point of the two air masses. Admiral Morison has calculated that the sea reached force 8 on the Beaufort scale, a formula for certain disaster for two vessels of such small tonnage as the *Pinta* and the *Niña*. Already one of the three ships that had left Palos, the *Santa Maria*, had been lost. Now the danger loomed that the other two caravels would vanish into the sea, and that a veil of silence would descend for all eternity over Columbus's deeds.

The storm, which was of a force never before seen, lasted three days and three nights, from February 12 to 15. The log describes its stages in great detail, starting with when "the sea began to swell and the sky grew stormy," up to the peak of the fury, with "the ocean . . . in fierce rebellion, such that we could neither advance nor make our way out of the waves attacking the caravels and breaking against them." There was "great suffering and danger," and "if the caravels had not been very good ships, and well repaired, they would surely have been lost."

The only chance they had was to have the ships lie to, sails shortened to a bare minimum, leaving just enough out to follow the sea and attempt to escape the storm. Such were Columbus's orders on the first night of the storm, when the ships were being tossed about like shoots of straw in a whirlwind. "Seeing that the danger was growing, the admiral gave in to the tempest," transcribes Las Casas from the log. The ships were no longer following a course. The officer on duty could only watch every billow as it approached, so as to confront it from the best possible angle. If a wave were to make the ship list sharply to windward, the *Niña*, which carried little ballast, might have easily capsized. And in those seas, the *Pinta* would certainly not have been able to pick up the survivors.

The *Pinta* also "went where the wind would take it." Clearly it was impossible to sail in convoy. At one point the *Pinta* disappeared from the *Niña*'s sight. For an entire night Columbus flashed signals from the ship's lamps. The *Pinta* responded faintly until the storm's force pulled it too far away. Fernando recounts: "Thus when day broke they found themselves completely lost from the other's sight, and each ship must certainly have thought the other had gone down."

The *Niña*'s crew, in terror, cried out for help from the powers above. The whole ship became a chorus of prayers and invocations. They vowed to make a pilgrimage to the Sanctuary of Saint Mary of Guadalupe in Estremadura, one of the most famous and venerated shrines in all of Spain. They drew lots to see who would lead the procession, trying in this pious manner to pass the time and forget the tempest, as much as this was possible. In a beret they put as many chick-peas as there were men on board. On one of the peas a cross had been carved, and the man who drew this one would lead the pilgrimage. The marked chick-pea fell to Columbus, most likely not by accident: once again, he probably wanted to maintain his preeminence. But since neither wind nor water showed any signs of calming down, the men vowed to make a second pilgrimage, and drew lots again. This time the "winner" was a sailor from Cádiz. Columbus promised to finance his trip, which was to be to the Sanctuary of Our Lady of Loreto, in the Papal States in Italy. The storm, however, kept jolting the ship so fiercely, pitching it from one wave to the next and soaking it through to the skeleton, that still more devotions were deemed necessary. "On the first dry land that they should safely reach, all the sailors resolved to go in procession, with only shirts on their backs, to the first church of Mary the Holy Virgin." Once again Columbus drew the chick-pea marked with the cross. There was probably a sailor skilled in games of chance manipulating the lotteries, which were beginning to seem fixed. Prayers were the only words audible on board. After two days and two nights in the middle of the hurricane, the men were no longer praying for anything but their souls: "No one thought any more about escaping the storm, which was so terrible that they all considered themselves doomed."

Even Columbus feared the worst. He later wrote that his doubt was blamable, since divine providence had wanted and guided his discovery, and would never have buried knowledge of the deed in the silent ocean, which had already been conquered. Columbus's greatest fear was that his fame would be eclipsed forever. While the elements were raging at their fiercest, and the ocean, as his son Fernando puts it, "was raising its head ever higher," the admiral hastily drafted a brief account of the voyage on leaves of parchment, which he wrapped in oilskin. This he put in a barrel which he tossed into the ocean. It was never found. Many forgers in the centuries that followed claimed loudly to have come into possession of the manuscript. A swindler from Wales put one such "copy" up for sale in 1892, the year of the most recent centenary. But who would believe him, when the text that he claimed was the original was written in English?

During the return voyage Columbus did write a letter recounting the story of his discoveries. It bore the title *De insulis inventis,* "On the discovered islands," and he hoped to send it to the court as soon as he arrived in Palos, as a public announcement of his achievements. He did in fact do so, and then had many copies made at court, which were sent to the most eminent persons in the kingdom. One of these copies, addressed to Luis de Santangel, who was in a sense the major financer of the enterprise, was printed in Barcelona in the same year, 1493, and rapidly disseminated throughout Spain and the rest of Europe. It constitutes the first instance of the news of a major event being distributed immediately after the occurrence. The style is brief and condensed. It could serve even today as an example of the work of a good reporter who knows how to present, comprehensively and succinctly, the events to which he has been a direct witness.

The sky began to clear up a bit by sundown on the fourteenth, the third consecutive day of severe storm conditions. The waves showed signs of diminishing in force. The winds had shifted and now came out of the east, blowing directly away from Spain. Columbus, however, did not dare maneuver the sails to exploit the wind, but just let the ship be carried along. On February 15, at sunrise, land was sighted ahead. Delivered from their anguish, the men began to speculate as to what shores they might be: some said Madeira, others believed they were nearing a promontory north of Lisbon, and still others even hoped it might be Castile. Columbus remained firm in his belief that the land sighted was one of the Azore islands. Once again he was correct: it was the island of Santa Maria, the southernmost of the archipelago.

Air and ocean were still so agitated that the ship had to wait a long time before dropping anchor. Columbus had initially had no intention whatsoever of stopping at the Azores, and indeed had wanted to avoid places under Portuguese dominion at all costs. But the ship as well as its men had emerged so bedraggled from the tempest that it would have been absurd not to land. The need for water, firewood, fresh food, and rest most of all, was too great. The night before going ashore Columbus finally slept, after four sleepless days. "His legs were all numb and aching from exposure to the cold and water, and from lack of nutrition."

Finding a place suitable for anchorage was in itself anything but easy. The island of Santa Maria has no natural ports, and the few spots where one can cast anchor become impracticable when the wind is blowing in from the sea. Columbus sailed up the coast to the island's northern side and there dropped anchor, more or less poorly, in front of a strand no more than half a mile in length. There was a village on the coast called Our Lady of the Angels. The fishermen who lived there were astonished to see a caravel arrive on their shores. None of them, they said, could ever remember having experienced a storm as violent as the one that had ended the day before. They thought it impossible for anyone at sea during that time to have survived.

In the village the Spaniards looked for new supplies of water and food. But first they fulfilled the vow made at sea, the third of the series. In Our Lady of the Angels there was a little chapel devoted to the Virgin Mary where the sailors went as penitents in procession to render thanks to the Madonna, after having removed all their clothing except their shirts. Columbus had prudently sent only a part of the crew ashore, with a good number of men remaining on board, as is commonly the case when ships lie at anchor. It was a wise decision. When kneeling in prayer, the sailors were surrounded by a crowd of islanders and taken prisoner. The island's governor, João de Castanhiera, was on the alert for illegal traffic of the sort that the Spanish continued to practice along the coast of Guinea despite the pledges made in treaties. The Azores, especially in stormy seasons, were an almost obligatory port of call for ships coming from Guinea. The sailors immediately spoke in their own defense, saying that they had come from the Indies, from the other side of the ocean, but everyone thought their story to be too farfetched to believe.

Governor Castanhiera also seized possession of the beached launch that had taken the sailors to shore, put it in the water, boarded it and headed straight for the *Niña* anchored not far away. Once he was within calling distance, he began to rail against Columbus, who had just witnessed the whole scene from the deck. "I am the Admiral of the Ocean Sea and Viceroy of the Indies, which belong to the Spanish Crown," Columbus shouted, leaning out toward the launch. "What right have you to detain my men?"

The governor started laughing. "And you introduce yourself from that little nutshell? An admiral does not go around in a wherry. As for the sovereigns of Castile, they are not my concern. This is Portuguese territory." Both men flew into a rage. Columbus flashed his credentials from the *Niña*'s deck, but refused to hand them over to the governor so that he could verify their authenticity. The governor in turn refused to free the men taken prisoner. Columbus replied that he would not leave the island until he had captured one hundred Portuguese subjects, whom he would then take back to Spain chained up like slaves. The bitter negotiations were broken off, among other reasons because the sea had become stormy again. The wind raged with such fury that one of the anchors' ropes snapped. Columbus tried to seek refuge in a more sheltered spot, and so set sail for the island of San Miguel, about forty miles away. But most of the crew's sailors by trade had gone ashore and had been taken prisoner. Those remaining on board were for the most part functionaries, civilians and Indians, along with only four or five crew members capable of manning the ship, clearly not enough for sailing in a storm. Thus the *Niña* lay to through the night, at the wind's mercy. The next morning it returned to Santa Maria.

A good night's sleep had brought some sense to the minds of the Portuguese. Two clergymen and two notaries came aboard the *Niña* to examine Columbus's recommendations. They were deemed valid, and the sailors were promptly released. On February 24, a Sunday, Columbus was finally able to set off again. In the Azores he had lost seven days and three anchors, as the wind kept breaking their ropes. He pointed the prow toward Cape St. Vincent, which was the course one had to take to go to Palos. Palos was eight hundred nautical miles from the Azores, a week's worth of sailing. But the stretch of ocean between the Azores and Iberian shores is always very stormy during the winter months, and was especially so during Columbus's return. After sailing barely two hundred miles east, the *Niña* ran up against another frightful storm whose clutches it did not escape until it was just a short distance from the Portuguese coast—not quite where Columbus had wanted to go, but farther north, near the mouth of the Tagus, on whose banks sits the city of Lisbon. For six days the vortex of the hurricane held the ship in its power. This time around, the center, the eye, of the Atlantic cyclone probably formed closer to the *Niña* than the previous one had done. This new misadventure really put Columbus's ship to the test: the *Niña* failed to hold its course and was forced to make port at the Portuguese capital, which was the last place Columbus wanted to land. And then, after so much damage, the fading cyclone's last gasp was a series of squalls that "shredded all the sails and once again put the ship in great danger." Morison eloquently describes it as follows: it was "as though an enemy fleet had fired upon the caravel from beyond the horizon." On March 4, amid lightning, thunder and whirlwinds, the ship came very close to land, to the rock of Sintra, which overlooks Cascais and the Tagus estuary. The *Niña* came very close to smashing against the rocks, which would have meant certain death for the entire crew.

Columbus slid past Cascais, from whose shores some fishermen spotted the little ship riding the storm, which was so fierce that "they spent the entire morning praying for the safety of those sailors." Anchor was finally dropped that same morning, in the channel that leads into the Tagus. The port where Columbus landed was—and still is—called Port Restelo. At that time it was outside the city, some four miles downstream. A large vessel flying Portuguese flags and armed with heavy artillery lay at anchor beside the *Niña* at the channel's mouth, as though guarding the port. The recent experience in the Azores counseled Columbus to exercise great caution. He hastened to send a letter to King John asking permission to sail upstream as far as Lisbon, leaving behind the distant, solitary berth where he was at that moment. He needed the services of a shipyard to get his vessel back in sailing condition after all the damage and abuse it had sustained during the two severe storms.

In the meantime, a launch set out from the nearby warship and came toward the *Niña*. It was carrying the ship's second in command, Bartholomeu Dias, who five years earlier had sailed around the Cape of Good Hope. Columbus and Dias together represented a glorious chapter in the history of navigation. In these strained circumstances, however, their discussion was limited to bureaucratic formalities and remained cold and detached on the part of each great navigator. Dias asked Columbus—with the tone of someone giving an order, this being his territory—to come on board the Portuguese ship to make a report to the captain. Columbus repeated the haughty pronouncement he had made in the Azores: I am Admiral of the Ocean Sea, and only force can separate me from my ship. Dias then asked to examine his papers. Once he was aboard, Columbus showed them to him. There was something quite extraordinary in what Columbus had achieved, and the Portuguese realized this. The commander of the warship decided to come aboard the *Niña* to pay homage to Columbus, "with great display and a fanfare of drums, fifes and trumpets." He put himself entirely at Columbus's disposal for anything he might need.

Two days later a gentleman of the court appeared at Restelo with a card from the king inviting Columbus to pay him a call. Columbus in a way dreaded this encounter because of all that had taken place between him and John II in years past. Yet he could not refuse. The king had granted the *Niña* permission to sail up the Tagus to Lisbon, and had also given Columbus unlimited credit at the royal shipyards for all necessary equipment and repair work.

In Lisbon there was an epidemic of the plague. King John had chosen as his refuge a monastery surrounded by a large pine forest, upstream from the city. Columbus went there under the escort of the king's men, and brought with him the handsomest and healthiest of the Indians that he had taken prisoner across the ocean. The meeting between the king and Columbus was charged with tension. America's discoverer had stood once before at the foot of that throne, a shunned petitioner. King John tried to determine just where, in the adventures that Columbus recounted to him, truth ended and deception began. He was skeptical about these Indies, and suspected that the Spanish expedition had come from Guinea, or from some other land belonging to Portugal. They were both very willful, passionate men. Columbus at the time was forty-two years old, King John thirty-eight. But the king barely lived two more years, never making it past forty.

With specific designs in mind, the king showed great magnanimity. He mentioned nothing of their past dealings, and received Columbus "with many honors, letting him sit in his presence with his head covered." An admiral's treatment. He congratulated him on the success of his voyage. Then, after a brief silence, he expressed his opinion that "according to the current treaty between Portugal and Castile, this discovery and conquest belonged to him."

(He was referring to the treaty of Alcaçobes of 1479, signed by his father. But the world had changed since then, and Columbus's enterprise upset the very terms of the question. The treaty of Alcaçobes was no longer a valid guideline.)

The admiral responded dryly that he had "no knowledge of that treaty." He knew that Spanish mariners were forbidden to sail to Guinea, and he had respected this prohibition. John II remained impervious. He let Columbus speak freely, but soon Columbus got carried away by pride, vanity and an uncontrollable desire to vindicate himself with this powerful man who had not believed in him. He punished him merely by showing him that he had been mistaken. It was a risky attitude to assume. The court chronicler Ruy de la Peña states that the gentlemen in the king's retinue who witnessed Columbus's bold impudence were quite nonplussed. They judged Columbus guilty of "discourtesy and insolence" and supposedly urged the king to execute "that braggart." "But the king," continues the faithful chronicler, "was a God-fearing man and would not listen to them." The Lisbon court was famous for its cruelty and bloodthirstiness. The dynasty had been threatened by too many conspiracies not to have had to resort often to violence. This same John II, "a God-fearing man," had with his own hand stabbed his brother-in-law, accused of plotting behind his back. Columbus might very well have been in danger for his life during the two days and two nights he spent in that monastery buried in the woods.

When he returned to Lisbon he found the *Niña* in perfect condition: new sails, a shiny new varnishing, rigging all back in working order. He weighed anchor at dawn on March 13, and set sail for Palos. He was still deeply concerned, however, about the fate of the *Pinta* and Pinzón. Whatever had happened to them? Could they possibly already have arrived back in Spain, and Pinzón already appropriated for himself the joy of announcing his achievement? He might by now be headed for the court, which from what Columbus had heard in Lisbon was presently in Barcelona. But if the news had already reached Spain via Pinzón, they would have known about it in Lisbon; something would have leaked out. King John, on the contrary, had seemed entirely in the dark on the matter.

The *Pinta* at that moment was no more than thirty or so miles away, though still behind him. Both Columbus and Pinzón were entirely unaware of each other's movements. After they got separated by the storm on the night of February 13, Pinzón never reached the Azores. He knew what sorts of procedures to follow when caught in a storm in those waters. He had to abandon temporarily all plans of sailing due east to Spain, and to try instead to climb farther north in order to get around the storm from above. Thus he ended up in Bayonne, in the Bay of Biscay, a long way from the Azores but not far at all from the Spanish coast. From Bayonne he sent a message over land to the sovereigns, asking permission to see them to tell them in person the story of the voyage. A reply arrived two weeks later, responding in the negative. The sovereigns maintained that it was up to the admiral to present an account of the voyage and enterprise. He was the man they wanted to see.

This happened in early March, and hence for the first half of the month the court clearly must have already known of the discovery, whether from Pinzón's announcement or from reports coming out of Lisbon. Pinzón left Bayonne and sailed straight down the Iberian coast on his way to Palos. He escaped the second storm, and did not stop in Lisbon. He had traveled faster than Columbus, though sailing a greater distance. But his disappointment over the sovereigns' refusal had robbed him of the joy of returning. Pinzón felt hounded by this Columbus, crushed by his arrogance. Of course, as far as he knew, the admiral's ship might have gone down in the hurricane, and Columbus with it. But he dared not hope for this, since on board the same ship was Vicente Yáñez, his dearest brother.

At dawn on March 15, 1493, Columbus entered Spanish waters after rounding Cape St. Vincent. He had the ship's guns fire a salute: happiness and triumph reigned on board the *Niña*. On the *Pinta*, however, just a few hours' distance behind it, anger and frustration were the order of the day. Life's double edge cuts deep: of one single event, one single achievement, it can make two camps of emotion and divide the memory of something accomplished by joint effort.

Once he reached the Saltes Bar off the mouth of the Río Tinto, Columbus had to wait for the tide to come in to sail upstream. When he could finally proceed, he passed again below the walls of the monastery of La Rábida, saw again the castle and houses of Palos and the Church of St. George, where he had gone to pray the night before setting sail. The ship's log, from which I have quoted at length, comes to a close with these simple words, related impersonally by Las Casas: "At midday [the admiral] entered the port of Palos, from where he had set off on August 3 of the previous year." The voyage had lasted eight months.

Chroniclers would remember for years the *bodas y banquetes,* the celebrations and feasts that livened many Palos evenings that spring in honor of the new heroes. For this was what the people considered the sailors returned from the Indies: heroes. They were the focus of everyone's curiosity and admiration, they and the strange people they had brought back with them as proof of their deeds, the silent Indians lost in a world that was also "new" in their eyes. People came from Moguer, Huelva and the entire Niebla country-side to stand in line to see them. Among the guests of honor the only one missing was Martín Alonso Pinzón. He arrived immediately after Columbus, on the evening of the same day, and straining his eyes from the Saltes Bar he noticed the *Niña* already at port, its sails furled. It was just before sunset, and the sky was still light. Instead of waiting for the evening tide to take him up the river, Pinzón went ashore on a launch, landing outside the city. He did not go to greet the admiral, nor even his own brother. He went straight to his house in the country between Palos and Moguer, went to bed, and within five days he was dead. Was it weariness? A broken heart? Envy? He probably feared that Columbus would have him imprisoned for desertion. What lay heaviest on his heart, however, was the Crown's slight, which had defeated all his hopes. However fair or unfair it may have been, there was now a great distance between him and Columbus, the distance between obscurity and glory. And in that abyss he died.

Columbus's glory was to be celebrated in Barcelona, at the royal court. By land, Barcelona was a good seven days away from Palos. Columbus had originally wanted to arrive in Barcelona from the sea, entering the port with banners flying, a proud victor over the ocean. But then Pinzón's arrival prompted him to move fast. Pinzón had disembarked and then disappeared. Columbus's mind filled with suspicions of outrages and vendettas that Pinzón could never have fostered. He did not learn of his death until later, and it wrung his heart when he did. They had shared the greatest adventure of their respective lives, had felt both love and hate for what each of them was to the other, and for what each had done. It is not uncommon to mourn the loss of an enemy. Part of oneself dies with him. What Columbus could not have known at that time was that the rivalry would not die with Pinzón. Through Pinzón's heirs, it was to haunt Columbus and his memory for the next three generations, for more than a century. And it was not so much the accounts of the voyage as the chronicles of the trial that created an image of Pinzón as a figure at least as glorious as Columbus, a Pinzón who was the real discoverer of America, as is written—in vain—on the monument in Palos.

To speed things up, Columbus went to Seville and waited for the royal messenger to arrive from Barcelona with permission to appear before the king and queen. Holy Week was under way in Seville, and Columbus entered the city on Palm Sunday, "with great honors." Attending Easter mass in the large cathedral, dark as a forest, he was showered with admiration by the townspeople. Everywhere he went with his escort of Indians and caged parrots, a crowd would follow close behind and women would watch from their windows, applauding him and pointing him out to others: he was the man who had reached the Indies by sea and had come back safely. Las Casas himself remembers witnessing as a child Columbus's appearances in Seville and feeling very excited about the wonderful tales told of the voyage and the Indians that he saw one evening passing through the gate of Las Imagines. His young companions had wanted to pinch them to see if they were real.

The letter came from the king and queen. The manner in which it was addressed gave Columbus good reason to feel proud: "To Don Cristóbal Colón, our Admiral of the Ocean Sea, Viceroy and Governor of the Islands discovered by him in the Indies." They were anxious to see him, and still more anxious to plan more expeditions across the ocean. "It is our desire that what you have begun with God's help should be continued and perfected. Come at once, and make haste."

Columbus left Seville immediately, escorted by his officers, servants and Indians. He brought with him many objects he had found in the islands: pieces of pure gold, amber, cotton, aromatic herbs, not to mention the colorful parrots and other birds "never before seen or heard of." Crowds of people flanked this spectacle as it advanced along the road between Seville and Barcelona. Columbus also passed through Córdoba, where he spent the night. He was welcomed by his sons and by his old friends from the druggist's shop. And of course by Beatrice as well, though this is never mentioned in the histories: better to hide past sins. Columbus considered Córdoba his home. The city honored him with great celebrations. Then the glorious procession crossed the Sierra Morena, went down to Valencia and then continued along the coast to Barcelona. It arrived there on April 20. Says Oviedo: "The court and the entire city went outside to welcome the admiral."

Isabella and Ferdinand waited for him at the royal palace, in the rectangular courtyard paved with stone that one must cross lengthwise to reach the palace entrance. The Royal Palace of Barcelona in the late fifteenth century was still the former residence of the counts of Barcelona, in the heart of the old city. It is a building made of gray stone and is not particularly grand in appearance, with simple, graceful arches in front of low, compact walls. To get to the palace one had to pass through the narrow streets of medieval Barcelona alongside the cathedral, the bishop's house and the old monasteries. In the company of courtiers and his train of officers and servants, Columbus crossed the dark little streets of the district on his way to the open courtyard in front of the palace. The courtyard was teeming with princes, grandees, nobles and dignitaries with their squires and families and *todo el boato*—all the pomp and splendor of the most famous court in Europe.

The reception was a public one. On one side of the courtyard, between the palace and the palatine chapel (dedicated to Saint Anne), a platform had been erected to seat the king, the queen and all the nobility. All except the sovereigns rose to their feet when Columbus entered, a custom usually reserved for the grandees of Spain. There were shouts, applause, and banners waving in the air. Armor and brocades sparkled in the April sun. The king and queen, together with court intimates, the Prince Juan and the highest officials, withdrew into the palace to the Great Hall, where the sovereigns sat on their thrones. Columbus was brought before them: he climbed the steps with proud bearing and solemn gait, the celebrated man of adventure crowned with a head of white hair accentuated by his still youthful face. He smiled broadly. He masked neither his joy, his pleasure, nor his pride: he had risked his life—and defeat—for this moment.

Ferdinand and Isabella rose to their feet, extending their hands to him. Columbus kneeled to kiss them, whereupon the sovereigns graciously asked him to stand and take his place with them and the Prince Juan. A chair was brought for him, a very rare occurrence in audiences with the king and queen. Columbus was treated almost as an equal, with one difference: his chair had no back to it.

For more than an hour the sovereigns besieged him with questions, asking for every last detail. They examined the strange objects he had brought, and had the Indians speak. Amid all that majesty, the Indians stood half-naked, painted, and according to Lope de Vega, *bozados*—"muzzled." A page carrying a trayful of gold bars circulated among the guests. Another went around with the wicker cages containing parrots with green and yellow feathers. Ferdinand and Isabella's eyes filled with emotion as they listened to Columbus describe his adventures in that winning, eloquent voice of his. When Columbus raised his eyes from time to time, he encountered Isabella's gaze. She seemed to be bursting with joy, and the gentle smile that Columbus thought he saw rise to her lips bore a hint of tenderness, ever so slight.

After the interview everyone gathered in the Chapel of St. Anne to recite the *Te Deum* in thanks. Columbus stood beside his sovereigns the whole time, honored and respected in every manner possible. When they went to eat dinner in the royal apartments, Columbus was served "covered"—that is, with a cover over his plate, placed there after the king himself had sampled his guest's food. This practice was called *salva* and expressed the highest regard, being usually reserved for persons of royal blood. A historian of the time, Gonzalo Fernandez de Oviedo, witnessed these events in person. His account of the festivities in Barcelona on Columbus's return is quite fascinating.

For Columbus, those April days were to be the summit of his success. Never again for the rest of his life would he experience anything like it. Someone once wrote that if he had been wiser and less ambitious, he would have stopped at that point and not sought further glory, honors and wealth. The person who wrote this did not know, or had forgotten, the sort of man Columbus was. There is no choice between wisdom and ambition for the sort of temperament that Columbus had in such abundance. The admiral had to keep riding his phantoms across the horizon, like Don Quixote his nag Rocinante. Both men saw things before them which no one else saw. Columbus could not quit before he had met the Great Khan, before he had found the source of gold, before he had converted the Indians.

Glory calls for more glory. In this sense, the enterprise seemed to be just beginning.

14
༄༅།

Second Voyage:
The Thousand Islands

The news that a man had discovered another world on the face of the earth spread with a lightning speed never before seen. Not even Caesar's death, or Charles Martel's victory over the Moslems—to mention two events that changed the course of history—became common knowledge as swiftly as Columbus's great find. Swiftly, that is, considering the manner in which information was disseminated before the advent of mass communication, which is a very recent development in history; whereas for thousands of years news was broadcast by such means as fire signals from elevated land, soldiers from Marathon running as far as forty kilometers, couriers on horseback carrying letters from one post stage to the next.

In the case of Columbus's discovery, it was not just the speed with which word got around, although it was rather extraordinary that within two months of his arrival in Barcelona the news had reached Rome, Florence, Basel and Paris. What was even more surprising was the readiness with which the minds and imaginations of his contemporaries embraced the event. They immediately realized that the world had become larger, and that this in turn would change human society and the world of the individual. There weren't even any reactions of incredulity, of the sort that almost always greet a new discovery. No, Columbus's adventure was immediately accepted as true. Perhaps it was a breakthrough that had been long awaited, hoped for, like the flash of lightning that promises relief from the summer's heat. Columbus lived at the same time as men such as Leonardo da Vinci and Michelangelo. The human mind was reaching ever higher; it was a time of prodigies. Columbus's own mind thrived in this atmosphere, drawing stimulation and inspiration from the prevailing mood. Should there be any surprise that the world welcomed his discovery, realizing at once that this propelled it into the future?

Indeed, there had been, so to speak, a pre-Columbian Europe as well, which came to an end on October 12, 1492, with the discovery of America. When we speak, however broadly, of a New World, we should bear in mind that Europe as well, from that moment on, became a new world. The term was first used by Pietro Martire d'Anghiera, a truly unusual man—diplomat, humanist, commentator, and a great disseminator of information; a kind of respected gossip. In a November 1494 letter Martire wrote: *"Colonus ille novi orbis repertor"*—"this Columbus, discoverer of a new world." A few years later Pietro Martire published a book in Venice called *De orbe novo,* "the New World." But Martire was not the only one to use the term; it came almost naturally to everyone, and we find it used by the pope in Rome, Ercole d'Este in Ferrara, the doge in Venice, Ludovic the Moor in Milan. Columbus himself, in a letter written several years later, spoke of an *otro mundo.*

But we should not think that these people therefore knew about, or even had an intimation of, the existence of a new continent. The New World was still, in everyone's mind, the outer reaches of Asia, composed of previously unknown islands extending far out into the ocean. Behind them supposedly lay the fabled hinterland full of wonders and riches, which Columbus believed he had briefly touched. No one had the vaguest suspicion that the discovered land could be anything but the Indies. Another quarter-century would pass before Magellan, with his 1521 voyage, solved the mystery of the oceans and continents.

Even confined to the "region of the Indies"—since no one knew of any other regions in that direction—the discovery was extremely significant in terms of what might be called the world politics of the time. Two great empires, Spain and Portugal, were competing for the rule of the seas. Every advance by one side or the other created diplomatic conflicts and a mutual distress over further consequences. We have already seen what happened to Columbus when he merely tried to seek safety in the Azores during the great storm; and how the King of Portugal had with difficulty contained his anger when he learned from Columbus how far he had ventured under the Castilian flag. After Columbus's return to Spain, the diplomatic dispute caught fire. Since there was so much land to discover across the seas, could any limit be placed on explorations by either power, Spain or Portugal? Or should everyone be allowed to follow his own fortune, come what may?

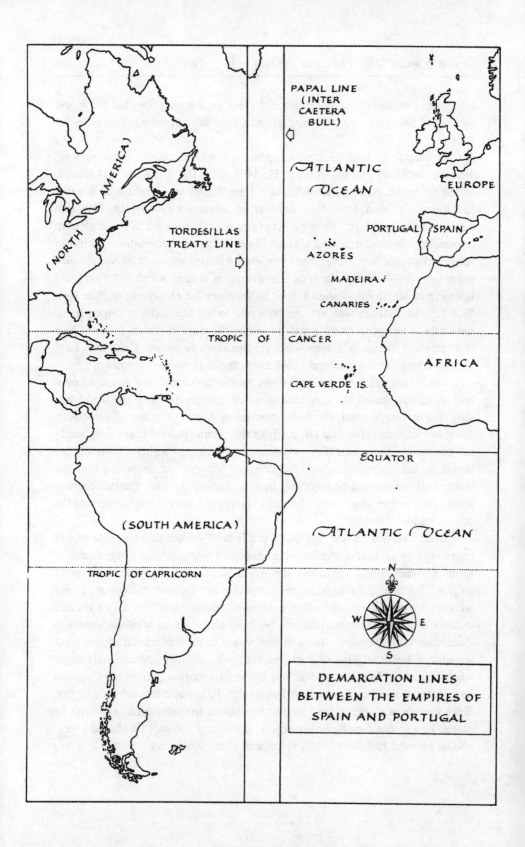

PAPAL LINE
(INTER
CAETERA
BULL)

ATLANTIC
OCEAN

EUROPE

(NORTH AMERICA)

TORDESILLAS
TREATY LINE

PORTUGAL SPAIN

AZORES

MADEIRA

CANARIES

TROPIC OF CANCER

AFRICA

CAPE VERDE IS.

EQUATOR

(SOUTH AMERICA)

ATLANTIC OCEAN

TROPIC OF CAPRICORN

N

W   E

S

DEMARCATION LINES
BETWEEN THE EMPIRES OF
SPAIN AND PORTUGAL

In Barcelona, during the days of celebration in honor of Columbus, a number of strange envoys from Portugal appeared. Many rumors began to circulate. Some said that John II was preparing an expedition to the newly discovered lands (according to the premise of freedom of action); others said instead that the King of Portugal was drafting a document that would assert his rights to all lands west of Africa and south of the Canaries. It was an ordering of the spheres of influence based on vague guidelines set forth in a papal bull issued about ten years earlier by Sixtus IV. In light of Columbus's discovery, however, this became an abuse of power of sorts, conveying the impression that the Portuguese wanted to conquer with official documents what Columbus had wrenched from the realm of the unknown with the boldness of his imagination.

The Spanish Crown had one great weakness in this conflict: Portugal possessed a much stronger fleet than did Spain, and John II was a powerful, ruthless ruler. If he so desired, he could make it very difficult for Spain to carry on regular traffic between Europe and the Indies. On the other hand, Ferdinand and Isabella also had one great strength: a year earlier Alexander VI Borgia had ascended to the papal throne. Borgia was a Spaniard and greatly indebted to the sovereigns of Castile and Aragon for their support of his election. The pope, as supreme authority, carried much weight in matters of determining the right to possession of newly conquered lands. Indeed, he carried all the weight. Over the years, the Holy See had established its right to determine, without appeal, the sovereignty of all land not previously under the rule of a Christian monarch. The Portuguese themselves had benefited a great deal from this arrangement, which had since become a firm cornerstone of international law. Their claims to the coast of Guinea, "all the way to the land of Indians who claim to worship Christ," had been codified by a series of papal bulls. The land of Indians who worshipped Christ corresponded more or less with Ethiopia, where according to an old medieval tradition, the legendary Prester John, a Nestorian of Christian faith, had converted the native population. (Though a legend in name, there must have been some grain of truth to the story if even today there still are Ethiopians who profess a Coptic Christian faith, an island in the Moslem sea that has surrounded them for centuries.)

The Borgia pope wasted little time. Within a space of two years he issued not one but four bulls, which defined, with progressive specifications, the boundaries of zones of influence across the ocean. It was an arduous task, dealing in such abstruse matters as the boundless solitudes of the seas, on which concrete decisions had to be made. The precedents were vague and ephemeral, the subject almost entirely unknown. Neither the pope, the Spanish sovereigns, nor the high officials of the two courts knew the first thing about geography. King John knew a bit more than they, but in substance, the charter was to be directed precisely against him. Rather than facilitating the task at hand, Portuguese knowledge of geography aggravated existing difficulties.

Pope Alexander VI asked for advice left and right. In Rome there was no lack of illustrious scholars ready to solve the riddles posed by the world's progressive enlargement. The pope also received advice from Spain, and the man he consulted above all others was Christopher Columbus, the only one who really knew anything about the matter at hand, the only one who had actually seen and crossed those empty spaces that now had to be in some way apportioned. In the end, all that was really expected of the pope was the establishment of a line, a line that would extend across the ocean and put all Portuguese claims to one side and all Spanish claims to the other. The line, *la raya*, was finally drawn on a map annexed to the *Inter caetera* bull solemnly issued in July of 1493. It was not soon to be forgotten, and was probably dictated, or at least suggested, by Columbus himself. He based his general outline on the trade wind front, thus translating a physical and meteorological boundary into a political one. The seaman and discoverer was now becoming an arbiter of world powers. He was truly at the pinnacle of his career.

The pope's *raya* was drawn one hundred leagues to the west of the Azores. Everything that lay to the west of the line, whether discovered or still to be discovered, belonged to Spain; everything to the east of it, to Portugal. Thus Portuguese claims to the African coast, the Azores, Madeira and the Cape Verde islands were respected. On the other hand, the bull clearly established the Spanish claims to Cuba, Hispaniola, the Bahamas and the other places that Columbus had found across the ocean.

The Portuguese were not satisfied. They wanted the *raya* moved farther west, and demanded greater clarification regarding the fate of territories in the southern part of the demarcation line. It was said that John II expected to find "very rich and profitable lands" between the *raya* and Africa, but even vaster and more fertile ones right in front of Africa, where, still unknown to the world, lay the land mass known today as South America. Moreover, the King of Portugal wanted to know how far in the direction of the Indies one could still speak of "west." If the Spanish could go as far as they wanted beyond the *raya* in an ocean considered their own exclusive domain, Columbus would be able to plant the Castilian flag almost anywhere, from China to Malay and beyond. This would severely compromise the eastern route to the Indies, which went in the opposite direction and followed a course around Africa which the Portuguese had been trying obstinately to establish for more than a generation until Bartholomeu Dias finally rounded the Cape of Good Hope in 1488. The road to the Indies had, so to speak, been opened. But how far would the Pope's *raya*—Columbus's *raya*—allow them to go?

Portugal's contestation was fierce. Grave consequences were intimated if things remained as they were—that is, unacceptable. Alarmed, the Spanish sovereigns consulted Columbus again. The Admiral of the Ocean Sea was in Cádiz getting ready for his next Atlantic expedition. They wrote to him asking for sound, expert advice amid all the uncertainty and ignorance around them. If he thought it necessary, they would ask the pope to "emend" the *Inter caetera* bull.

On September 26 Pope Alexander VI issued a "bull of extension," *Dudum siquidem*. But nothing came of it. Portuguese opposition remained unchanged, since the bull explained very little beyond what the previous one had said. Columbus suggested that the Pope's *raya* be considered a sort of general guideline, and that the two kingdoms, Spain and Portugal, negotiate between themselves a treaty specifying the manner in which the guideline was to be applied in actual practice. This resolved the dispute. The sovereigns of the two countries met at Tordesillas on June 7, 1494, after a long period of negotiation. By then Columbus had already gone back to America on his second voyage, but the treaty of Tordesillas remained, in spirit, his creation. The key to the agreement had been to move the western limit of *la raya* 270 leagues, an amendment of roughly 600 miles in the ocean. The pope's *raya* ran roughly along the 38th meridian, that agreed upon in Tordesillas along the 46th meridian, a difference of eight degrees longitude. All lands and islands to the east of that meridian were to belong to Portugal, all lands and islands to the west, to Spain. The line in effect divided the ocean into two sovereign zones. Spain would devote itself to overseas enterprises, while Portugal in effect would stick to its African route to Asia.

The boundaries, in any case, remained vague. The longitudes weren't even measured with any precision. Nevertheless, the pope's *raya,* as amended at Tordesillas, served for three hundred years as the legal and moral basis for the Spanish conquest of the Americas. The only American land that lay outside its demarcation was eastern Brazil, which, because of the 8-degree adjustment agreed upon at Tordesillas, ended up falling within the Portuguese zone. These decisions, distant in time and inexact in their formulation and authority, managed to shape the destiny of nations and peoples over the centuries. Columbus, in any case, had not been mistaken. Here he had spanned the Atlantic just once, and already he had succeeded in giving Spain the largest empire the world had ever known.

Now he was getting ready to go back. This time, however, he went not for the purpose of random discovery but with a precise plan to bring some of the old world to the new. It was Spain's first act of colonization in America. The swiftness with which Columbus set such massive and troublesome under-takings in motion itself indicates a new rhythm of existence, an acceleration of the slow tempo of medieval life. For his first crossing, once he had obtained royal consent, it had taken Columbus only a few weeks to rig out the fleet, set a course and draw up a plan of navigation toward unknown lands. For the second crossing, which would transport hundreds of men across the ocean to found the first cities, he needed only five months from the day of his triumph in Barcelona. This means that one year after the discovery of the first trace of America, the first colonizers, gold seekers and adventurers were on their way to settling the new land, led by Columbus in laying the foundations of an emigration from one continent to the other that from this moment forward became unstoppable. That was the way he wanted it, and that was the way he conceived the fulfillment of his dream. And indeed, that was what happened. Whatever one may say about Columbus and about what happened after him, one thing is undeniable: America is truly his child.

It became even more so on the second voyage, though the second was less thrilling, lacking that breath of poetry that rendered the first immortal. On the second voyage, Columbus took 1,200 men to America on seventeen ships—a real armada compared to the three caravels of a year earlier. Their destination was the island of Hispaniola, which was considered the focus of the search for gold and had very fertile land for cultivation. There these men would found new cities and inhabit them. They were all volunteers. They were not going to America to satisfy some temporary urge to explore, but to stay. With them they brought provisions for several months, after which they would have to depend on the products of the land that they themselves would work. The fleet carried grain seeds and cereals, grapevines and many animals for breeding, from horses to sheep. To make sure that the men did not get carried away by the greed for gold—*la golosina del oro,* Lope de Vega calls it —specific periods were established for searching for the metal, and the rest of the time was to be devoted to agriculture. Joining the expedition were dozens of skilled farmers who would instruct the others, and technicians trained in irrigation systems, locks and canals. Everything seemed logical, perfectly laid out. Even too much so. Projects always look so grand in the planning stage. But how often does reality belie them?

America's evil was an ingrained evil: gold. The feverish greed that it inspired was irresistible. It promised too rapid, too easy a wealth. The talk of farming and colonization was all well and good, but how many of those men would have crossed the Atlantic if gold had not dazzled their eyes? There was also much talk of converting the Indians. It was a subject which the sovereigns took very much to heart. Even Columbus sincerely felt it to be their debt to God. Yet of all the men who went on the second voyage there were only two friars, in addition to several lay brothers trained in catechism: a negligible rear guard in an army on the march toward wealth.

To rig out so many ships, to organize so many men, to prepare in a short period of time the provisions, equipment and all the other things necessary for so long and crowded a voyage, a good administrator was needed. The king and queen, who anxiously oversaw the preparations of the expedition, entrusted this task to Don Juan Rodríguez de Fonseca, archdeacon of Seville, a man "very skilled in worldly matters." De Fonseca became a kind of superintendent of "Indian affairs." He made his headquarters in Seville, and took on two close collaborators: a treasurer, Francisco Pinello, and a chief accountant, Juan de Soria, a courtier from the chamber of the Infante of Spain. All told, they constituted a rather dreary trio, and moreover had little experience in seafaring matters. De Fonseca saw his principal duty as spending as little money as possible. He was a tightfisted administrator, and was only interested in this aspect of his office. Pinello obeyed him as a good bureaucrat obeys his boss—who for Pinello was certainly de Fonseca and not Columbus. As for Soria, the most dangerous of the three, he insinuated himself into Columbus's plans for glory as representative of a court ill-disposed to recognize the admiral's merit and greatness. There was a feeling of distrust—that old prejudice against the foreigner who wants to give orders in another man's house—and above all an unfathomable gulf of antipathy between the petty concerns of these officials and Columbus's spirit of adventure. The three of them went so far as to claim that the admiral had granted them discretionary authority over his spending requests. The admiral of the Ocean Sea! How dared they trample on his dignity, his prerogatives? Columbus took umbrage, never stopped brooding over it, and tried to elude all control that he considered improper for a person of his stature. Indeed, he thought he belonged more to the class of kings than subjects: he was King of the Indies, Spain's third or fourth most powerful ruler. His similarities to Don Quixote reemerge every time Columbus soars on the wings of his imagination. America was his Dulcinea, and no one was permitted to insult her by neglecting what had to be done for her. Too many times de Fonseca and his two stooges let themselves be cheated by ship chandlers, taking aboard weak barrels, wine that quickly turned to vinegar, old nags instead of Andalusian horses. It was the same old story of incompetent management and the swarm of profiteers buzzing around the honey of easy deals. But it is the kind of story that Don Quixote rejected, and did not want to hear about. And the same was true for his precursor Columbus, knight-errant of the seas.

(The sovereigns, who received reports from de Fonseca and confidential communications from Soria, began to realize that Columbus had a tendency to rebel against all authority. And since in the final analysis there was only one irreducible authority in Spain, which belonged to them, they could not help but feel a certain irritation at this fact. They were rather familiar with the early signs of insubordination. Time and time again they had had to subdue it on their way to ruling all of Spain. They certainly were not going to let Columbus break the tradition. For the moment he was useful to them, but that was all.)

The second voyage left not from Palos, which was too small a port to accommodate a fleet of such magnitude, but from Cádiz, a haven of incomparable beauty which extends out into the ocean like a giant lizard. Columbus arrived there in August, raising up a storm because things were not moving as quickly as he would have liked. He wanted to set sail at about the same time of year as the first voyage, hoping to encounter the same wind and water conditions that had favored the first crossing. Instead he did not set off until the end of the next month, on September 25, 1493. Joining him on the new expedition were some of the men and ships that had made the first voyage. Actually, only one ship was returning: the excellent *Niña* that had carried him through the Atlantic storms, now rechristened as the *Santa Clara.* Of the men, the entire Niño family of Moguer came along, forever faithful to Columbus. On the other hand, not a single Pinzón went this time, as though the bitter dispute between that family and Columbus had not ended with the death of Martín Alonso, head of the clan and the admiral's rival. Among the voyagers there was also Pedro de Las Casas, father of Bartolomé who was to become the most thorough and scrupulous of Columbus's biographers, and two very valuable chroniclers of the journey: the ship's doctor Diego Álvarez

Chanca, who sent a report to the town council of Seville that has survived to this day, and the Savonese Michele da Cuneo, whose letters to various friends in Liguria have been published in the *Raccolta Colombiana di Genova* (Columbian Collection of Genoa). We are fortunate that these firsthand documents still exist, since the log that Columbus kept during the second voyage was lost in its entirety.

Columbus took his place of command on a new flagship which also bore the name of *Santa Maria*, only to be later changed to *Mariagalante* in homage to the navigational excellence it demonstrated during the voyage. It was larger than the first *Santa Maria*, and provided the admiral with quarters more befitting his rank. The ship's master was Antonio de Torres, brother of Prince Juan's wet nurse and a person who would figure prominently in the vicissitudes that lay in store for Columbus. But the day of departure from Cádiz was a day of celebration, a continuation of Columbus's triumph. The ships were all bedecked with standards and banners flapping in the wind in such number that they became entangled in the rigging. Prince Juan came in person to witness the event. He went to watch the procession of the seventeen ships from the very top of the lighthouse in the castle of Santa Catalina on the outermost projection of land in the port of Cádiz. Carried by a good strong wind, the fleet soon disappeared in the direction of the Canary Islands. The adventure was beginning again.

Things were going so well that they covered the stretch of ocean between Cádiz and the Canaries in only seven days. By the beginning of October Columbus was at his cherished island of Gomera, seeking final provisions for the crossing. Upon arrival he had been welcomed with fireworks and gun salutes ordered in his honor by the no less cherished Beatrice de Bobadilla, governor of the island and as winsome as ever. Her black hair seemed aflame. Was it Columbus that made it so? A hero of the seas, such as Columbus had become, appeals to feminine sentiments. But you will remember that there had already been something between the admiral and this Beatrice, something that eluded the pryings of chroniclers, as true love stories always should. In commenting on Beatrice's conduct in Gomera, Michele da Cuneo said that "our admiral had once been in love with [her]." With all his sailing, they saw each other no more than a few days out of the year. A few days and a few nights, and no doubt Columbus spent a few more this time around with the lady of Gomera.

In the meantime the seventeen ships lying at anchor in the port of San Sebastián were being loaded with all sorts of good things: plants, seeds, and animals—including eight sows from which many of the pigs in America today are descended. The stop in Gomera was leisurely and unhurried. It wasn't until October 13, after having lost some time in the belt of calm air that almost always surrounds the Canaries, that the fleet finally lost sight of land off the island at Hierro. October 13, one year and one day after the landing at San Salvador.

The course that the admiral set was again a westward one, though this time it was one rhumb to southwest from the start and hence a more southerly course than the first one. Columbus had so often heard the natives of Hispaniola speak of splendid lands that lay to the south and east, in an arc of countless islands, that he had felt even then a desire to explore them, to give more new names to unknown lands. He wanted to arrive at a list of one hundred islands, which he would unveil to the world, having salvaged them from ignorance. It would be the prize of his dreams, the verification of truths ignored for years and years which he had had the perseverance to redeem from the void.

He was anxious to return to Navidad to rejoin the companions he had left there on the shore. By now they had probably already found the source of the gold, the seal of his victory. But he was also avid for more discoveries. He felt the wind blowing from astern, pushing the ship swiftly forward. At those low latitudes the trade winds blew at full force, the fleet sailing right in the middle of their favorable course. The crossing was an exceptionally easy one. The fleet encountered only a few hours of stormy weather at the end of the voyage, a wild barrage of rain and wind. It happened at night and struck with such sudden force that a few sails were torn away and a few spars broken. By morning it was over. Chanca, the physician, writes, "The sun rose on a sea as smooth as polished marble."

Blue marble—that intense blue that the ocean assumes in tropical regions—adorned with flying fish, the suite of trade clouds overhead and the seventeen white-sailed ships spread across the horizon, youthful, festive and impatient. At nightfall the ships would all close in around the flagship like birds returning to the nest, since nighttime navigation had to be carried out in as tight a formation as possible.

During the final days of the journey Columbus saw some of the same signs of land that he had seen the first time around: the sea's altered aspect, the flight of gulls, the thickening of the clouds indicating hilly terrain ahead. America, for the second time, lay before him. The crossing had taken only twenty-one days. It had been an easier voyage than the first, along a more

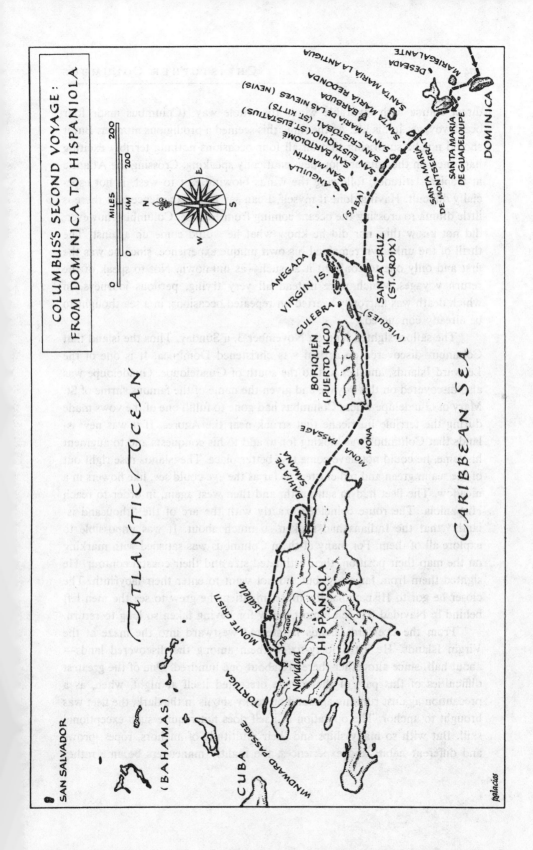

COLUMBUS'S SECOND VOYAGE:
FROM DOMINICA TO HISPANIOLA

MILES

KM

SAN SALVADOR

CUBA

WINDWARD PASSAGE

(BAHAMAS)

TORTUGA

Navidad

Isabela

MONTE CRISTI

RIO YAQUE

HISPANIOLA

BAHIA DE SAMANA

MONA PASSAGE

MONA

BORIQUÉN
(PUERTO RICO)

CULEBRA

VIRGIN IS.

(VIEQUES)

ANEGADA

SANTA CRUZ
(ST. CROIX)

CARIBBEAN SEA

ATLANTIC OCEAN

SABA

SAN MARTIN

ANGUILLA

SAN BARTOLOMÉ (ST. BARTS)

SAN EUSTAQUIO (ST. EUSTATIUS)

SAN CRISTOBAL (ST. KITTS)

SANTA MARIA DE LAS NIEVES (NEVIS)

BARBUDA

SANTA MARIA REDONDA

SANTA MARIA LA ANTIGUA

SANTA MARIA DE MONTSERRAT

SANTA MARIA DE GUADELOUPE

DOMINICA

MARIGALANTE

DESEADA

palacios

direct course with favorable winds the whole way. (Columbus made four ocean voyages in his life. At the time, this seemed a prodigious number. But it should not be surprising that on all four occasions nothing terribly exciting happened on the outward journey, nautically speaking. Crossing the Atlantic at tropical latitudes, following the winds blowing east to west, is not especially difficult. Having done it myself, I can say from experience that there is little drama to crossing the ocean, coming from Europe. Columbus, however, did not know this, nor did he know what he would come up against. The thrill of the unknown remained his own unique experience, since he was the first and only one to confront it as such—as unknown. Not to speak of the return voyages, which were instead all very trying, perilous journeys, in which death was narrowly averted on repeated occasions, in a sea thought to be already conquered.)

The sailors sighted land on November 3, a Sunday. Thus the island that Columbus discovered on arrival was christened Dominica. It is one of the Leeward Islands, and lies just to the south of Guadeloupe. Guadeloupe was also discovered on this voyage and given the name of the famous shrine of St. Mary of Guadelupe where Columbus had gone to fulfill one of the vows made during the terrible hurricane that struck near the Azores. If it was new islands that Columbus was looking for to add to his conquests and to augment his fame, he could not have come to a better place. The islands rose right out of the sea in green and red clusters as far as the eye could see, like flowers in a meadow. The fleet had to sail north, and then west again, in order to reach Hispaniola. The route coincided exactly with the arc of the "thousand islands" that the Indians had spoken so much about. It was impossible to explore all of them. For many of them Columbus was satisfied with marking on the map their position, their estimated size and their coastal contour. He sighted them from far away, but did not want to enter their labyrinth. The closer he got to Hispaniola, the more impatient he grew to see the men left behind in Navidad. He felt almost guilty for having taken so long to return.

From the Leeward Islands he steered westward into the maze of the Virgin Islands. He listed forty-six of them among the discovered lands— about half, since altogether there are about one hundred. One of the greatest difficulties of this part of the voyage presented itself at night, when, as a precaution against running aground on rocky shoals in the dark, the fleet was brought to anchor. The operation in itself does not require such exceptional skill. But with so many ships and their multitude of anchors, ropes, prows and different habits and experiences, the nightly maneuvers became rather complicated. The men had to use extreme skill and expertise to avoid collisions.

Occasionally, when they came upon passable havens, the crews would go ashore to look for provisions, especially fresh water. They had something of an adventure on Santa Cruz, an island right outside the Virgin Island group. A team that had disembarked was pursued on their way back to the ship by a canoeful of natives who began assailing them with arrows arched high in the air. It was the first real attack made by Indians. Two Spaniards were wounded, one of them fatally. The canoe was rammed and capsized. The Indians fled by swimming to a rock, where they were quickly surrounded by Spaniards. Pietro Martire had the event recounted to him, and later described it as follows: "The Indians fought bravely until they were overpowered and captured. Once on board, they struggled like Libyan lions in chains. There wasn't a single man who could stand the sight of them, so horrific, menacing and cruel an appearance had nature given them." Martire called them "cannibals," which at the time was simply the name of a tribe, the Canibs or Caribs, already mentioned here as man-eaters. They wore their hair shaved clean on one side of the head, and streaming down in long black strands on the other. They had dark skin, which was painted red. They made a very deep impression on the Spaniards, who had found their first enemies.

Leaving the Virgin Islands behind, on November 19 the fleet reached the large island of Puerto Rico, which the natives called Borinquén. The Indians who had accompanied Columbus during the first voyage began to recognize their home territory. It was they who pointed out the course to take along Puerto Rico's southern coast. The island provided a magnificent sight but was surrounded by coral reefs, which Columbus rightly feared. He was now so close to Hispaniola that he could not allow for any more delays.

On November 22 the fleet entered the strait that passes between Puerto Rico and Hispaniola. On the twenty-third it was already in Samaná Bay, where Columbus and Pinzón had stopped one year earlier: thus the second itinerary closed the circle begun by the first. The memories abounded. And there was Monte Cristi, just two dozen miles from Navidad, little more than a half day of sailing. At Monte Cristi a team sent ashore to get water found two corpses tied to each other, up the Yaqui River. They were in a state of advanced decay and unrecognizable, but one of them bore the remains of what appeared to be a thick beard.

The news provoked alarm and anguish. Columbus hurried toward Navidad, but the sun set before the ships could approach the coast. They were right where the *Santa Maria* had sunk. Columbus did not dare go any farther. But from where the ships were at that moment, the men in Navidad would be able to see the fire signals, which were promptly lit, and to hear the cannons, which were then fired. But no response came from land. A Genoese chronicler named Syllacio described the emotions of the Spanish at that moment: "A sadness and profound grief seized their hearts."

Not one of the forty men left behind in Navidad was still alive. The fortress built from the planking of the *Santa Maria* had been razed to the ground. The site was strewn with ashes and refuse, the corpses scattered about a radius of several miles. Perhaps they had been caught trying to flee. Columbus's great friend, the cacique Guacanagarí, sent representatives with gifts and words of condolence. They said that he was wounded and lying in his bed. He had been struck by a Carib arrow when trying with his men to defend the Spaniards of Navidad from their common enemy. The Caribs, terror of the islands: it was always they. Was he telling the truth? Columbus and Chanca the physician, when walking along the shore—with its fine white sand and turquoise sea, and solitude still unaltered by the centuries—came upon an abandoned village in which they found a few remains from the pillage: scarves, clothes, one of the anchors of the *Santa Maria*. The Indians continued to blame the Caribs. But they also complained that the Christians had taken too many women, at least two or three to a man. "Which led us to believe," wrote Chanca, "that the unexpected problems had arisen because of jealousy."

To get a clearer picture of the matter, Columbus and his men decided to accept Guacanagarí's invitation to pay him a call in his village. They found him lying in a hammock, wounded in the thigh. He stuck by his story of Caribs that had come ashore to exterminate the white men. Columbus was puzzled. He listened and tried to understand, to imagine how the tragedy might have occurred. In the meantime Chanca, on the pretext that he was a doctor, began to unwrap Guacanagarí's leg. There was not the slightest trace of a wound, "though the cacique," writes the doctor, "with foxlike shrewdness pretended to feel very sick."

What to do? Some, including the Benedictine friar Father Buyl, advised Columbus to have Guacanagarí put to death. Only capital punishment could serve as a strong enough example; indeed, it was imperative, they said. But Columbus had more faith than they in the fundamental goodness of human nature. They had never really established guilt; the lie about the leg wound was not enough. He refused to condemn Guacanagarí to death.

The truth came out a little bit at a time, like all painful and complicated truths. Using the information provided in the texts of Las Casas and Fernando Columbus, the facts may be reconstructed as follows: Shortly after Columbus's departure, arguments and fights broke out among the Spaniards within the enclosure at Navidad. The reasons were many: the desire for freedom; the right to go beyond the fort and explore the island; the need for women; the lust for gold. Everyone wanted to do these things independently, without the restriction of authority or the responsibility toward a collective goal. The brawls resulted in a few deaths, tempers raging out of control. Actual bands of plunderers were formed, which roamed the countryside and sacked the villages, forcing the native women to go with them and searching everywhere for gold. Pedro Gutiérrez, the king's majordomo, and Rodrigo de Escobedo, who had been the first fleet's secretary and had drawn up the deed of the landing at San Salvador, were the most active leaders of the forays. Guacanagarí's Indians had no way to defend themselves. But when the gangs passed over into the territory of Caonabó—the other cacique of Cibao, whom Pinzón had dealt with on the first voyage—they encountered much fiercer resistance. Caonabó captured Gutiérrez in an ambush and had him executed on the spot. Then with an enormous force of men he descended upon Navidad, where a garrison of only ten men remained, presided by Diego de Harana. They were all slaughtered. A few tried to escape by throwing themselves into the sea, but they soon drowned. Having meted out this severe punishment to the Spaniards, Caonabó returned immediately to his villages. Soon other Indians from the area arrived in Navidad, also seeking vengeance. The small groups of Spaniards hiding out in huts with their booty of women and small supply of stolen goods were flushed out and killed. Everyone had quickly learned how it was done.

Guacanagarí was not lying when he said he had tried to save the white men. He had gone to alert Diego de Harana of what was about to happen, when he came up against Caonabó's squads, who wounded many of his men. This was the truth. And it had changed a timid, unaggressive people, the "good savages" initially hailed by Europe, into fierce defenders of their independence, which had been violated by sailors come from afar whose sudden presence was neither welcome nor desired.

The massacre at Navidad marked a turning point in the history of relations between Europeans and Americans. Columbus realized this immediately, with his usual quickness of perception. He understood that the myth of the good savage was over, and that the colonization of the new lands would henceforth be a long, hard struggle. The time of discovery, of peaceful exploration of the islands and seas, was also over. The happiness and magic of the meeting between the two worlds had ended at Navidad.

15

Columbus Cannot Find the Indies

The Navidad massacre had strangely little effect on Columbus. He showed no emotion. He ordered his men to search for gold that the dead might have buried if they had found any from following his directions. But tatters of old clothes were all they turned up. A hasty funeral service was held, and then without even bothering to look for all the bodies or clear up the matter with Guacanagarí to determine just who was guilty, the fleet set off from that cruel site to found a new city. Columbus seemed impassive. His presence had been needed at the scene of such troubling events. But was Columbus really a man of action? When faced with unpleasant situations, he usually preferred to move on. He escaped his troubles by leaving them behind. The man of imagination is seldom a man of action when the action expected of him does not fall within the scope of his fancy. At that point he prefers to turn away and look ahead, where the purity of imagination remains as yet unsullied, like snow atop a volcano.

The city that was to be settled by all these men still crowding the decks would have to be built somewhere not far from the gold mines—that is, not far from where the gold mines were believed to be, since Columbus thus far had no indications as to their location aside from the Indians' vague, deceptive words and gestures and Pinzón's more precise mention, one year earlier, of a certain valley and a certain river. Columbus found what he thought he recognized as the right landscape; in its foreground was a wooded peninsula with a long, flat bank tracing a very wide arc. It would even serve as a good shelter for the ships. It seemed to him a suitable place for founding the city. He decided without further delay that this was the place to disembark, and went ashore on January 2, 1494, the start of a new year. He had the men and animals disembark. The city's foundations were laid at once, the first seeds planted. He named the city after "his" queen, Isabela.

Like all hasty, ill-considered decisions, the choice of this site for the new city was a disastrous mistake. Isabela rose up on the banks of a river, the Río Bajabonico. But it was not a navigable river, and it ran along the periphery of a marshy area that was anything but fertile and anything but healthy. Here too the natives claimed with assurance that there were gold mines nearby. They even offered to take the Spaniards to them. As Columbus was anxious to get down to business, he immediately organized a group of men for this purpose. They set out on an inland expedition on January 5, just a few days after debarcation.

Command of the group was given to Alonso de Ojeda, a prominent figure in the history of Columbus's voyages and the Spanish exploration of America. Las Casas says of him: "He was very devoted to the Virgin Mary, but was always the first one to spill blood whenever there was any dispute or conflict." Ojeda left with a squad of twenty men accompanied by Indian guides. The going was not easy, and there were some several dozen miles to cover. First they had to cross a group of mountains, climbing up narrow paths. Then they came to a large valley whose slopes glistened with brooks flowing down from the heights. The streams, said the Indians, carried gold in their waters. Still higher up in the mountains there were veins imbedded in the rocks. But Ojeda looked no farther. He was satisfied with the traces and fragments of gold that he saw at the streams' outlets, and in a nearby village he traded a few bells for three rather large gold nuggets. He returned to Isabela two weeks after setting out. Illusions were revived.

Michele da Cuneo relates that "the admiral has written to the king that he hopes soon to be able to send him as much gold as the iron produced in the mines of Biscay." But not that soon, however. Rain and bad weather plagued Cibao, swelled the rivers and soaked the marshes. Several hundred men— some authors say 200, some 300—fell ill before the end of January. It wasn't so much the bad weather that brought on the illnesses as the change of climate and diet, the type of labor demanded of the men, the haste with which they carried it out, and the mephitic fumes of the swamps. The new arrivals were also subjected to massive attacks by mosquitoes and other insects carrying unknown germs. The number of sick kept increasing, and soon half the settlement's population was ailing. Isabela seemed more like a hospital than a city of conquerors. Dr. Chanca was working so hard that he asked that his salary be doubled.

The major problems were due to diet. The rain and humidity had spoiled a good deal of the provisions brought over from Europe, limiting the food sources to fish and manioc, the tuber which yielded the flourlike substance from which cassava bread was made. Half of America at that time was living on manioc. It is not very nutritious and even less digestible. The Spaniards had no choice but to acquire a taste for it, or at least get used to it. They hated it. Cassava bread, to them, was like poison. I once tried some myself, in a village not far from where Isabela once stood. The bread I had, however, was cooked with great care, over hot coals. It was like unleavened bread, but somewhat mealy in texture and without much taste. As a change of pace it might even be pleasant, but as daily sustenance it would be nigh intolerable.

Faced with this spectacle of devastation, Columbus decided to send most of the ships back to Spain to get badly needed assistance. Only five caravels stayed behind, while the other twelve set off for home. He put them under the command of Antonio de Torres, his second-in-command on the outward journey. Columbus also gave him a report to be delivered to the king and queen. In it, he explained why he had to send back the fleet with so little gold on board. De Torres was bringing back a quantity estimated at about 30,000 ducats in value, a laughable sum in light of the cost of the enterprise and the expectations it had raised. In the report the admiral asked that three or four caravels be sent back to Hispaniola with fresh victuals, medications for the sick, footwear and clothing, mules and other work animals. And just so that the prospect of gold would not be forgotten, he also asked for one hundred skilled miners, to be recruited in the region of Estremadura. Torres's fleet left on February 2. Columbus estimated that they would be back within three or four months with the necessary reinforcements.

In the meantime he busied himself trying to establish a safe route to the gold mining area. Other expeditions were sent out, always led by de Ojeda, until finally Columbus decided to go there himself with escort and standards, and a group of carpenters, woodsmen, masons and hoers. He had decided to build a fort at the entrance to the mining area. The sight of the beautiful valley beyond the first set of mountains filled him with wonder. Las Casas has him say that "one might have thought we had come to a corner of paradise."

The convoy went as far as the Jánico River, which is well inland. Today, near the river, there is a group of cabins that has kept the name of Fortaleza —"fortress"—over the years, and they stand more or less on the spot where the fortress was built. Several years ago the current Dominican government began a series of excavations. The first traces of foundations were discovered, and from all evidence the fort appears to have been rather large and solid. The construction plan was drawn up by Columbus himself, who supervised the beginning of the work and then returned to Isabela, leaving fifty men behind in the command of Pedro Margarit. The fort was named San Tomás. It was supposed to become the center of mining operations in Cibao. But no one knew quite where the gold was, if there was any at all. True, the Indians queued up at San Tomás, bearing gold nuggets, fragments, chips and small objects. But where did the gold come from? From the sands of the rivers or from actual mines? Columbus had never taken the trouble to find out. When, after some time, he was told that the equivalent of 2,000 castellanos' worth of gold had been collected, he cheered up. But this was hardly an impressive sum, and Columbus was well aware of it. He had finally realized that Cibao was an indigenous name and had nothing to do with Marco Polo's Cipango. He was still dreaming of Japan's palaces and their roofs of gold. Where were they? And where were the Indies, the continent that always seemed within reach but always managed to elude him?

At Isabela, the river had overflowed its banks, the provisions were finished, and the men were throwing away their manioc flatcakes. The sick were beginning to die. Everyone wanted to go back to Spain. They would look at Columbus, their admiral, and ask him what he intended to do. The grumbling and criticism were growing. Columbus, as usual, remained secretive and reserved. He trusted no one, and distrust only breeds more distrust. He had a squabble with Father Buyl, who accused him of skimping on rations. A message came from San Tomás in which Margarit said that all the Indians had fled the area after receiving word that Caonabó, the terrible cacique who had led the slaughter of the Spanish at Navidad, was on his way there with many men, perhaps for another massacre.

Columbus sent Ojeda to the fort with new supplies of victuals and ammunition. The natives of Cibao were getting restless. There had been a few instances of plunder by the Spanish, and a few thefts by the Indians. Ojeda had the thieves' hands cut off, but only the hands of Indian thieves. The situation was tense, and rebellion was in the air, both in Isabela and in the mountains around Fort San Tomás. A strong intervention was needed, something that would restore order.

What did Columbus do? Once again, he left. He went off in pursuit of his Asian chimera, seeking proof that he had reached the Indies. It was no longer

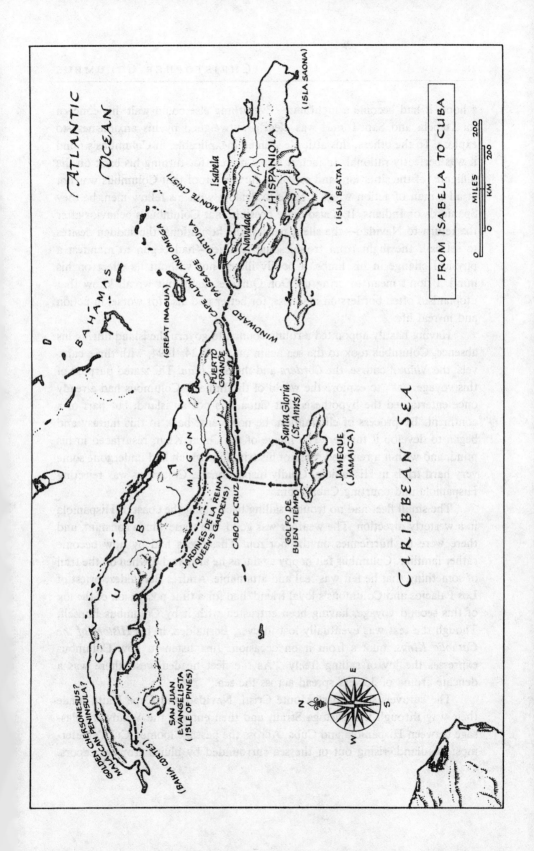

ATLANTIC OCEAN

(ISLA SAONA)

HISPANIOLA

(ISLA BEATA)

Isabela

MONTE CRISTI

Navidad

TORTUGA

CAPE ALPHA AND OMEGA

WINDWARD PASSAGE

(GREAT INAGUA)

BAHAMAS

PUERTO GRANDE

SANTA GLORIA (St. Ann's)

M A G O N

JAMEQUE (JAMAICA)

CABO DE CRUZ

GOLFO DE BUEN TIEMPO

JARDINES DE LA REINA (QUEEN'S GARDENS)

CARIBBEAN SEA

C U B A

SAN JUAN EVANGELISTA (ISLE OF PINES)

GOLDEN CHERSONESUS?

MALACCAN PENINSULA?

(BAHIA)

(CORTES)

FROM ISABELA TO CUBA

MILES 0 200

KM 0 200

N E S W

a hope; it had become a nightmare. Everything else could wait: his concern
for Isabela and San Tomás was clearly outweighed by his anxiousness to
explore. To the others, this attitude seemed inexplicable; in Columbus's mind
it was perfectly rational. In fact, it was a pretext for turning his back on the
difficulty of the situation, and serves as further proof that Columbus was not
at all a man of action when it came to dealing with his fellow men, be they
Spaniards or Indians. It is also quite possible that Columbus's behavior after
the return to Navidad—the silent pauses, the hesitations, the sudden desires
to set sail, the flight from troublesome realities—had begun to manifest a
physical change in his limbs, a bodily illness not without its effect on his
mind. I don't mean to bring up Don Quixote again, but we all know that
utopianism often borders on madness, for better and also for worse, in fiction
and in real life.

Having hastily appointed a ruling council to govern the island during his
absence, Columbus took to the sea again on April 24, 1494, with three caravels: the *Niña* of course, the *Cordera* and the *San Juan*. The stated purpose of
this voyage was "to explore the world of the Indies." Columbus had already
once entertained the hypothesis that Cuba was not an island, but part of a
continent. By process of elimination, he now came back to this fantasy and
began to develop it further. The image of the Great Khan resurfaced in his
mind, and with it a renewed sense of his triumph, which had undergone some
very hard trials in Hispaniola. Coldly dispassionate, Columbus was rejecting
Hispaniola and courting Cuba again.

The small fleet had no trouble sailing back along the coast of Hispaniola
in a westerly direction. The weather was good, the trade winds constant, and
there were no hurricanes on the horizon. These seas had by now become
rather familiar. Columbus felt happy again, as he always did when on the trail
of something that he felt was real and attainable. Andrès Bernaldez, priest of
Los Palacíos and Columbus's loyal friend, had for a time possession of the log
of this second voyage, having been entrusted with it by Columbus himself.
Though the text was eventually lost forever, Bernaldez, in his *History of the
Catholic Kings*, quotes from it on occasion. Just listen to how Columbus
expresses the joy of sailing freely: "As the fleet headed west, there was a
delicate aroma of flowers spread across the sea."

The caravels sailed past Monte Cristi, Navidad and Cape Haiti, made
their way through the Tortuga Strait, and then entered the Windward Passage between Hispaniola and Cuba. Across the passage loomed Cuba's outermost headland, rising out of the sea surrounded by bluish tropical vapors.

Columbus named it Alpha and Omega, the world's beginning and end. If Cuba formed part of the Asian continent, this promontory would have to be its westernmost extremity. Bernaldez, probably taking his cue from the lost log, gives the following explanation: "Point Alpha and Omega is the outermost point of the mainland, corresponding to Cape St. Vincent in Portugal on the other side of the ocean. If one were to begin walking eastward from Cape St. Vincent, one could eventually reach Cape Alpha and Omega without crossing any part of the Ocean Sea." In Columbus's mind, this was exactly how it was. Yet in the middle of it all lay America, unknown and unimaginable. And because of it, Columbus never succeeded in finding the Indies. America was in the way.

(Today Cape Alpha and Omega is called Punta Maisí, and all manner of craft cruising the Caribbean waters sail around it with ease. It would take many years, however, from the time Columbus christened the promontory, before anyone could disprove the opinion expressed by Father Bernaldez.)

Once across the passage, Columbus had to decide in which direction to continue his exploration, whether to sail along Cuba's northern or southern coast. He had already seen part of the northern coast on his first voyage, when sailing down from San Salvador. On the other hand, he knew nothing about the southern coast. Orthodox Church doctrine taught that the most precious things are found under the hottest skies. Ferrer de Blanes, a Catalonian cosmographer and frequenter of the court, maintained that "most good things come from the hottest regions, and under equatorial skies one finds the most highly prized merchandise, precious stones, gold, spices, drugs." Given what he was looking for, Columbus went south.

He came to Puerto Grande, which today is called Guantánamo Bay, site of a U.S. naval base. The sea was full of sargassos, the beaches crawling with iguanas, which the Spaniards cooked on spits though they had never seen anything like them before. On May 3 the caravels reached Cape Cruz, the island's southernmost point (though Columbus still did not know, and would not in any case have believed, that Cuba was an island). The Indians there ran out onto the beach to look at the ships. When asked about gold, which had become the admiral's obligatory first question, they went on at great length. They indicated that there was gold in great abundance in an island not far from there. They called this eldorado Jameque—Jamaica. Jameque sounded a lot like Babeque, which brought to Columbus's mind the memory of his adventures of two years earlier. Without even pausing to think twice about it, he raced down to Jamaica at once. He clearly was not in the most rational state of mind, nor the most stable. He was wavering between gold and the Indies. Jamaica, however, "a most pleasant island," proved to be a land of little favor. The natives, a silent lot very much on their guard, wore no gold ornaments on their persons. There was no gold to be found in any of the places where Columbus stopped. He wandered along those shores for six or seven days, then turned around and sailed back to Cuba, to Cabo de Cruz.

He proceeded along Cuba's southern coast and soon found himself surrounded by a myriad of islands. Bernaldez writes: "The sea was full of islands in every direction, each of them green and covered with trees, the most splendid islands that the eye could ever behold." In a single day, Columbus counted more than a hundred of them. As there were too many to name them individually, he gave the archipelago a collective name, Jardines de la Reina, "The Queen's Garden."

The navigation was becoming rather difficult, the ships passing dangerously close to the land rising up all around them. The waters were full of perils—shoals, banks, reefs, currents, tight passages—and the men had to be on their guard every step of the way. It is quite remarkable that Columbus managed to get his caravels through those waters unharmed. There were some frighteningly close calls: more than once, the ships "touched ground." At one point the *Niña* got stuck in mud for many hours. Endless natural obstacles had to be overcome, not to mention the psychological obstacles. Sea legends had always told of unending shallows at the world's outer limits—which indeed was where everyone thought they were, since Columbus said as much, corroborating legends so old that they were accepted as true.

Once out of the island maze, Columbus had to do battle with storms. Every evening, writes Bernaldez, "frightful clouds would gather in the east," and until the moon had set on the horizon strong gales would rip across the sea, inundating the caravels, never missing a single day. The men grew weary from all the hardship and danger. They were also discontented, and did not hide their feelings. They wanted to turn back, since it was a long and difficult route and the provisions were by now nearly exhausted and clearly would not be enough to allow them to proceed any farther.

Columbus, as usual, remained silent. He had no hopeful promises to offer his sailors, as he had had in the trying days before the first landing, at San Salvador. This time he was looking for something that continually eluded him, something he did not know where to find. Untiringly, he kept asking the natives, every time he went ashore, whether Cuba was an island or a continent. Bernaldez remarks: "They were simple, ignorant people; they thought the whole world was made up of islands." Every now and then, however, one of their answers shone like a flash in the dark. For example, one old native, shaking his head and extending his hand westward, told Columbus that the coast was very, very long, and that not even within a period of forty moons could one reach the end. Forty moons, hence forty months, or almost. Columbus calculated that the coast must be more than three thousand leagues long, or ten thousand miles. Who had ever heard of an island more than ten thousand miles long? In his discussions with the natives, Columbus had heard them refer to the region in which they found themselves as Magon, Magon province. Was this not similar in name to Marco Polo's Mangi? Columbus often let himself be fooled by similarities of name. This time, however, there were too many elements of coincidence, and he was tired of always looking and never finding.

Thus after much reflection and not a little dreaming, Columbus finally convinced himself, once and for all, that he had arrived in the Indies. In his mind, this long "peninsula," the Cuban coast, corresponded exactly with the Malay Peninsula, "the Golden Peninsula" as the ancient Greeks had called it: it was a peninsula "beyond the Ganges," halfway around the world. The sun ran half its daily course over that part of the world that preceded the Golden Peninsula, half over the part that followed it. The globe's surface from Cádiz to the Ganges was presumably equal in extent to that from Cuba to Cádiz, since Cuba after all "was" the Ganges, the Malay Peninsula, the Indies. The inspired, fantastical state of mind in which Columbus found himself was such that he took his thought to be the reality. It simply could not be otherwise.

We find proof of this in the events of the following morning, June 12, 1494. The ships were anchored off the island of St. John the Evangelist (now called the Isle of Pines), which is located near the end of that strip of land where Cuba tapers off into its westernmost point. Seen from the inlet where the caravels were moored, the coast seemed to turn southward, more like a peninsula than a promontory. In fact the island came to an end only about one hundred miles away. If Columbus had continued sailing in that direction he would have realized that Cuba was not a continent; moreover, he would have gathered valuable information that might have taken him as far as the Yucatán and the splendor and wealth of Mexico, which was very close by. Then he would indeed have been in a position to scoff at all criticism of his enterprise. His vindication lay within reach. The American continent was little more than a stone's throw from his ships.

But Columbus had entrusted his fate to his dreams, to the utopia in his mind. He had plunged headlong into their abyss with no intention of coming back out, though he probably would not have had the strength to do so had he so desired. He called for Fernando Pérez de Luna, public notary of Isabela and fleet secretary, and gave him specific instructions. In this exertion of authority Columbus appears to have been quite lucid. He told de Luna to consult one by one all the pilots, officers and sailors of the expedition, to board each of the three caravels to question them in person, and to ask them —I quote Bernaldez here, though the facts are borne out by Las Casas, Oviedo and all the other writers of the time—"if they had any doubts as to whether this land was the continent of the Indies, at that point where it begins for those arriving from the sea and ends for those arriving by land." Every man questioned was to express all doubts or differing opinions to the notary, who would then record them. Those with no doubts or differing opinions would then take an oath, swearing that they had reached the Asian continent and that they had come to this conclusion on their own. The oath could not be changed once it was recorded. Anyone who violated it was subject to punishment ranging from a fine of ten thousand maravedis to having his tongue cut out.

To us this seems the height of absurdity, Columbus's wildest act of arrogance yet. One wonders if it was brought on by his physical and mental condition, by that touch of madness twisting through his mind. Actually, Columbus had reached the limit of the imagination and could no longer distinguish it from reality. Nothing new had happened to make him abandon the conviction that drove him on. He also remembered being told of a similar action by Bartholomeu Dias when the two had met in Lisbon two years earlier. Dias had made his men sign a document when, after having rounded the Cape of Good Hope and set a course for the Indies, they had forced him to turn back. Dias, however, had indeed sailed around the Cape of Good Hope, whereas Columbus made his men swear to things that they had not seen or experienced, things that existed only in his imagination.

It should be said, however, that everyone complied without a word of protest. They wanted to turn back, and it appeared that they had to take this oath in order to do so. In any case, the crew's opinion on the matter was for the most part in agreement with Columbus's hypothesis. They too had heard the mention of forty moons, and no one imagined that an island could possibly be so long, just as no one thought of doubting the old Indian's word. The oath was even signed by Juan de la Cosa, the famous cartographer traveling aboard the *Niña*. A number of years later, when tracing his famous map of the world, Juan de la Cosa changed his mind and represented Cuba as an island. But for many years, the oath of "the Golden Peninsula" confounded geographical understanding all over the world. It wasn't until 1516 that maps ceased to represent Cuba as part of Asia.

Was Columbus therefore entirely at the mercy of his daydreams when he had his men all sign that incredible declaration? Not everyone thinks so. Riccaro Bacchelli, in the valuable little book mentioned earlier, maintains that Columbus's action "was not an instance of irrational, despotic, antiscientific behavior, as people said, but rather an excess of rationality, a geographical fanaticism." According to Bacchelli, Columbus had more trouble combating his own doubts than those of his officers and sailors. He wanted to unburden himself of this worry. His was the excess of a reasoning mind which, once it finds a shred of evidence, feels horror at the thought of falling back into uncertainty. "Truth can be loved even through error," warns Bacchelli. It is a profound statement, one that encapsulates all of Columbus, the audacity of his mind and the passion of his convictions. That oath was certainly an act of courage, but it was also an act of stubbornness and pride, qualities that Columbus also possessed in excess. More important, the method by which that declaration was extorted belonged to an epoch against which Columbus had fought bravely and desperately. Now it was as if he had fallen back into the Middle Ages, after apparently having left them behind. Perhaps when judging Columbus we should always take care to remember that his feet were still planted on medieval ground.

The day after that unforgettable declaration, the fleet began to make its way back. But Columbus took a long time before heading directly to Isabela. He wandered from one shore to the next, apparently planning a punitive expedition against the cannibals, who he thought inhabited Puerto Rico. To him this was yet another object of glory to present to his sovereigns. But, as Las Casas tells us, "the admiral fell into a pestilential sleep that robbed him of all his faculties and strength, so that he seemed as though dead. Everyone thought that he would not live another day." Such were the effects of the disease that would accompany him for the rest of his life, a form of gout or podagra aggravated by widespread rheumatic affections and an overall change in his metabolism. Gregorio Marañon, a Spanish authority on rheumatism and all related afflictions, made a careful scientific study of the Columbus case. He defined Columbus as the "martial" type, because of the congestion that often turned his face the color of Mars, and the helmet of prematurely white hair that adorned his head. The ships returned to Isabela on September 29 after five months of nearly fruitless wanderings, the admiral lying ill on board. He had to be carried off the ship, and then remained bedridden for many weeks.

De Torres had not yet returned from Spain, but Columbus was instead pleasantly surprised to find that Bartholomew, his dearest brother, had arrived. Bartholomew had heard in France of his achievements and had done all he could to try and join his brother on this journey, but had not made it to Cádiz in time. Thereupon, with the Crown's permission, he brought together a small fleet of three caravels and set off for Hispaniola to join his brother. He would never again leave his side. Bartholomew did not have quite the original personality that Christopher did, but he was a strong-willed man with an innate sense of authority, a gift his brother did not possess in such abundance. Now his brother lay abed, drained of strength and besieged by serious problems: Isabela, a lifeless, unhealthy city, was going to ruin; the inland area as far as the fort of San Tomás had become unsafe and was the scene of numerous ambushes and clashes; the source of gold seemed to have run dry.

What to do? Columbus gave full powers to Bartholomew, appointing him *adelantado* of the colony. The title of *adelantado* was given in Spain to provincial governors and imparted full authority on them. It was a much-desired title which only the sovereigns had the power to grant. Columbus, acting as Viceroy, had assumed their prerogative as his own. The sovereigns, however, had not approved of the decision, and thus it amounted to a violation of their legal authority. Columbus was wrong to overestimate the autonomy of his office, and to take royal consent for granted. He thus helped to revive the criticism and the displeasure felt in his regard, which would seriously threaten his position in the Indies as the Spanish presence there increased.

Thus he ought never to have placed his brother in a position of such high authority. Columbus's insecurity regarding his status as a foreigner of which he never quite managed to rid himself, condemned him to a life of painful solitude and a mistrust that weighed heavily on all his choices and decisions. He was unable to resolve these problems except by surrounding himself with people in whom he had absolute trust, people from either his immediate family or his closest circle of friends. For example, he ought never to have given command of the fort at Navidad to Diego de Harana, cousin of Beatrice. Harana had not been the right man to ensure the safety of the fort, either by temperament or experience. Now, on a larger scale, he was making the same mistake with Bartholomew, even though Bartholomew was of a different stamp and character from de Harana. The citizens of Isabela were already speaking ill of this viceroy who always hedged when it came to taking action, and who left them and their troubles behind for months at a time, making no effort at all to remedy their situation. When Bartholomew was suddenly appointed *adelantado* just after his arrival from across the sea, they became furious and openly hostile to Columbus and his family.

At San Tomás things were no better. Relations with the natives had deteriorated considerably. They no longer brought gold to the Spaniards, and Margarit's men did not know where to look for it. They would scatter into small groups with the sole purpose of acquiring food in whatever manner possible; whereas their task had been to explore, not to plunder. The natives put up resistance and clashed with the Spanish, who also fought among themselves. Bartholomew summoned Pedro Margarit back to Isabela to have him explain his conduct as commander of the fort. Margarit, a quick-tempered, violent man, rejected all criticism. He banded together with other malcontents and organized a kind of mutiny, seizing Bartholomew's three caravels in order to sail back to Spain. One of the rebels was Father Buyl, who reproached Columbus for being too soft with the natives. They were still "outside Christ's law," and did not deserve to be treated as brothers.

Once back in Spain and inside court circles, Margarit and Father Buyl, more than anyone else, started a flood of slanderous reports about Columbus. The picture they painted was that of an ambitious, incompetent, arrogant man who thought himself the equal of a king. They said that the much-promised gold was a lie and that the Crown was throwing its money to the wind by financing so vast an enterprise. They were exaggerating. But as we all know, calumnies always leave doubt and perplexity in their wake. These slanders were seeds that fell on fertile ground at court, where many wanted nothing more than to find stains in Columbus's glory, which they could not bear.

Another new year arrived, 1495. De Torres had finally returned from Spain with caravels laden with food. This relief alleviated the situation in Isabela to a degree, but relations with the natives were becoming more and more hostile. After Margarit's departure, the fort's garrison had fallen into a state of total anarchy. The men had given themselves over to violence, and the natives responded with insurrection. Each day brought nothing but more deaths on both sides.

The situation deteriorated to such an intolerable degree that in March, Columbus and his brother decided to lead, personally, a punitive expedition with the purpose of crushing the revolt. They left Isabela with a large force of armed men bent on vengeance. Beyond the mountains they clashed with a massive formation of Indians; Las Casas asserts that there were at least ten thousand of them. But the Spaniards' crossbows and harquebuses quickly put them to flight, as did the horses, animals which the Indians had never seen before and which in their terror they thought comprised single creatures with the men on their backs. The natives scattered into the valley. Yet they stubbornly continued laying ambushes for the Spanish, raiding their encampments at night and setting fire to their food depots. They fought like guerrillas, dragging out the conflict as though it might never end. Ten months passed, almost all of 1495, before this first colonial war could be considered won. The redoubtable Caonabó was also brought into it, and was eventually taken prisoner and put in chains. It was a hard-fought campaign, inspired above all by Bartholomew Columbus, who drove his brother to act and to persevere. The expeditionary force was implacable. In his *History,* Fernando Columbus describes the people as so submissive after the storm of punitive violence "that a Spaniard could venture alone wherever he pleased, enjoy the products of the soil and the local women free of charge, and have natives carry him on their shoulders for as far as he should so desire."

Hundreds were taken prisoner. Columbus had already proposed that caravels full of natives to be sold as slaves in Spain be exchanged for the caravels laden with provisions for Hispaniola. It was one way to pay back the expenses, since he still had not found any significant quantities of gold. The Indians were viewed as man-eating pagans captured as enemies during what could be termed a military operation in circumstances of war. The morality of the time allowed for non-Christians taken prisoner during war to be treated as slaves. This principle had been widely accepted in the past in regard to the Moors of Spain. The sovereigns, however, were reluctant to acknowledge the right to enslave these new savages from across the ocean. These people were not God's enemies, they simply did not know Him. And it would be much more commendable to convert them into Christians than to make them slaves.

Columbus, however, acted too hastily in this matter and thus committed yet another serious blunder in this unhappy period of his life. Without waiting for word from the court, he loaded five hundred slaves onto de Torres's ships, which were getting ready to return to Spain. The slaves seemed to him a seal of victory, a mark of great power. He was giving the Spanish nobility the opportunity to buy slaves at a good price. Their souls were sold at the market in Seville, where they were displayed in the nude for buyers to choose. Andrès Bernaldez saw them on the seller's block. Two hundred of them died within a short period of time.

In effect, the message that Columbus's action conveyed was that there was much less gold in "those Indies" than Marco Polo and Mandeville had led one to believe. He tried nevertheless to wring as much gold as possible out of the natives of Cibao by imposing a heavy tax on them. Every three months, every male Indian more than fourteen years of age had to produce enough gold to fill a small flask. Harsh fines and other forms of punishment were leveled against those who failed to comply. But the strategy failed miserably. There wasn't enough gold to meet the tax's requirements. The natives fled into the mountains with their families and prepared another desperate uprising. Their hate for the Spanish swelled like a river in spate. News of these developments reached Spain. Father Buyl and Margarit then peppered this information with their own comments. The whispering at court began to grow, expressing a weariness with these Indies and all their problems.

Columbus himself was given an accurate picture of Castile's less than enthusiastic sentiments toward his discoveries when a special envoy of the Crown arrived unexpectedly in Isabela "to see and report." His name was Juan Aguado, and he was a majordomo of the court. He came equipped with credentials authorizing him to interrogate the settlers of Isabela and to have the notary record their statements. He had come to investigate the discontent and its causes, and to ask the Spaniards what they thought of the conduct of Columbus and his *adelantado,* Bartholomew. In sum, Aguado had come to check up on the "foreigners."

Columbus was furious. Aguado arrived when he was still waging his campaign against the natives of Cibao. Columbus was so displeased by the presence of an investigator on his turf that for two months he questioned the validity of Aguado's papers and debated whether he, as viceroy, should acknowledge them as valid. Columbus would receive him, hear him out, send him away, and then put him off. He kept him from carrying out his duty. Aguado in turn would taunt him, letting him know that the sovereigns were not at all pleased with him. He told Columbus that he had learned, from talking to some of the men, that he no longer commanded the respect and obedience that he once had. These courtiers were very clever in their insinuations. Columbus, with his silent, offended pride, was defenseless against the likes of Aguado. His attempts to humiliate Aguado proved fruitless. Indeed, the very presence of this majordomo come to investigate was itself enough to humiliate him, Columbus, a viceroy spied on by the lackeys of the court.

America's discoverer was not in much of a state to put up with all this. His pride, haughtiness and self-consciousness rose up in revolt and carried him away to those solitary, rarefied regions of the mind where he increasingly sought refuge from the contradictions of real life. He did indeed feel humiliated. But, as Las Casas tells us, since he firmly believed that no man could humiliate him except himself, "he dressed himself in brown cloth, being a devout worshipper of St. Francis; I myself saw him in Seville right after his return, dressed almost like a friar."

Shortly after Aguado's arrival, Columbus decided to return to Spain, in Franciscan garb, to clear up all controversy surrounding him. But just as the ships were preparing to set sail, a violent hurricane struck Isabela. (The word "hurricane" comes from the native Taino term *hurakán,* which means "sudden storm.") All the ships in port were lost except for the old and glorious *Niña,* which withstood the storm's fury because it was the smallest ship, and maybe the strongest. But Columbus needed at least one other ship in order to sail back to Spain, so he had another caravel built right there on the spot, in part from the wreckage of the destroyed ships. The new caravel was ready by the first days of March. It was the first ship to be built on this side of the ocean, and was given the emblematic name of *India.*

Two hundred Spaniards, almost all of them sick and the rest weary or unhappy, boarded the two small vessels along with thirty Indian prisoners, one of them Caonabó. It is difficult to imagine just how crowded the two caravels must have been, each carrying four or five times their usual limit of about twenty-five men. And yet they set off just the same, loaded down like beasts of burden. Isabela was a dying city. Before leaving, Columbus had sent out some of his men to look for a more suitable site for a new capital. It had already been decided that this city would be built on the island's southern coast. Isabela would be permanently abandoned and all its inhabitants transferred to the new site by inland routes. What remains of Isabela today? I have been to the banks of the Bajabonico where the "city" once stood. Today it is just a field by the sea, entirely deserted. The ocean's waves break softly on the beach, which is covered with dense green shrubbery that turns into a forest just a few hundred yards from the shore. It is a lonely, fragrant, strangely fascinating place. Only a few stones here and there remain to remind us that here once stood the first colony of Europeans in America.

The return voyage was a long one. Columbus went well out of his way eastward until he came to Guadeloupe. He needed more provisions for all the people he was carrying on board. To make it possible for them to sleep, it was necessary to establish two shifts: half the men would lie down on the deck while the other half waited in the corners, on the quarterdeck and even in the hold. Conditions were very harsh. Many men died at sea, one of them Caonabó, the great enemy, whom Columbus now would not be able to present to the king and queen, as Roman generals used to do with barbarian prisoners yoked to their chariots.

There also were a few storms to contend with which shook the very entrails of the ship's suffering human cargo. Columbus at one point sighted the Azores but was unable to approach them. In any case, he did not want to repeat the adventure of the first return voyage. The *Niña* and the *India* entered the port of Cádiz on June 11, 1496. Columbus unfurled every one of the few banners that he had, but this time his homecoming was hardly a glorious one. No one awaited him; there were no honors, no applause. Lying in port were three caravels ready to set sail for Hispaniola with victuals and livestock. The men on board those ships watched the newly arrived voyagers disembark. They had faces the color of lemon and saffron. They had come from the Indies. Suddenly the thought of going there no longer seemed so appealing.

16

*Third Voyage:
Columbus Is Put in Chains*

The first thing Columbus did upon arriving in Cádiz was to send a letter to the king and queen requesting an audience. Then he went on to Seville, which after Córdoba was the Spanish city where he felt most at home and had the most friends. He liked to hide away in its cathedral's dark recesses and then go out and lose himself in the city's bright and noisy streets. He frequented streets like Calle de Genova and Calle Sierpe, where many people with the same origins as he had shops, people such as the Centuriones and the Spinolas, who were very much interested in what was happening across the ocean.

He lived at the house of a friend, the same Father Bernaldez, parish priest of Los Palacíos and chaplain to the archbishop. Bernaldez at the time was writing his highly accurate *History of the Catholic Kings* and had very close ties to another friar who served as a valuable adviser, Father Gorricho, a Carthusian monk at the monastery of Las Cuevas just outside the city. In those days Seville had more monasteries than houses; and Columbus preferred the company of friars to that of nobles. They were better educated, led simple lives and believed in compassion.

Columbus was in need of compassion. He was sinking ever deeper into a pit of loneliness. He believed his misfortunes to be a form of punishment from providence for the excessive pride he had shown in his moments of glory, and for his lack of love for his fellow man. Thus he continued to go about Seville in a Franciscan robe with "the knotted cord of devotion" (as Bernaldez described it), his beard uncut and his white hair unkempt. One day someone in Calle Sierpe began to rail against him. Columbus was insulted and mocked by many. He was the man who had promised wealth and had not produced it.

He had disappointed many hopeful people. His fiercest detractors accused him not only of having been mistaken, but of having deceived them. They called him Admiral of the Mosquitoes.

He unburdened himself with Bernaldez and with one or two other friends that he trusted. He told them about everything: the agony of Navidad, the misfortunes at Isabela, the voyage to Cuba, the oath that he had made the crew take. He claimed to be certain that Cuba was part of the Asian continent, and that by sailing farther in that direction one would reach Cathay, the richest region in the world. Bernaldez, however, was anything but convinced of this. In his opinion, one had to sail westward another thousand leagues, perhaps more, to reach the Indies. Columbus's ocean was too small, its dimensions erroneous.

On July 12, one month after his arrival, Columbus received a reply from the king and queen. They would receive him as soon as he was fit to travel "without inconvenience, [they] having learned that [he] had suffered great distress over the recent course of events." The court at the time found itself in the environs of Madrid, but was in the process of moving to Burgos. Columbus left for Burgos, taking the road to Mérida and Salamanca, and carrying a great quantity of maps and documents with him. He was hoping to set many things straight. His frame of mind was already that of someone who has to defend himself, to plead his case.

The royal family did not arrive in Burgos until October. Isabella was first to arrive, Ferdinand joining her later. They were both extremely busy, the king with the war against the French, who had invaded Roussillon and were threatening Perpignan; the queen with the preparations for three upcoming marriages: all three of her children were about to forge important dynastic alliances in the nuptial bed with the great powers of Europe.

When Columbus finally met with the sovereigns, the first part of the encounter was pure spectacle: there was the usual show of Indians and parrots, a few more gold nuggets and a necklace valued at six hundred castellanos hung from the neck of Caonabó's brother. This latter object was the *pièce de résistance*. During the trip to Burgos, every time Columbus's cortege was about to enter a town or city where crowds had gathered to see the Indians, the necklace was removed from a saddlebag that Columbus carried himself, and then placed around the cannibal's neck. Once they were out of the populated area, it was removed and put away again. Ferdinand and Isabella seemed satisfied and amused. They praised Columbus, and showed him great courtesy. He came away with the impression that despite the court's hostility toward him, which it did not hide, the sovereigns' continued favor would guarantee him a future rich with further exploits and victories. He was counting heavily on his powers of persuasion, and his passion. But he was in poor health and still bitter inside. Though it is difficult to know exactly what transpired during his interview at Burgos, Columbus apparently did not state his case as well as he had in the past. His reflexes were slower this time.

Indeed, things were not quite as promising as Columbus believed. The court's ill will toward him had made some inroads. It was no longer at the stage of malicious gossip. The testimonies, protests and damning reports had been piling up. People spoke of Columbus as a terrible governor, an inefficient leader unable to exert his authority. They also said he was a poor navigator, lost in mirages and utopias for which he was willing to sacrifice all. The sovereigns listened to these complaints, taking into account such factors as enmity and invidiousness, and still they came away feeling admiration and gratitude toward Columbus. But something remained. They had received Aguado's report from Hispaniola, which led them to think that they had to consider this Columbus in a new light. For example, they could no longer ignore the continual failures of his relations with others, his inability to win people's confidence. It had happened too many times: with Pinzón, Fonseca, Father Buyl, Margarit, and now Aguado. Could all these men be malicious, treacherous and unbearable human beings, and only Columbus fair-minded and without fault? Judged on the basis of character and disposition, Columbus did not make out well at all. The king and queen knew from experience that overly proud men always create trouble.

As for everything else, what sort of proof did Columbus have of actually having reached the Indies and found the source of gold? Very little indeed. One could only take his word concerning the Indies. He said that Cuba was a continent; but this was only a presumption, not a proven fact. At Burgos he brought out figures of all the miles he had traveled and all the islands he had discovered: seven hundred of them, each with its own name. He began to name them all, reciting the list like a rosary and watching the faces of his king and queen with eyes full of reproach. The sovereigns interrupted him, telling him to stop. He had done well to discover these places, they said, but what had he found there?

They came back to the question of gold. Columbus talked about the mines in Hispaniola. He described the wild landscape without roads, the sick Spanish colonists and the treachery of the natives. The colony's means were insufficient. The sovereigns objected that there were five hundred men living in Hispaniola, all of them paid out of Castile's treasury. How much longer would the kingdom have to bear this load, which Columbus now wanted to increase, before it could be repaid? Months? Years?

Then there was the problem of the slaves, which could not be ignored. Columbus had indirectly proposed reimbursing a portion of the expenses by selling the captured prisoners as slaves. (Paul Claudel, in his *Columbus,* has the monarchs respond to this idea with a cry of horror: "You had no gold, so you paid back your promises with men's souls!") Ferdinand, a rather callous man accustomed to matters of war, was inclined to accept the proposal and sell the slaves. He only had to verify that they were indeed enemies captured in battle. Isabella was firmly against it. Her moral sense was far stronger and deeper than the king's, and she instinctively opposed all commerce in human beings. The Church's upper echelons advised prudence. Theologians and canons were consulted. Those who came out in favor of the proposal appealed to pragmatic, though utterly inhumane, arguments: they said that the slaves, once in Castile, would learn the Spanish language, through which they could then be trained in the Christian faith and eventually baptized. The goal of such an approach could not be questioned. But the price of conversion was the loss of freedom. These arguments, which were discussed during the Burgos meeting, pointed to a larger, more serious problem looming in the distance like an island sighted through mist from afar. It was a question that distressed Isabella more than anyone else, as well as a few truly religious souls among Columbus's own friends, men such as Las Casas and Bernaldez. Columbus's two voyages had left these people with the impression that Spain, possessed of the violent, aggressive spirit of an old and corrupt Europe, had invaded a virgin land inhabited by a sedentary race of people. What right had the Spanish to occupy those lands, other than to bring the gospel to them? If this was their only purpose, then, as Las Casas strictly maintained, the Spanish had to behave like Christians. So much for slavery.

At the end of the Burgos meeting, Columbus requested permission to prepare for a third voyage across the ocean. His cause was supported by the court cosmographer Jaime Ferrer de Blanes, mentioned above, who had come to enjoy considerable influence with the king and queen. De Blanes had been assigned the task of overseeing the observance of the stipulations made in the treaty of Tordesillas, by which the imaginary line first put on the map by the pope separated Portuguese and Spanish zones of dominion. Recently, news had been coming from all over that the King of Portugal was certain that directly across the ocean from Africa, to the south of all the lands thus far discovered, lay a large continent. Columbus himself had repeatedly heard the Indians speak of a large land mass south of the islands. If this was true, the pope's *raya* would ultimately determine whether the hypothetical continent fell to Spain or to Portugal. These matters had to be looked into, maintained Ferrer de Blanes, and the best way to do so was to go and see for oneself.

This was the basic purpose of Columbus's third voyage, which came to be called the *rumbo austral,* the southern voyage, as it ventured south of the equator. The course was entirely different from those of the two previous voyages, though the final destination remained Hispaniola, where Columbus's brother had already established the new city of Santo Domingo. Columbus was still viceroy and governor of the Indies. These titles and privileges were confirmed at his Burgos interview, during which the sovereigns also ratified the appointment of Bartholomew as *adelantado* of the Indies.

The fleet of the third voyage left from Sanlúcar de Barrameda, the port at the mouth of the Guadalquivir. It consisted of six vessels, three of which were to sail directly to Hispaniola with victuals and fresh supplies; the other three, under Columbus's command, would head south on the *rumbo austral.* It was late May, 1498, a peaceful time of year when the bright sky made the placid river's waters gleam, warming the winds between its banks and brightening the nearby mountainside with its white houses lying in the shade of fig and olive trees.

The convoy set sail for Madeira, and called at Porto Santo. On this same island as a young newlywed, Columbus had first begun to pursue his dream, albeit somewhat timidly. Twenty years had passed, and yet it already seemed as if his whole life had been used up. Columbus went to the Church of Porto Santo and had a Mass said for his wife's soul. Before leaving Seville, he had had a deed of majorat drawn up for the benefit of Diego, the only son born of their marriage. Upon Columbus's death, Diego was to receive his patrimony, privileges and title of Admiral of the Ocean Sea. One of the obligations that Diego would have to meet was to turn over a certain sum to the Banco di San Giorgio for Genoese charities. This was one of the very few recorded connections between America's discoverer and what was in all likelihood his place of birth.

After Madeira, the ships went on to the Canaries, dropping anchor in the now familiar haven of San Sebastián, below the walls of Gomera castle. Of the things he did during this stay on the island, Columbus in his log said only, "We stocked up on cheeses, of which there is a great deal down here of good quality." No mention at all of the lovely lady governor. Did their brief idyll already belong to the past? (As I have quoted here from the log of the third voyage, I should give a brief explanation. It was actually more of a report of the voyage than a ship's log. Columbus dictated it to, or had it copied by, Bernardo Ibarra. The text was eventually lost. Las Casas, however, consulted it at length, and my quotations are drawn from his book.)

The six ships split up in Gomera, three heading west to Hispaniola and Dominica, the other three heading south, in the direction of the Cape Verde Islands. Columbus's plan was to descend to the latitude of Guinea, where the Portuguese had found gold. According to Aristotle's teachings, lands located at the same latitudes yield the same products. Once it reached Guinea's latitude the little fleet would turn its sails and set a westward course. Columbus could in this way pursue two goals: that of discovering whether and where the continent dreamed of by King John actually existed, and that of making new inroads in his quest for gold, which had thus far proved all too fruitless. Columbus was well aware that these attempts were mere stabs in the dark, not based on any solid evidence or previous experiences. "I believe that the course I am following," he writes in the log, "has never been taken by anyone else, and that these seas are utterly unknown." He feels a certain pride at finding himself once again face to face with the unknown. The voyage took on a shade of the mysterious, and Columbus had always been fascinated by mystery. His own mind resounded not a little with echoes of the mysterious.

The Cape Verde Islands were a disappointment. "Their name is deceptive," he noted, "since they are rather arid and contain nothing green [verde] that I could see." All that he found there were wild goats, large tortoises, and lepers. Meanwhile the heat at sea was becoming unbearable. It was July, and they were near the equator. Six years had now passed since the landing at San Salvador, and here was Columbus, getting on in years, once again in the middle of the Atlantic and still without a real understanding of the geography. He had the vague impression that he was navigating somewhere between Japan and the Philippines. His mirages remained Cipango, Cathay, the Indies —the "distant Occident." The sun was so hot that people feared the ships might catch fire. Columbus thought of St. Augustine's "burning seas," but he had never believed in them and was not about to change his mind. Nevertheless, the hoops of the casks on board broke and spilled their precious contents of wine and water. The food was beginning to spoil. The ships found themselves in the hottest, calmest region in the entire ocean. Unable to advance for lack of wind, they lay still beneath the sun's scorching rays.

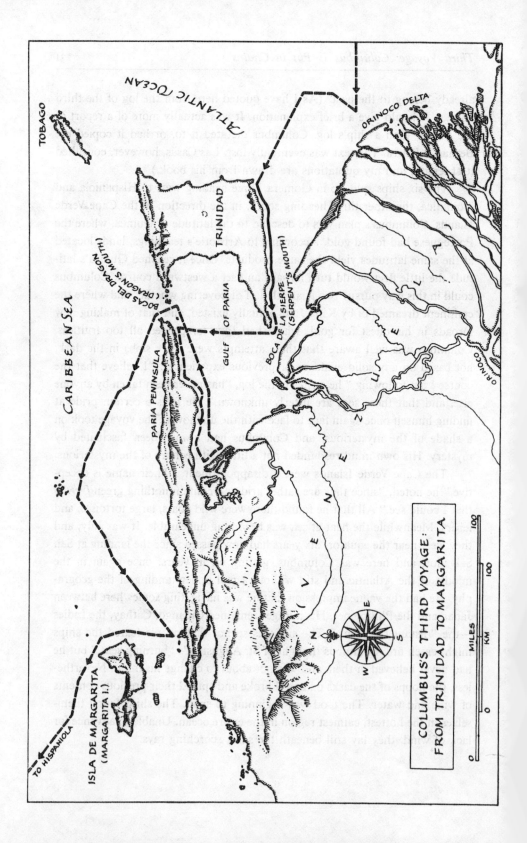

TOBAGO

ATLANTIC OCEAN

ORINOCO DELTA

TRINIDAD

CARIBBEAN Sea

BOCAS DEL DRAGON
(DRAGON'S MOUTH)

GULF OF PARIA

BOCA DE LA SIERPE
(SERPENT'S MOUTH)

PARIA PENINSULA

V E N E Z U E L A

ORINOCO

N W E S

ISLA DE MARGARITA
(MARGARITA I.)

TO HISPANIOLA

COLUMBUS'S THIRD VOYAGE:
FROM TRINIDAD TO MARGARITA

MILES

0   100

KM

0   100

Luckily rain and wind soon arrived and carried them away from there. The crews were so exhausted that Columbus judged it necessary to abandon the southerly course and head directly north. If he had continued along the course he had begun he would have reached the Amazon River basin and discovered that "continent to the south" whose existence the Portuguese had sensed. Now the fleet sailed more or less parallel to South American shores, though from a good distance. Wanting to return to more familiar waters, Columbus headed for Hispaniola. There was a shortage of water on board the ships. The admiral was suffering from his gout and unable to sleep at night, and his eyes were always red and tired. The idea of the continent to the south had lost its urgency and now faded in the distance behind them.

On July 31 the crew sighted land to the port side of the ships, three peaks rising up from a surrounding island. For this reason Columbus named the island Trinidad, the name it still bears today. The crossing was over. The crews celebrated their arrival with much rejoicing, chanting the *Salve Regina.* As the ships approached the coast a large swarm of Indians set out to sea and sent a hail of poison arrows out to greet the newcomers. No one disembarked. The three ships circled part of the islands and entered the Gulf of Paria, which opens out in front of the mouth of the Orinoco River on the coast of Venezuela. The promontories and bays that Columbus could see from his ship were part of the South American continent. But he was so accustomed now to the orgy of islands through which he had been wandering for much of the past six years that he believed every new promontory he saw to be another island.

The waters in the Gulf of Paria are generally very rough, because of the strong currents running through it and the proximity of the ocean, into which it flows through a turbulent little strait that Columbus named "Dragon's Mouth," *Bocas del Dragón.* He refrained from drawing near to land, because of conditions unsuitable for landing and because of his worsening health. He sent a few teams of explorers ashore, however, primarily to replenish fresh-water supplies, for which there was desperate need. On land, the sailors found plants quite unlike those growing in the Antilles—corn, for example. But more importantly, they met Indians who wore huge pearls on their arms. On nearby islands such as Margarita (which owes its name to the fact that *margarita* means "pearl" in Spanish), there were whole beds of pearl oysters growing attached to mangrove branches submerged in the water. For more than a century, Spain made great profits from these pearls, which Columbus was the first to find but did not pay much attention to, anxious as he was to return to Hispaniola. Two years later Alonso de Ojeda, one of his lieutenants in Isabela, led an expedition into the Gulf of Paria. He did not let the pearls get away.

Taking advantage of clear skies both during the day and at night, Columbus took many bearings with the quadrant. They were only approximate readings, to be sure, and quite likely erroneous. But judging from the manner in which the North Star moved, he believed himself to be in a different hemisphere, a judgment consistent with the cosmographical notions of the time, according to which the Earth's two hemispheres were not exactly the same. The northern hemisphere was thought to be perfectly round, the southern not entirely round. Ptolemy and a number of other ancient philosophers also believed this to be true. In the account of his voyage, Columbus wrote: "I had always read that the world, land and water, was spherical. But I found so many differences in the sky that I began to form various notions of what it meant to be spherical without being round." He likened the northern hemisphere to a half ball, and the southern one to a woman's breast, nipple and all, with the nipple being "the part that is highest and closest to the heavens, and is found below the equinoctial line in this Ocean Sea, at the far end of the Orient."

Another aspect of the Gulf of Paria's environment that seemed entirely new to Columbus was its great quantity of fresh water. To reach the salty water of the sea one had to go some twenty miles off the coast. A river whose waters reached so far out to sea must be very powerful. One could assume, then, that no island could be vast enough to contain a river so large. Was it therefore a continent? Columbus's imagination raced off in an unexpected direction. He wrote: "The Scriptures tell us that in the Earthly Paradise grows the tree of life, and that from it flows the source that gives rise to the four great rivers, the Ganges, the Tigris, the Euphrates and the Nile. The Earthly Paradise, which no one can reach except by the will of God, lies at the end of the Orient. And that is where we are." Where the dawn of Creation took place. In Columbus's image we find exaltation, mysticism and the certainty of being predestined to make discoveries of the most extraordinary sort. Once again we find madness as well, and genius, the imagination's indispensable trigger. "I believe that all this water might indeed come from there, though the place be far away." He had not quite reached the Earthly Paradise, but he saw traces of it; he sensed its proximity and could situate it in the regions of his world.

The suspicion that he might be at the edge of a continent did, however, emerge, though in a rather vague fashion. In a note made on August 14 and cited by Las Casas, Columbus writes: "I believe this land may be a great continent that has remained unknown to this day. Reason bears this out, in light of the immense river and the sea of fresh water formed at its mouth." Las Casas maintains, though he draws the conclusion on his own, that before quitting the coast "Columbus understood that a land so vast could not be an island, but only a continent." The hypothesis is consistent with the assertion in the Book of Esdras, so precious to the admiral, that the world is six parts land and only one part water. But the reader should be wary here of jumping to false conclusions. Columbus had no idea he had discovered a "new" continent; rather, he believed himself to be at the outer edge of a world that the ancients had known about, but were unable to explore in its entirety. He imagined the Venezuelan coast to be part of the Chinese province of Mangi, in the country's southernmost part. He saw it as part of the same continent of which he thought Cuba to be an extension, and believed that the two regions probably joined somewhere. Columbus's mind had never left Cathay and the Indies. It had only ventured beyond its expectations and caught a glimpse of the exceptional size of this continent on the ocean.

But he delved no further into the matter. At the time he was roughly where Güiria is today, some 450 miles east of Caracas. He set sail from there, without looking any further into the great wealth of pearls, or into the prospects of discovery presented by the continent. He was, in a sense, turning his back on good luck, and indeed his luck turned bad from this point forward. He drew one final conclusion from these explorations as soon as he had left the Gulf of Paria and found the trade winds again, which carried him swiftly to more familiar seas. He concluded that "going south one goes upward, and going north one goes downward." And so he went down to Hispaniola, arriving on August 11, 1498, after nearly three months of travel that had taken him close to the equator.

Columbus did not know exactly where to find the new city that had been built in his absence in Hispaniola. Before leaving Isabela he had given his brother Bartholomew instructions to look for a suitable location on the island's southern shores, somewhere not far from the mines of San Cristóbal, which had just been discovered at the time, and from which they hoped to extract a good deal of gold. Other stipulations that Columbus had made to his brother were that the city be built in a well-sheltered haven where ships could land, on a navigable river along which the gold could be transported. They had decided together to name the city Santo Domingo, in memory of their father. After which Columbus had left for Spain, leaving the matter behind him.

He met up with his brother at the Isla Beata, a small island off Hispaniola's southern coast, about halfway down the coast. Bartholomew then escorted him to Santo Domingo, which was about a hundred miles from there. Columbus arrived there on the last day of August, 1498. He was seeing Santo Domingo for the first time. It was a cheerful place on the Ozama River, a wide tropical river with low banks and a peaceful current flowing amid green shrubs and grasses. A dull silence reigned over the site, broken only by the cries of birds in the swamp and by the sea. Bartholomew had settled the town's inhabitants—some two or three hundred men—on the Ozama's left bank. On the right bank there was a native village, which the experiences at Navidad and in Cibao had counseled the Spanish to keep at arm's length. No houses or buildings had yet been built in stone. The Spanish lived in wooden houses with thatched roofs of palm leaves. A rather solid fence surrounded the compound, and a small fort had been built overlooking the river to protect it. The settlers had already begun the work of gradually replacing the wooden houses with solid stone constructions. The surrounding region was rich in quarries that yielded a stone of a lovely color ranging between green and pink, and sometimes light gray. These were to become the hues of the city of Santo Domingo, and we still find them today in the district known as the colonial quarter. Every trace of the Columbus era is religiously preserved, to the point that one can say without exaggeration that Santo Domingo is the most Columbian city in the world, whether for the constructions left over from that era, starting with the cathedral facing the ocean, or for the time that Columbus spent there, two whole years of his life—a considerable amount, since he spent most of his life wandering, across the seas or from one city to the next.

Columbus felt proud and satisfied. This was his realm, he was its viceroy. He hoped to find peace and quiet here, a place to rest his tired eyes and his rickety limbs devastated by arthritis, rheumatism and worsening gout. But Bartholomew had terrible news for him. The first days after Columbus's departure had been very, very hard. After their long march through the center of the island after abandoning Isabela, the settlers were immediately faced with hostility from the Indians. There were numerous clashes, with dead and wounded on both sides. Others continued to die from privation and hardship as well; food was always very scarce, and hunger the worst of counselors. Discontent grew rampant again, spreading like an epidemic. The viceroy's arrival brought a brief period of revived hope, but the resentment soon returned, finding in the two "foreigners" a larger object on which to focus itself. Actually there were three of them now, since around this time Columbus's younger brother, Diego, also settled in Santo Domingo. He acted as deputy when Christopher and Bartholomew went inland to kill Indians. To most of the Spanish settlers, this trio, with its small court of self-interested faithfuls, seemed rather arrogant, suspicious and loath to communicate with the rest of the colonists, their ostensible companions in this adventure. The "foreigners" shut themselves inside their own circle; they gave only orders, especially the order to work. And not all were willing to comply.

Francisco Roldán, a man of the viceroy's household who had served as *alcalde* of Isabela (a kind of mayor), became leader of the most disgruntled and seditious of the men. There was open rebellion. About a hundred men took Roldán's side, all of them ready to do anything to change the situation. Bartholomew tried to placate them by offering them the services of slaves to release them from hard physical labor. But this did not suffice. Bartholomew's appointment to the office of *adelantado* had now been officially confirmed, sealed by royal hand. To oppose him, and even more so his brother the viceroy, was in effect to oppose the king and queen, whom they represented in office and person. Nevertheless, the rebellious group grew in size. Roldán established a kind of alliance with the Indians, who saw him as championing the cause of better treatment and a suspension of the burdensome tributes that Columbus continued to exact from the males of each tribe.

Roldán formed his most solid alliance with the inhabitants of the Xaragua region, which lay roughly in the area of the modern-day boundary between Haiti and the Dominican Republic. Roldán and his men went there to live, deserting Santo Domingo. It was an act of revolt. Many of his followers were criminals released from prison to fill out the ranks of colonizers, which were growing thin because of all the talk of danger, hardship and adversity that had spread throughout Spain, with Columbus as scapegoat.

But there was also something different, even unusual, about Roldán's revolt. Roldán had what we might today call a romantic disposition; he was very attracted to the beauty of the land and the gentleness of the Indians' customs. His sentimentalism had a social side to it. He preferred the savages and their way of life to the rules and obligations of the city. He had made himself leader of the commonest men in a revolt against the gentlemen surrounding Columbus. Columbus wanted to found a colony and to resolve problems of organization and exploitation in a manner serving the interests of the Crown. Roldán wanted only to immerse himself in the enchanting paradise of this New World and to create something along the lines of an independent, Hispano-Indian state, with plenty of friends, servants and women. His rebellion was a spontaneous one, a desire for freedom, the freedom of natural forces. In Xaragua, the young noble women would appear at ritual celebrations lying nude on a litter of roses, covered only by garlands of flowers. Why stay with Columbus, who was so moody, so harsh, so proud?

Columbus, moreover, never understood Roldán, and never knew how to deal with him. Alas, those sudden flashes of understanding that used to dispel the shadows of his existence no longer occurred. Poetry had abandoned him, that particular poetry that brings the human mind to understand itself and others. He now lusted for power, prestige, wealth. Poetry, if anything, had gone over to the other side, since it always stands by simple men and abandons the overly ambitious.

At first Columbus tried to exert his authority as viceroy. How could a handful of mutineers stand a chance? When it came down to counting those truly faithful to him, however, there were only about seventy men left who would stand by him. He grew afraid, tried to buy time. He had a proclamation posted on the cabins, which permitted all those colonizers who wanted to return to Spain to do so. They would be provided with ships and provisions for the voyage. A general amnesty was also declared for all past actions, promising in the future a justice that was "humane and reasonable." Together with these proclamations, which were almost a kind of repentance for what he had done in the past, Columbus sent a message to Roldán inviting him to discuss the matter. In his letter he called Roldán "dear friend" and implied that he would keep his title of *alcalde.*

Before he would come to Santo Domingo, Roldán wanted a safe-conduct. It was granted him. The meeting was long but without anger. It did not, however, lead to any specific arrangement: Roldán returned to his paradise, where Columbus would eventually send a delegation with the draft of an agreement. The revolt had now lasted six months. The agreement, which was made in late 1498, provided for the return of the rebels to Spain with their slaves and women, free of all accusation. Anyone who wanted to stay would be granted land free of charge in Xaragua. Under these conditions the rebels signed a deed of surrender. Roldán was named *alcalde mayor,* one grade higher than his previous title. After his pardon he was undecided as to whether he should go back to Spain or stay in Xaragua. There were no more reprisals or disputes to fear. Columbus's capitulation had been total.

Columbus's plan was to make it easier for the subversives to leave Hispaniola. He wrote a letter to the king and queen describing Roldán's uprising and what had ensued. He made a point of emphasizing that in his opinion they were, for the most part, ex-convicts, and that one could not hope to colonize the Indies with men of their sort. He asked the sovereigns to send to Santo Domingo, with each new dispatch of ships, fifty men of proven worth, in exchange for whom he would send back to Spain the sick and unreliable. He also asked them to send "pious and zealous" priests to the Indies. After Father Buyl's departure, all religious matters were left in the hands of one friar, Roman Pane, who by himself had succeeded in converting a dozen Indians. But more than this could not be expected of him.

This is followed, in the letter, by some rather vague and incoherent proposals regarding the colonization of the Earthly Paradise. Columbus hoped to return to Paria, to add to the garland of conquests that he had "bestowed" on Spain those places where "God's seal" still shone. Isabella was very upset, practically terrorized by the letter. The sovereigns were left with the impression "that he was no longer the same man." He had always been given to fantasizing and daydreaming, but now he seemed to have gone mad. They had noticed a change during the meeting at Burgos. Columbus had seemed to possess neither the lucidity nor the self-confidence that in the past had enabled him to overcome all obstacles.

He made one final request in the letter, one which provided another clear indication of his perplexity: that he be sent a wise administrator of justice. He was even ready to pay such a person out of his own pocket. "I may be mistaken," he protested, "but it appears to me that princes ought to protect their governors for as long as they keep them, since without protection, all is lost." Columbus was not a subtle man. His gambit appeared imprudent, to say the least. Nor, like all people who presume themselves to be infallible, was he very wise. The fact was that his influence at court was disappearing. The sovereigns were inclined to believe that he and Bartholomew had created a chaotic situation in Hispaniola, and did not know how to remedy it. Ferdinand did not want to incur further debts by sending more ships, supplies and men in support of an enterprise that seemed unable to get off the ground. Isabella was disappointed in the meager success of the plan to save souls, on which all justification of conquest was based. Columbus, undaunted, continued to send slaves to Spain, against the queen's wishes. This offended Isabella, who had been Columbus's strongest, most loyal supporter in the past, the only one who had understood him and shown faith in him when all the rest had turned their backs on him.

But she had been young then, full of hope and perhaps not unmoved by a few tremors hidden away in the remotest recesses of her heart, where passions are born. Now Isabella was a fifty-year-old woman wasted by power and crushed by misfortune. Of the three children that she happily married off in 1496, the last happy year of her life, two died very suddenly, like flowers nipped in the bud. Don Juan, who had taken Margarete von Hapsburg as his wife, died at the age of nineteen. Shortly thereafter her daughter Isabella, who had become Queen of Portugal by marrying the young Prince Manuel, perished while giving birth to the heir to the throne. This sacrifice proved to be for naught, since the child died at two years of age. The dynastic alliances were thus thrown into disorder, and with them the policies of their respective governments. For Isabella, however, these were deep personal wounds that struck the very core of her being. "Her health and her life were cut short," writes Bernaldez, "for from that time forward she lived without joy."

As for Columbus, she left it to her husband to say that "he was a good admiral but not a good viceroy." She probably felt the same way. She had heard too many rumors portraying the admiral's conduct as that of a weak man. The malcontents and rebels called him a tyrant. One can impose one's will either through strength of character or through the violence of power. Pietro Martire was told by veterans of Hispaniola that "those two"—Columbus and his brother, the "foreigners"—"were always quick to torture, hang, and behead." The worst that was said was that "they behaved like enemies of the king and queen." How could the sovereigns of Spain tolerate that a man who acted as their "enemy" go unpunished, especially when everyone was talking about it, thus casting doubt on their very authority? Ferdinand certainly would not tolerate it, given his character and his general lack of sympathy for Columbus. Isabella, drowning in grief, could only nod assent. Las Casas frames for posterity the moment in which Columbus lost out: "Indignant, the king and queen decided to take away his government."

The man they chose to carry out the decision was an old officer of the crown, Francisco de Bobadilla. They were well familiar with his loyalty, integrity and firmness of character. Bobadilla knew only how to obey. He was a Knight of Calatrava, the oldest chivalric order in Spain: he stood at the top of the sovereigns' list of those who had served them dutifully without ever saying a word, asking for neither honors nor favors in return. Oviedo calls him "a great gentleman loved by all." Bobadilla, a man of the court, did not like Columbus. He considered him an outsider, however bold and successful. He left for Santo Domingo armed with supreme judiciary powers, the same that Columbus had wanted granted to his "wise administrator of justice." Bobadilla was sent to him as the very man that he himself had requested.

But Bobadilla had different cards up his sleeve. He was empowered to arrest "all persons in rebellion against the authority of the sovereigns," to sequester their belongings and to have all fortresses, houses, ships, arms, ammunition and "everything belonging to the Crown" turned over to him. At the last moment the king, and especially the queen, hesitated a bit, searching for further proof in the testimonies of those returning from Santo Domingo. Finally they gave Bobadilla the go-ahead, in the summer of 1500. He was carrying a letter from the king and queen to Columbus. It was addressed to "Our Admiral of the Ocean Sea and of all the islands and the continent of the Indies," making no mention of the titles of viceroy and governor. Columbus's fate was sealed.

Upon arriving in Santo Domingo, the first thing that Bobadilla saw, on the shores of the port, was a gallows from which hung the corpses of two Spaniards. Las Casas gives us this description: "They were still fresh, having been hung just a few days before." There had been a new uprising, led by one of Roldán's lieutenants, Adrian de Muxica. But when Muxica was captured and condemned on the spot to the gallows, the sentence could not be carried out immediately because no confessor could be found in all of Santo Domingo. When the priest finally arrived, de Muxica refused to confess, saying that he had in the interim forgotten all his sins. Columbus, in a rage, had him thrown into the sea from the top of a tower.

Bobadilla was horrified. He learned that five other Spaniards were awaiting execution, scheduled for the following day. Columbus and his brother Bartholomew were absent, patrolling the inland areas with their men and looking for rebels. Don Diego, the youngest brother, had stayed behind in Santo Domingo. Bobadilla ordered him at once to turn all prisoners over to him. He showed the royal papers authorizing his request. Don Diego refused to do as he asked as long as the admiral was away. The dispute, which was repeated numerous times, drove Bobadilla to exasperation. He had the colony's entire population gather in the Church of Santo Domingo (not the lovely cathedral that one sees beside the ocean today, since in 1500 it had not yet been built), and asked Diego Columbus, in the sovereigns' name, to obey his orders. No one raised any objections. Bobadilla seized the citadel, took possession of the house that Columbus lived in as governor, sequestered all his papers, letters and everything else that he found. To arouse popular sympathy in his favor, he announced that everyone could keep as much gold as they wanted, except for a much reduced tribute that they had to pay to the crown. Don Diego, who had refused to obey his orders, was put in fetters.

When Columbus returned to his capital and was greeted by all these unexpected, incredible new developments, his shouts of protest and indignation resounded all the way to the river. Bobadilla could show his credentials as much as he pleased! Mine, screamed Columbus, are much more valid; it is you who owe me obedience. But while Columbus carefully refrained from taking any action, Bobadilla, backed into a corner, declared Columbus his prisoner. And since Columbus responded to everything with a shrug of the shoulders, saying that no one would dare lay a hand on him, Bobadilla responded to his provocation by ordering that irons be placed around his wrists and ankles. The Admiral of the Ocean Sea, in chains! Such a thing was unheard of, inconceivable. Indeed, when the moment came to put the chains on him, no one had the heart to do it. "Respect and compassion"—I quote from Las Casas again—"prevented those present from acting." Unfortunately, one can always find a willing jailor. Columbus's cook was the man who finally put Columbus in chains, and he did so "with an expressionless face, as though he were serving some new, dainty dish."

With the three brothers imprisoned in the citadel and under close watch, Bobadilla assumed full powers as special delegate of the Crown. He opened an inquest into the conduct of Columbus and his *adelantado* Bartholomew. It was swiftly conducted and swiftly concluded: the admiral was too much of a burden to Bobadilla, who was after all just a simple court official. Indeed, the conclusion of the inquest was that the brothers Columbus should be taken to Spain to undergo a regular trial. Bobadilla was ridding himself of the admiral, passing him on to more powerful hands.

In chains, Columbus left Santo Domingo in early October of 1500, on board the caravel *La Gorda*. Once out at sea, the ship's commander, with great respect, offered to release Columbus from his fetters. Columbus refused: "I have been placed in chains by order of the sovereigns," he said, not without pride, "and I shall wear them until the sovereigns themselves should order them removed."

And so he did. He wore the chains at his feet during the entire crossing, which was a swift one without any navigational difficulties, and when he disembarked in Cádiz in late October, he was still in chains. The last time he had arrived in a Franciscan frock, this time in a criminal's fetters. Were they proof of his humility or his pride? By now Columbus valued those chains very highly; he considered them his most precious possession. Even after they were removed, he always kept them close to him, and requested that they be buried with him.

As soon as he went ashore he secretly passed a letter to a young officer who during the voyage had shown him friendship and respect. The letter was addressed to the sister of Antonio de Torres, Doña Juana, who resided at court. Doña Juana had once been the governess—*l'aya*—of Prince Juan, in whose chamber Columbus's sons, Diego and Fernando, had served as pages. Columbus had intimate ties with the prince's *aya*. And Doña Juana had a close relationship with the queen, of which Columbus was well aware. The letter he was sending to her was part of a carefully plotted strategy. Columbus could unburden himself of his great bitterness by turning to Doña Juana, the person most likely to understand him. And through her he could speak indirectly to the queen, open his soul to her. Columbus was confident this plan would work.

The letter began with the most flattering of openings: "Most Virtuous Lady." He lamented the great outrage to which he had been subjected, "the great insult and ingratitude." This was the point he most wanted to stress, the sovereigns' great indebtedness to him for the things he had achieved and for the injustice with which they had repaid him. He listed all his deeds in the letter, achievements carried out "by divine will." He had brought "another world" into the king and queen's domain, "which shall make Spain, once deemed poor, the richest of all countries." And: "I have put under the sway of my kings more land than there is in Africa and Europe, more than one thousand seven hundred islands." (The number of islands that Columbus boasted of as the patrimony of his discoveries steadily increased as he advanced in age and his memory faded.) "Not even if I had stolen the Indies, or had given them to the Moors, would I have been treated so dishonorably! In this undertaking I have lost my youth, as well as my due honors."

Youth and honors. His youth was beyond recovery; it remained inaccessible, behind him, and all he could do was to look back on it with regret. The same was true of his triumph over the ocean, his great season of glory. But his honors, his "due honors," had to be returned to him, along with the other titles and tributes that Columbus firmly believed belonged to him. This was the purpose of the letter to the "Most Virtuous Lady." Columbus landed in Spain, humbled by his fetters. But his pride in his rights, his privileges and his future remained intact.

17

Fourth Voyage:
The Entire Fleet Is Lost

At Cádiz, and then Seville, where Columbus requested to go right after his arrival, the admiral in chains was a painful sight. Yet he walked through the streets impassive, pride in his eyes, dragging his chains behind him with such a clamor that all who passed turned around to look.

At Seville he was taken in by the monks of the Carthusian monastery of Las Cuevas, having been invited there by his friend Father Gorricho. King Ferdinand and Queen Isabella were in Córdoba. When they learned of Columbus's treatment they showed surprise and irritation with Bobadilla, who had gone to extremes in carrying out their orders. They certainly had not expected the admiral to be subjected to the humiliation of chains. They immediately ordered him to be set free, and sent him by courier, as Córdoba is not far from Seville, a purse with two thousand ducats "so that he could appear in court in a state befitting a person of his rank." This decision, its tone, and the invitation once again modified Columbus's state of mind. He now felt a mixture of newfound gratitude, lingering bitterness and above all a desire to protest and to demand reparations for the wrongs he had suffered.

He was so caught up in his misfortunes that it did not occur to him that justice could wait. In the sovereigns' minds, Columbus's case was certainly not among the primary concerns of state. The admiral had to sit patiently for weeks and weeks at the Las Cuevas monastery. Long waits are an excellent antidote to fits of anger and rage. The king and queen were well aware of this; they did not receive Columbus until shortly before Christmas, in December of 1500. They received him at the Alhambra in Granada, amid Oriental opulence. Columbus had to walk through the large, stately room to reach the thrones at the back, where the king and queen sat in royal splendor. When he finally stood before them, the admiral remained silent a long time. Then he could only fall to his knees and burst into tears.

The sovereigns bade him rise and speak freely what was on his mind. Columbus spoke at great length, somewhat confusedly, but with a grace and charm that still shone through the disorder of his speech. He said that his errors had been made in good conscience. For years he had proved his loyalty, many times over. He assured them profusely that this had not changed, and would never change. Writes Madariaga: "He loved them with a passionate hatred."

Then, changing the whole tone of his speech, Columbus went into a vehement tirade of protest against Bobadilla for all that Bobadilla had taken from him: the office and authority which was due him by right and which the Santa Fé pacts, signed by the sovereigns themselves, had defined as "perpetual," and the possessions confiscated as though he, Columbus, had wrongfully enriched himself. He mentioned the chains, which had been recently removed but would weigh on his heart forever. The grievance was so strident, so aggressive, that the sovereigns must surely have thought that faced with such a man, Bobadilla had no choice but to put him in chains. They had received Columbus with open, generous minds, but the encounter did not alter the opinion they had formed of him as a poor governor and administrator of justice, and now he even appeared more generally to be a person disagreeable to listen to.

In response to Columbus's requests they were politely evasive. Columbus wanted nothing less than Bobadilla's head! Such a recourse had never even entered the sovereigns' minds. They told him only that they would look into the question of his possessions. And Oviedo, whose text is quite impartial in its description of the interview at the Alhambra, tells us that "never did they promise that he would be reinstated as governor."

Curiously, Columbus came away from the discussion rather satisfied. He felt he had given their highnesses a piece of his mind. He now expected Bobadilla to be recalled and reprimanded, and every right and office that he had enjoyed before Bobadilla's arrival in Santo Domingo to be reinstated: in other words, he expected everything to go back exactly to how it was before 1500, an absurd presumption. But Columbus not only had an exaggerated opinion of himself, he also possessed an unshakable sense of optimism, which is really just the other side of stubbornness. His optimism never abandoned him, not even during the darkest, most trying moments of his life, of which he certainly had not seen the last with the humiliation of the chains. Indeed, in the years to come, as he remained forever lost in his dreams and drifted farther and farther away from reality, his imagination began to lose its edge, its force, its impetus toward shaping the future. And in losing its vigor— because of his advancing age, his infirmity, and his continual disappointments —Columbus's imagination turned more and more into a vehicle for mad ravings. In his mild delirium he came to believe that he had been chosen by God for his exploits, that he was a kind of messenger sent to earth by God to show the world how great He was. He attributed his successes to the divine mission for which he had been destined. Columbus the man might be fallible, but God could never be.

He also projected these convictions—or delusions—into the future, when passing long weeks in the fragrant gardens of Granada as he awaited the sovereigns' decisions. He started compiling a Book of Prophecies, collecting passages from the Bible in which he found some connection to his discoveries and designs. If he had once been able to fulfill biblical prophecy by shattering the ocean's barriers, who was to say that new exploits, foreseen by the scriptures, were not within his grasp? His life was steered by providence. Where would it take him next?

The redemption of the Holy Sepulcher had always been a goal of his, something hidden between the lines of the agreements he signed with the sovereigns, of the letters he exchanged with them, and even of the conversations he had had with them, especially with Queen Isabella. In the Book of Prophecies the liberation of Jerusalem from the Infidels became an urgent mission for the man chosen by destiny. He had conquered new regions of the world, opening the door to gold and riches. Yet he had done so not to satisfy men's greed: those riches were to go toward the reconquest of the Holy Lands.

He sent the Book of Prophecies to the king and queen along with a letter. Columbus was well aware that Ferdinand did not like to read; he was counting, rather, on the mystical tendencies of the queen, with whom he had spoken on many occasions of this dream of Jerusalem. In the letter he underscored Isaiah's prophecy: "The Lord shall hold out His hand a second time to rescue those of His people remaining in Assyria and Egypt, and in the islands of the sea." These "islands of the sea" he had already taken care of. Then he quoted Jeremiah: "At that time they shall call Jerusalem the House of the Lord, and all peoples shall be gathered there."

Could there be any doubt of his mission? As far as Ferdinand and Isabella were concerned, he never found out, since they never read the letter from their admiral, much less the Book of Prophecies that came with it. As time went by, they always had something more urgent to attend to than those bothersome and faraway Indies or the wanderings of Columbus's mind. The friars of Las Cuevas, and perhaps those of La Rábida as well, his old friends, tried to help him. The wall of indifference that the sovereigns had erected was not insurmountable. The admiral kept waiting.

In the meanwhile, other things were occurring which managed to turn even his attentions away from those unlikely future exploits in Jerusalem, of which no more mention was made. These new developments included a spate of new "discoverers" who had set out on the trail that Columbus had blazed eight years earlier; as Las Casas put it, "they were encroaching on his islands." The Indies were no longer a hunting preserve accessible to him alone. These expeditions were authorized by royal permits, granted under the stipulation that they would keep to maritime routes "away from the islands discovered by Admiral Columbus." This led the new explorers to venture for the most part farther south, to South American shores; they were still unsure whether they should consider this land Asia proper or an outlying extension of it. Thus Peralonso Niño, who had been helmsman of the *Santa Maria,* made a courageous expedition and discovered the estuary of the Amazon River. At around the same time Rodrigo de Bastidas was sailing from the coast of Venezuela to the Gulf of Darien, roughly the spot where the Panama Canal is today. Ships were also heading north in search of new shores, once they had crossed the Atlantic. While Cabral, a Portuguese navigator, was discovering the coasts of southern Brazil, the Venetian John Cabot went looking for the "seven cities" of the North on behalf of Henry VII of England. The colonial era had begun; and all the claims and conquests made by the European powers were based on the seafaring exploits of these brave explorers. Starting, of course, with Columbus.

Among the first "invaders" of Columbus's solitary realm was one of his own former lieutenants from the time at Isabela, Alonso de Ojeda, rebel slayer and slave hunter, a person apparently more gifted with the sword than with the sail. He had managed to get hold of both the map that the Admiral had made of his third voyage, and a copy of the letter that he had sent to the king and queen containing a description of what he had found: the so-called Earthly Paradise, which interested Ojeda not a bit, and the marvelous pearls of those waters, which instead whetted his greed not a little.

Ojeda had served for a while as secretary to de Fonseca, who had become

Bishop of Badajoz but was still chief administrator for the Indies and, deep down, still Columbus's enemy. Ojeda asked him for a permit to sail to the Gulf of Paria, for the purpose of exploring more closely what Columbus had neglected. De Fonseca gave him his authorization. This happened in 1499. Among the men Ojeda took with him, either on this expedition or, more likely, on later ones, was a Florentine who had taken up residence in Seville and worked for the commercial bank of Giannetto Berardo Berardi. His name was Amerigo Vespucci. He had never before crossed the ocean. But it was in the cards that he should enjoy the honor of having the continent across the ocean named after him. Ojeda profited from the pearls, Vespucci from a travel diary, which he may have backdated to around the time Columbus sailed to those same places, and which oddly makes no mention of the name of the commander leading the expedition. His name, however, Amerigo Vespucci's name, is there without fail. Ten years later, with Columbus dead and nigh forgotten, Europe named those lands America. It is an almost unbelievable story, which I shall return to.

With the rash of new discoveries, the geographer Duarte Pacheco Pereira felt confident to put forward the hypothesis that "a continuous land mass" extended uninterrupted from Labrador to the Río de la Plata, from 70 degrees latitude north to 28 degrees latitude south. Columbus shuddered at the news of each new development. His sense of ownership of the Indies was so strong that, as Las Casas observes, he felt plundered, despoiled of his property.

He began to study very carefully all the accounts of voyages made by "the others" across the ocean. He meticulously drew a map of the explored lands with as much detail as possible. It should have become clear that this was a new, unforeseen continent. Yet Columbus clung desperately to his Asian hypothesis, and simply could not let go of it. It had been the dream of his youth; how could it founder so suddenly? How could the ancients, the prophets, the classical authors and cosmographers all have been unaware of the existence of another continent, after all the experiences accumulated in Europe over so many thousands of years?

Studying the routes taken by the new explorers, Columbus noticed that they had all neglected the entire area west of the islands discovered by him. Most of the voyagers who had crossed the Atlantic after him directed their explorations southward, a few of them northward. But no one had continued sailing westward. Columbus still believed that Cuba was a province of the Chinese Mangi, the outermost point of the Golden Peninsula, an appendage to the Asian continent, extending out into the ocean. Between Cuba and the Gulf of Darien—which washes the shores of the Isthmus of Panama, not yet known as such—stretched a large, enclosed body of water that had never been explored. *That* was where the westward passage to the Indies must be— a narrow waterway between the ocean's two seas, where Marco Polo had gone. With a last spurt of imagination Columbus realized that if he could discover this passage he could sail around the globe and return to Spain from the East. He anticipated Magellan in this idea. But Magellan succeeded because he went looking for the passage south of the equator. Columbus never crossed that line. He was convinced that the passage was north of it. And thus his last throw of the dice failed.

On September 3, 1501, while Columbus was engrossed in his new plan, the sovereigns announced their decision regarding the requests he had made during their meeting at Granada almost a year earlier. Columbus would no longer be governor of the Indies. In his place they had appointed, as "governor and supreme judge of the islands and terra firma of the Indies," Nicolás de Ovando, knight commander of Lares, whom Las Casas called "a very wise man." Ovando was given neither the title of admiral nor the office of viceroy, but it was clear by now that Columbus's duties and privileges had been annulled, for all intents and purposes. The only concession made to him was the release of his possessions, which Bobadilla was to make available, and the right to send a confidential secretary to Santo Domingo to ensure that he received his due share of duties on commercial gains and gold production. To this task Columbus appointed Alonso de Carvajal, who had stood by him during the years in Hispaniola. Carvajal carried out his orders in such scrupulous and meticulous fashion that Columbus soon became a fairly wealthy man.

With this income and the formal distinctions that he still enjoyed, he could easily have retired to a life of idle luxury, with a handsome pension and a castle in Andalusia. The king and queen would not have denied him a recompense of this sort; on the contrary, according to what was said at the time, they had certain people suggest this solution to him as a very dignified manner in which to spend the rest of his life. Columbus was fifty years old then, already a rather advanced age for one with so much sailing experience and afflicted with illnesses slowly sapping his vital strength. If he had been a sensible man he would have contented himself with his solid prestige and wealth. But he was not a sensible man, and would not have discovered America if he had been.

Instead, upon receiving the sovereigns' reply Columbus felt two different emotions. The first was satisfaction at the thought that his privileges had not been permanently revoked. He was deluding himself, but his optimism let him believe that sooner or later he would get them back. God does not tolerate injustice, he thought; and was he not a man of God? His second feeling was one of restlessness and impatience. His plan for finding the passage to the Indies filled him with excitement. He would have liked to depart immediately: he felt suddenly overcome by a nostalgia for sailing, by a desire to flee to the sea's cherished solitudes, far from the murky jealousies of the court, which had entangled him like spiderwebs. And deep down he was actually convinced that if he could make new, important discoveries, this would bring about a reconsideration of whether to reinstate his titles and privileges.

He drew up a plan for a voyage, which he then sent to their majesties. He wrote to them repeatedly, imploringly, sending message after message. But nothing came of it. He was finally told that his plan had been lost. He redrafted it. The sovereigns at last made a gesture of response on March 14, 1502. They were in favor of the voyage, and were giving their approval. Perhaps they had realized that this might be the best way to rid themselves of such a bothersome petitioner.

The sovereigns' letter was extremely courteous, considering it was addressed to a discharged viceroy. They declared that his having been treated as a prisoner greatly aggrieved them, though it was already two years since this had happened. Royal sentiments are strangely slow to manifest themselves, except for indifference. The letter added that the king and queen still desired and willed that the admiral be treated honorably, "always and everywhere." They were even examining the matter of his privileges, a rather touchy subject. These were to remain intact, but until they should be reconfirmed—and this was the only certain thing—Columbus was forbidden to exercise them.

As though in exchange for what they had taken away from him, their majesties consented to Columbus's projected voyage, stating explicitly that it would be done at their expense and in their service. They allocated ten thousand ducats for Columbus's purposes, to cover the expenses of preparation. Columbus was to focus his attention above all on gold, silver, pearls, precious stones and spices. He was absolutely forbidden to send back natives as slaves. The letter made no explicit reference to Columbus's main goal, the search for the passage to the Indies, but it was implied in the general instructions. Columbus was also forbidden to land at Hispaniola; only on the return voyage could he call at port there, though only for a brief stop, "if this should appear necessary."

Columbus was so carried away by enthusiasm over his new project that he paid little attention to the prohibitions enumerated in the letter. It was easier to steer around official language than around islands in the sea. What interested him most was the implied reconfirmation of his privileges, which according to the royal letter had been only temporarily suspended. He would know how to act accordingly. In the meantime Ovando, the new governor, had already left for Hispaniola at the head of a superb fleet of 32 ships, 2,500 men, and 12 Franciscan friars. Antonio de Torres was appointed commander-in-chief of the whole force. Bobadilla had been ordered to return to Spain as soon as Ovando arrived to take over. (Oviedo says of Bobadilla: "He had performed his duties fairly.")

Now it was Columbus's turn to weigh anchor. He left from Cádiz on May 9 of the same year, three months after Ovando. His fleet, however, was considerably more modest and actually quite similar to the one with which he had first crossed the ocean. It consisted of four caravels, a flagship whose name is not known, the *Santiago* (nicknamed the *Bermuda* by its owner Francisco Bermudez), the *Gallega,* and the *Vizcaína.*

Columbus did not captain the fleet because of his still ailing health and advanced age. The post of first pilot was assigned to Juan Sánchez, who had landed on American shores in 1499 with Ojeda. The fleet's command was entrusted to Diego Tristan, a loyal companion of Columbus during his exploits on sea and on land. On board, Columbus brought along Fernando, his youngest and favorite son, who was barely fifteen when they set sail. His brother Bartholomew also came along, reluctantly boarding the *Santiago,* where he served, for all intents and purposes, as captain. The *Gallega*'s commander was Pedro de Terreros, who had taken part in all of Columbus's ocean voyages, and the *Vizcaína*'s a Genoese named Bartolomeo Fieschi.

They reached the Canaries without difficulty. This time Columbus steered clear of Gomera, whose lady governor had herself advanced a bit in years and was now remarried. He took on his final supplies and provisions at the Grand Canary, stopping in the bay of Maspalomas. Then he plunged into the Atlantic for the fourth time, setting a course for Dominica, the landing spot of his second voyage. He erred slightly in direction, eventually landing at an island next to Dominica, the considerably larger island of Martinique. It was the fastest of all the voyages made by Columbus. It took barely twenty days, which even today would be considered fast for a sailing vessel.

They stayed three days in Martinique. Finally Columbus succumbed to the temptation to head for Santo Domingo, despite the prohibition. He knew the route well. He retraced the passage inside the arc of the Leeward Islands, sailed along the coast of Puerto Rico, then sheered south until he sighted the large estuary of the Ozama river. He saw the first stone buildings of "his" city rise up in the distance, as Ovando had already set the construction in motion.

From the coast Columbus sent word to Ovando that he needed to enter the port, in order to replace the *Santiago* with some other ship that was prepared to leave. The *Santiago* had too wide a keel and "sides too small to support its sails." He also alerted Ovando to the fact that a cyclone was about to strike that part of Hispaniola, and he feared that his caravels might not survive the storm if they weren't brought to shelter. Ovando had received very strict orders from the king and queen. He refused Columbus access to the port, making no mention whatsoever of the alleged cyclone, as though this were just a ruse on the admiral's part.

Columbus was not mistaken. He was quite familiar with the warning signs of these oceanic terrors, having twice experienced the explosive force of the tropical *huracán*. In both cases he had just barely escaped. The signs were the same this time: long, oily waves coming from the north, an unevenly rising tide, a heaviness in the atmosphere, short, violent squalls blowing intermittently. Columbus could also feel the storm in the joints of his painful, rickety bones. He did not want to take any chances. Refused entry at Santo Domingo, he immediately went to take cover in the haven of Puerto Hermoso just a few leagues away. And there he waited.

While his ships were pulling away from Santo Domingo, the fleet that had brought Ovando two months earlier was leaving the port to begin its voyage back to Spain. Here Columbus was frantically looking for shelter, and the fleet commanded by de Torres was heading out to the open sea unconcerned. No one had wanted to heed the admiral's warnings. Many considered him a daydreamer given to wild ideas that were not worth listening to. But they were wrong this time. The hurricane descended on the waters of Hispaniola just as Columbus had said it would. The large fleet was at that moment crossing the Mona Passage, which leads out into the ocean. A violent northeast wind suddenly assailed the ships, tossed them into a whirling, churning sea which seemed to rise up from the depths like a mountain. Several ships sank immediately, while others that had managed to pull in the sails were dashed against the coast and reduced to splinters. No one survived. There had been twenty ships. After only a few minutes of the storm's fury, the sea was empty, strewn with flotsam that was quickly swallowed up by the raging waters. The fleet's flagship, where de Torres had sat in command, had been carrying aboard Francisco de Bobadilla, the man who had put Columbus in chains, as well as Francisco Roldán, who had led the revolt against him in Hispaniola and was about to return to Spain free of guilt and accusation, after Columbus had paid dearly for all involved. Bobadilla and Roldán, his two most bitter enemies! Bobadilla, who had dared to take him prisoner and shackle him in irons! They had sunk to the ocean's bottom, returned to nothingness. Had Columbus been right to believe that divine justice was infallible? And was this not further proof that God was behind him?

Columbus's four caravels, prepared for the storm, emerged from it relatively unharmed. When the cyclone reached its peak of intensity the night of August 30, it seemed that it would uproot the ships' anchors. But Columbus had the cables reinforced with all the available chains on board, and the small fleet survived. Only the *Gallega*'s launch was lost. After the hurricane passed, everyone rested up, regained his strength and then set about making the necessary repairs. Then the fleet went a short way down the coast in search of fresh supplies of water, wood and food, most of the latter coming in the form of fish, which was abundant and quite good, according to Fernando Columbus in his memoirs. Around the middle of July the fleet finally set off to look for the passage to the Indies.

Columbus's initial intention had been to land at the coast near Margarita, the island of the pearls. That was where, on his previous journey, he had felt compelled to leave the continent behind, driven by impatience and illness to sail to Hispaniola without further delay. On the present voyage he had planned not to head back out to sea after Margarita, but to sail westward along the coast until he found the strait he was looking for. This route would have been feasible had he had the resolve not to sail north of Dominica, or Martinique, where he had landed after crossing the ocean. Instead, nostalgia had taken him back to Hispaniola. Now he was too far north of the projected course to follow it any longer. Thus he decided to sail directly into the still unfamiliar western zone of the Caribbean, in the hope, which he believed to be well founded, of finding terra firma in that direction as well. He still thought that Cuba was a peninsula of the Asian continent. If he sailed past Cuba, he thought, he would find that continent. And then by hugging the coast, he could set out in search of the passage leading to the Indies.

That was his plan. Unfortunately, the caravels quickly ran into an area of dead calm and barely moved for two weeks, carried only by currents toward Jamaica and the group of islands that lie to its east. They managed to pull out of it by late July, still 1502. Soon thereafter, Columbus reached the island of Bonacca, now called Guanaja. Only a few miles away was the rocky coast of Honduras. Columbus had America before him.

He landed at Bonacca, and a number of his men went ashore with Bartholomew. It soon became clear that they had come to a different world, a civilization more advanced and more refined than that of the islands thus far discovered. Here the natives knew the crafts of weaving and metalworking. They had large cauldrons for melting copper, they dressed in nicely woven and colored tunics and covered themselves with cotton blankets. The women wore shawls similar to those of the Moorish women in Granada. They also possessed weapons—hatchets and long wooden swords with sharp edges of flint. They drank fermented beverages. They traveled the sea in large canoes hollowed out from single tree trunks. They were far more developed than the Arawak and Carib peoples that Columbus had encountered in the "thousand islands" of his previous voyages.

The stretch of Honduran coast that lay opposite Bonacca had belonged to the Mayan empire of the Cocoms until 1485, when that empire collapsed. But Mayan civilization continued to dominate the region. Since it was Bartholomew who gathered information on shore and brought it back to Columbus, who had not disembarked, posterity has criticized the two brothers for failing to take advantage of the great opportunity within their grasp. If they had only gone a bit north from where they were, they would have reached the Yucatán and discovered the Mayas. The inhabitants of Bonacca, which was just a small, distant outpost of the empire, had, through gestures, given Columbus's men indications of the wealth and industry of the people that lived to the west of them. Columbus may have been tempted to go in that direction, but whenever he was unsure of something he always settled the matter by making a brusque decision, usually shunning any new attractions that might induce him to change his plans. The imagination cannot go beyond itself. At that moment he was looking for the passage to the Indies, which was already in itself a fantastical project. He persevered in his intent. And in early August he reached the Central American coast at Cape Honduras.

From there he began a long, hard journey eastward along the coast, sailed entirely in tacks and against the wind, with the trade winds blowing head on and the caravels forced to zigzag in the opposite direction. It was a slow, painful, unending voyage. The small fleet was pounded by rain and storms almost the whole time. After leaving Cape Honduras to sail along the

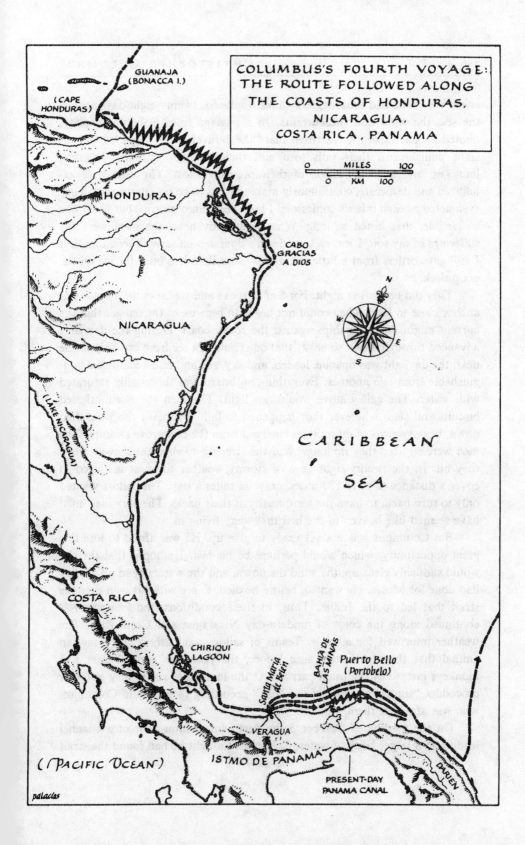

COLUMBUS'S FOURTH VOYAGE:
THE ROUTE FOLLOWED ALONG
THE COASTS OF HONDURAS,
NICARAGUA,
COSTA RICA, PANAMA

MILES
0   100

KM
0   100

GUANAJA
(BONACCA I.)

(CAPE
HONDURAS)

HONDURAS

CABO
GRACIAS
A DIOS

NICARAGUA

(LAKE NICARAGUA)

CARIBBEAN

SEA

COSTA RICA

CHIRIQUI
LAGOON

Puerto Bello
(Portobelo)

BAHIA DE
LAS MINAS

Santa Maria
de Belen

VERAGUA

ISTMO DE PANAMA

DARIEN

(PACIFIC OCEAN)

PRESENT-DAY
PANAMA CANAL

palacios

coast, the crews had to struggle without respite for twenty-eight days against the sea, the wind and the currents. In a passage from Columbus's diary, quoted by Las Casas, it is written that "the caravels were subjected to constant punishment, their sails torn and their anchors, shrouds, hawsers, launches, and a good portion of their provisions lost. The men were exhausted and desperate, continuously making vows to go on pilgrimages. They even acted as each other's confessors! I have seen many storms, but never one so terrible, that lasted so long. What wrung my heart the most were the sufferings of my son. I was sick, at death's doorstep on several occasions, but I still gave orders from a little cabin that the sailors had built for me on the poop deck."

They did not sail at night. For fear of rocks and shallows the ships lay at anchor close to land. They could not heave to because of the danger that the current might dash the ships against the rocky coast. During the day they advanced through a rain so heavy that one could not see from one ship to the next; the daylight was opaque, leaden, and sky, sea and rain became indistinguishable from one another. Everything on board was thoroughly saturated with water. The galley stove would not light. The men ate worm-infested biscuits and slept wherever they happened to fall. Whenever the wind died down, huge swarms of mosquitoes emerged from the mangrove swamps. The men were so tired they no longer had the strength to shoo them away when they bit. In the twenty-eight days of stormy weather the fleet managed to cover a distance of only 170 miles, only six miles a day. The sailors wanted only to turn back, to have the wind finally at their backs. The very idea must have seemed like heaven in the hell they were living in.

But Columbus was not yet ready to give up. He was afraid to lose this great opportunity, which would perhaps be his last. He hoped that the sky would suddenly clear up, the wind die down, and the waters open up as they had done for Moses. He wanted, before he died, to see with his own eyes the strait that led to the Indies. Thus, in these conditions, the four caravels continued along the coast of modern-day Nicaragua and Costa Rica. The weather improved for a while. Teams of sailors went ashore: they saw an animal that they had never seen before, the puma, as well as deer and monkeys instead of the usual parrots. At the mouths of rivers they also saw crocodiles "similar to those of the Nile," according to Fernando Columbus, who was afraid of them.

On the evening of October 5 the fleet came within view of a channel leading to a larger body of water. Columbus thought he had found the strait he was looking for. He was once again fooled by indigenous place names. The natives called the region Chiguara, and when they pronounced the word Columbus thought he heard the name of Champa, Marco Polo's Cochin China. Everything corresponded to his imaginary geography of the world. Thus the caravels entered a small arm of the sea very near the shore, so narrow that "the foliage of the trees touched the ships' rigging." Everyone thought they would soon see the ocean appear "on the other side." Instead all they found was a large lagoon, a splendid sheet of turquoise water surrounded by very high mountains. The sea ended abruptly at the foot of the mountains. The lagoon was called Chiriquí Lagoon. It was a great disappointment after so many battles with the wind and storms and so long and hard a voyage.

But it was a stunningly beautiful place, and they stayed there for many days to give the crews a hard-earned rest. A great deal of gold circulated among the local natives, in the form of large disks which both men and women wore around their necks and willingly gave away in exchange for little necklaces and bells. Exploring all the local villages, the Spaniards managed to buy up most of their gold. In a letter written to the king and queen in 1504—which came to be called the Lost Letter—Columbus informed his sovereigns that he had learned of the existence of great quantities of gold not far from there, in the valley of a river called Veragua. It thus seemed to him reasonable to believe that he was, at that point, at the end of Ptolemy's Golden Peninsula. Thus the long Asian peninsula stretched from Cuba, its northern point, down to the places where Columbus had just landed: Cochin China, with the Moluccas and their pepper probably not far away. The natives had made it clear to him that the Chiriquí Lagoon was located in an isthmus between the seas, and that on the other side of the mountains, about a nine-day journey on foot, lay the shores of another ocean.

Thus Columbus now had within reach both of his goals: gold and the passage to the Indies. The latter, unfortunately, seemed limited to land. Once he felt certain that he was on an isthmus, Columbus at once abandoned his search for the precious strait. He hadn't the proper means to cross the mountains, as Balboa did in 1513, ten years later, when he sighted the Pacific Ocean from high up in the mountains. Having reached what is today one end of the Panama Canal, Columbus ceased looking for his channel and concentrated his energy on the search for gold.

What the natives had told him was true. About twenty miles east of the lagoon there was indeed gold—pure gold, which the Indians extracted from the ground using only knives as tools. The region in which the mines were found was called Veragua. The name was preserved down through the history of Columbus's family, as his descendants were given the title of dukes of Veragua, a title later passed on to the house of Alba, which still retains it today. Yet aside from the future title, Veragua meant nothing but bad fortune for Columbus. To repeat, there was gold there. And there may still be today, despite numerous attempts at exploitation after Columbus, all of them failures as well. But the habitat is wild and inhospitable, consisting of high mountains covered entirely with an impenetrable tropical forest. In the valleys that lead to the deposits—the Veragua and Belén river valleys—the climate is unbearable. A good deal of the soil is alluvial and pounded by frequent and heavy rain which the terrain is unable to absorb. Thus the rivers often swell and overflow, inundating everything. To create conditions stable enough to permit the proper functioning of a mining industry would require large investments, perhaps so large as to render inadequate the value of the exploitable gold.

Nevertheless, for several months Columbus stubbornly tried to overcome the obstacles presented by the soil, the climate and even the natives, who were more warlike in these parts than elsewhere, and as usual had been provoked by the conduct of the Spanish. It was a real battle—against the jungle, the floods, the Indians. The expedition reached the gold deposits numerous times, but every time was forced to abandon them because of adversity. Columbus planned the foundation of a new colony here and had already given it the name of Santa María de Belén, Our Lady of Bethlehem, having discovered those valleys on the day of the Epiphany in 1503. The men even built a number of houses and a storehouse, and were erecting a fortress of which Bartholomew would take command, as he intended to remain at the site with about fifty men and a caravel, the *Gallega*, at his disposal. In the end, however, the project foundered. The water level of the Veragua dropped all of a sudden, and the ships could no longer leave the estuary because at the outer bar there was only two feet of water.

The natives came in bands to attack the trapped caravels. They wanted to get rid of the intruders. The Spaniards went ashore in armed groups to scatter the howling gangs, chasing them away from the ships, which were waiting for the right moment to take to the sea. After two days the river began to rise again, and the ships, tugged by launches, made it out to the open sea. Only the *Gallega*, left behind for use by Bartholomew and his men, remained anchored in the river. In the struggle with the Indians, which had its moments of drama, Bartholomew was wounded. Elsewhere, the flagship commander Diego Tristan, together with a team of sailors, had stayed ashore to get final supplies of water. On their way back they fell into an ambush. Tristan was killed by a javelin through the eye. All the men with him also died. The Indians tossed the corpses into the river, which dragged the lifeless bodies down to its mouth pursued by flocks of vultures.

Columbus came down with malaria. He raved deliriously, standing on the quarterdeck of his ship. He raved and cried. All hope was lost, and life itself was slipping away from him. He decided to leave it all behind: the gold, Veragua, the newly founded colony. A brave man by the name of Diego Mendez managed to bring the entire garrison, along with their provisions, out to the ships on a crude raft that he steered past the sandbars. The *Gallega* was abandoned, empty, at the river's mouth. On April 16, 1503, Easter Sunday, the three surviving caravels put Veragua behind them forever. Columbus promoted Diego Mendez to the rank of flagship commander in place of the unfortunate Tristan.

What was Columbus to do next? There was only one thing he could do: head straight back to Santo Domingo, to repair the rather wasted ships and from there return to Spain. His undertaking had failed. But the modest task that lay ahead of him was hardly an easy one. The first problem was the uncertainty as to what course to follow. All the ships' pilots maintained that Hispaniola was due north of the coast they were about to leave. Columbus thought instead that northeast was the direction to take. He maintained that to the north lay Cuba, not Hispaniola. He was right, of course.

The second problem consisted in the terrible damage that a certain small mollusk had inflicted on the ships' hulls. Whole colonies of shipworms had invaded the submerged part of each caravel during the long stay in Veragua. Once they had penetrated the hulls there was no stopping them. As they are wont to do, they had set about boring through the planking until it was little better than a sieve at keeping out water. The fleet had now been at sea for more than a year. Fernando Columbus, who was on board, later wrote: "The entire crew, using pumps, pots and other receptacles, was unable to remove all the water coming in through the holes made by the shipworms." The *Vizcaína* was the first victim of the tiny destroyers. Columbus, whose insistence on sailing east along the coast had prevailed, was forced to abandon the ship in the haven of Puerto Bello after just a few days of sailing, as the water had nearly reached deck level. The fleet was now reduced to just two caravels. With difficulty they made it as far as the Gulf of Darien, which is near the narrowest part of the Isthmus of Panama. They were sailing against both the

wind and the current, whose combined negative effect would have been difficult for even ships in good condition to overcome. The ships' pilots, still
clinging to their earlier hypothesis, insisted that the fleet by now must be at
the longitude of the Antilles and managed to persuade Columbus to quit the
present course. The flagship and the *Santiago* came about and headed north,
leaving the continent behind them.

Columbus may have given in, but he had not changed his opinion. Indeed, the first land sighted was that of the Cayman Islands, which are small,
low-lying islands full of turtles. The Caymans lie between Cuba and Jamaica
—in other words, off course for someone going to Hispaniola. A bit farther
on, the two caravels reached the archipelago that Columbus had named "the
Queen's Garden," off Cuba's southern coast. In the letter to the sovereigns in
which he told of the vicissitudes of this voyage, Columbus made a point of
saying: "On May 13 I arrived at the province of Mangi, which is part of
Cathay." He still had not abandoned the belief that Cuba was part of the
Asian continent. His blindness is almost touching.

As a storm was about to break out, the ships took shelter between islands, their men "full of anguish and hungry," as Fernando tells us. The
storm was a violent one. The *Santiago* broke its moorings and went crashing
into the flagship, shattering the stern almost as far as the rudder. The anchors
no longer held. Columbus's ship lost three of them on the treacherous coral
bank, and was left with only the so-called sheet anchor. The rain swept down
in torrents, whipped about by a violent wind. The weather did not improve
for six whole days. Thus, with his two dying ships "riddled with more holes
than a beehive," Columbus set out again. Hispaniola was still two hundred
miles away. There was no way that the ships, their sails ragged and yards
unsteady and their keels taking in more water with each passing hour, could
possibly cover that much distance. The only hope was to set a course for
nearby Jamaica, as a favorable wind was blowing that way.

The vessels were as though mortally wounded, no longer able to keep the
sea. The three pumps were in use day and night. When one of them broke it
had to be immediately repaired and replaced in the meantime with any available receptacle. The water began to rise in the *Santiago*'s hold at such an
alarming rate that Columbus gave the order to brace the yards and head for
Jamaica at once. On the morning of June 23 the ships staggered into a haven
identified as Puerto Bueno, near the middle of the island's southern coast.
With a superhuman effort the crews managed to keep the two caravels floating for the entire day of the twenty-fourth. On the twenty-fifth, they sailed

another dozen miles westward, as far as the bay of Santa Gloria, which Columbus had already explored during his second voyage. Fernando described the final landing of the moribund ships: "Once inside the bay, being no longer able to keep the ships afloat, we pushed them onto the shore and dragged them as far from the water as possible, beaching them one next to the other, side by side, and propping them up from each side to prevent them from listing. On the decks, and on top of the forecastles and aftcastles, we built cabins to lodge the men, making them strong enough to serve as protection and shelter from Indians."

Thus the last fleet ever commanded by Columbus met its end, and his last voyage, by far the most trying, also came to an end, though an inconclusive one, with the admiral facing the prospect of living out his last days cut off from the rest of the world, where no one would know what had happened to him until years, even decades, after his death. This did not happen. Nevertheless, in Jamaica Columbus lived through an adventure that would have broken the spirit of just about any man who did not possess his power of will, his unshakable optimism, and his presumptuous faith in God as his own personal ally.

The chances of any explorers' landing on those shores or sighting the castaways from the open sea off the Jamaican coast were practically nonexistent. No Spaniard had been to Cuba or Jamaica for ten years. Columbus had gone to those places in 1494, but had made it known that the land contained no gold, so who would have had any reason to go there? There were not even any launches left, which Columbus's men might have used in a desperate and unlikely attempt to reach Hispaniola. The shores of Hispaniola were two hundred miles away from the bay of Santa Gloria, and Santo Domingo five hundred. The two islands lay next to each other, but were divided by a rather wide channel swept by ocean winds and currents and perpetually rough waters that a small coastal craft would never have been able to cross.

The essential problem was returning to Santo Domingo. If it was not resolved, they would all have to live out their lives in Jamaica. But there was another, more immediately urgent problem than this, that of living. Living meant eating, feeding a hundred hungry men stranded on a deserted beach. The ships' food supplies were exhausted. Only half a mile away was the large Indian village of Maima, where they could obtain sustenance in exchange for the usual knickknacks. But Columbus remembered all too well what had happened on his previous visit to Jamaica, ten years earlier, in the very same area. The natives had shown that they could respond to plunder and aggression with violence. The Spanish had had to take to the sea to escape the Indians' assaults. This, of course, was no longer possible. If they did not succeed in establishing as civil a relationship as possible with the Indians, there would be no escape for the castaways of Santa Gloria, and the natives' fury would quickly overwhelm them. The tragedy of Navidad served as a reminder. But how could Columbus prevent his men, who were "disobedient by nature," from going around stealing food and molesting women? He found a way. Fernando tells us, "No one was allowed to leave the ships without permission." Columbus made them all stay on board as if they were sailing. Then he sent Diego Mendez and three other men to the Indian villages. Mendez reached an agreement with the caciques, who promised to provide the Spanish daily with cassava bread and to allow them to fish and to hunt. In exchange the Indians received a few glass necklaces, falcon bells, and several pairs of scissors, which went to the most important chiefs. For several months at least, the problem of hunger had been resolved.

Which left the problem of getting back to Hispaniola. Aside from the vain hopes for a miracle, the only chance lay in making a desperate attempt to cross the channel. Columbus called aside Diego Mendez, who had proved his courage and loyalty many times in the past. He told him that he wanted to equip a large canoe with special rigging so that it could keep the sea even far off shore. Would Mendez feel up to trying to reach Hispaniola? There he would tell the colonists about the castaways in Jamaica, and then organize a rescue mission.

Mendez responded that reaching Hispaniola in something so small as a canoe, using oars to cross the channel between the two islands, would be more than difficult: it would be impossible. Columbus insisted that it was possible. Mendez suggested that they call all the men together, explain to them that this was their only hope for salvation, and ask if anyone wanted to volunteer for the mission. According to Las Casas, Mendez concluded by saying, "If they all refuse, I shall risk my life in your service, as I have done before."

The meeting was held. No one came forward. Mendez prepared to depart. On the canoe selected for the mission they nailed boards across the prow and the stern, to prevent water from entering. Then they set up a mast with a sail and filled the boat with as many provisions as they could fit in the small space. Six strong-armed Indians were put at the oars.

The first attempt at departure failed when, along the last stretch of Jamaican coast, Mendez and his men were attacked by other natives and forced to turn back. On the next attempt an escort under Bartholomew's command was to accompany Mendez as far as the strait. The failure of the first attempt proved a blessing in disguise, however, when Captain Mendez found a partner willing to follow his example in Bartolomeo Fieschi of Genoa, who had commanded the *Vizcaína* abandoned in Panama. A second canoe was fitted out, and the number of Indians aboard each boat increased to ten. The two canoes doubled the odds that at least one would make it across the strait to Hispaniola.

The story of the voyage was recounted by Fieschi to Fernando, who retold it in his book. The channel that had to be crossed was one hundred nautical miles wide, all of them open sea, a daunting task that appeared nearly impossible for boats so light and fragile. Morison called it "one of the most daring adventures in the history of the sea." No wonder Diego Mendez wanted a canoe carved on his tombstone.

It was July. The tropical sun blazed down on the ocean. The two Europeans had to stay awake the whole time, even at night, because they could not trust the Indians, who had come not of their own accord but by coercion. The Indians began to crack under the pressures. In the middle of that vast stretch of water, with the sun beating down unshielded, thirst became hard to resist. The Indians immediately drank up their rations, as well as the small reserves that the two captains had set aside. One native died of thirst and was thrown into the sea. Others lay as though lifeless at the bottom of the canoe. Those who kept rowing were withering from the heat. The boats advanced slowly, trying to avoid contrary currents. The two sails were also of little use, being too small and unaided by any wind. Thus the first day passed, then the second and third. Three-fourths of the way across the channel—about twenty-five miles from the coast of Hispaniola—they expected to encounter the islet of Navassa, a rock that rises straight up out of the sea. But after three days on the sea they still saw nothing on the horizon. Mendez and Fieschi feared they might have passed it, or drifted off the proper course. After sunset, however, as the moon rose, they saw a dark bluff looming in the distance ahead. They had reached Navassa. At daybreak they disembarked and went looking for rainwater that had collected in the hollows in the rock. They drank their fill, experiencing "one of the happiest moments" of their lives. They rested until sunset, and by the next morning they were already in sight of Cape San Miguel, Hispaniola's westernmost promontory, in what is present-day Haiti.

It was still three hundred miles to Santo Domingo. But the dangers and difficulties of the open sea were behind them now. The canoes were fine for coastal travel, though rather slow. The two commanders arrived in Santo Domingo in September. They lost more time trying to get in touch with Ovando, who was somewhere inland, and still more time endlessly negotiating over the authorization to send a boat to rescue the castaways. Ovando was an indecisive, fearful man. Such behavior as his often creates suffering when it involves other people. He hedged and hesitated for months, up to the new year—1504—and beyond. What was Columbus to think, stranded on a stretch of beach in Jamaica and entirely in the dark as to everything?

In the meantime, in Jamaica many things had occurred to worsen a situation already fraught with anguish. A revolt had broken out among the sailors, who were still confined to the beached ships by the admiral's strict orders. As long as the hope that Mendez would reach Hispaniola remained alive, they were impatient and did little more than grumble. But with the arrival of the new year after months of fruitless waiting, their hopes vanished and rebellion erupted. The revolt's leaders were the Porras brothers, Francisco and Diego, men with connections to the court who were hostile to Columbus and intolerant of his authority. Forty-eight sailors joined the conspiracy, roughly half the castaways. They decided to go to Santo Domingo themselves, imitating Mendez. Crammed into about ten canoes, they set out to sea singing. But they hadn't the courage to confront the channel when they found its waters all agitated, so they turned back, stopping at a village on the coast. From there they returned to Santa Gloria, thieving and pillaging along the way. Francisco Porras was captured by Bartholomew, sword in hand, and taken aboard in irons. The others surrendered.

Then it was the Indians' turn to show their discontent. They had been providing food for the Spaniards for almost a year now and were growing tired of it. They became discourteous and began refusing things asked of them. They seemed to be considering seizing the ships and slaying the white men inside, who were getting weaker each day. Columbus then resorted to a stratagem truly worthy of his genius. He had read in the almanac of Regiomontanus that a total eclipse of the moon was expected for the night of February 29. Thus at sunset that night he called all the region's caciques and other notables together and made a brief speech, whose content was conveyed to the Indians through an interpreter of sorts. The Christian God who lives in the sky, he said, rewards the good and punishes the wicked. He is very angry with you for neglecting to feed us according to our agreement. Look up to the sky now, and see what happens. God will send a warning of the terrible punishment that he has in store for you if you do not mend your ways.

The Indians did not believe him for a minute. They thought it was a joke. They snickered and laughed. But when the moon began to darken, shrinking behind the earth's moving shadow until it seemed to disappear inside a hole in the sky, the caciques and their comrades were filled first with wonder, then fear, and finally out-and-out panic. They began weeping profusely and making promises, which Columbus made them repeat. The eclipse was in fact coming to an end, the moon reappearing in the sky.

The situation in Santa Gloria improved, but there was still no news of Mendez. By now Columbus was in despair. March went by, then April. Finally in June, when it was no longer expected, the rescue mission arrived. Diego de Salcedo, a friend of Columbus from Santo Domingo, whom Columbus had granted a trading monopoly on all soap, came in person to take the admiral to safety. He had rented a large caravel at his own expense, which he brought along with the smaller caravel that he normally used for his personal business. Columbus could now rejoin the world. The ordeal was over.

On June 28, 1504, Columbus and his one hundred companions headed back to Hispaniola. The two ships propped up on the beach, looking like two strange, unlikely monsters, soon vanished from sight. Once in Santo Domingo, the admiral was received with great deference and respect by Ovando, the man administering what should have been his governorship. Ovando begged him to stay as his guest. But at the same time he had Porras released, claiming that the events in Jamaica were not under the admiral's jurisdiction. Columbus, disgusted, asserted that Ovando had violated his privileges.

On September 12, 1504, his body wasted and his spirit humbled, Columbus set off for Spain on his last ocean crossing. Twelve years had passed since the landing at San Salvador which had opened the doors to a new world, a world in which Columbus would never again set foot.

Right before Mendez had left Jamaica on his daring mission, the admiral had given him several letters with instructions to deliver them once in Spain, if Mendez happened to get there before he did. One of these letters was addressed to the sovereigns, the "Lost Letter" already mentioned, so called because it was lost and later found again after a long time. Las Casas, who saw the original, quotes from it at length in his book. It is the desperate cry of a man who feels abandoned by all. I present only one passage here, to bring to a close the overseas adventures of this book's protagonist:

"Until now I have always taken pity on my fellow man; today, may

Heaven have mercy on me, may the earth cry for me, as I wait for death alone, sick and racked with pain. I am so far away from the Holy Sacraments that if my soul should here leave my body, not even God would remember it. Those who love charity, truth and justice, let them cry for me now."

18

༄༄༄

A Hero Buried
Too Many Times

When Columbus landed in Spain at the end of his last ocean voyage, he was near the end of his rope. Yet he was hardly a doddering old man. He was barely fifty-three years old, an age at which one's powers begin to wane but are still far from disappearing altogether. But Columbus suffered terribly from gout, arthritis enfeebled his limbs, and feverish deliriums overcame him from time to time. These ailments were the legacy of his adventures: the Indies, the long ocean voyages, the swamps on land and the storms at sea. Not to mention the storms in his mind and heart. He had suffered great anguish and disappointment, injustices and calumnies, the pain of incredulity and the poison darts of envy. Many had betrayed him. In the past, upon returning to Spain, he had been buoyed by the rapture of triumph or the fury of pride. This time he was returning with yet another failure behind him, another luckless adventure. He had nothing to show or the prove, aside from the self-justification emphasized in his letter to the king and queen: "If I have failed at some things, it is because they were impossible, or else far exceeding my knowledge and power."

When he stepped ashore he could barely move. He was transported to Seville, where he moved into a rented house in the parish of Santa Maria, surrounded by servants and financially well off. Near him he always kept a little strongbox full of gold coins. Yet he complained that the money he had was only a fraction of what was due him. He wrote to his son Diego: "What I am losing from the dues that Their Highnesses had originally promised me amount to ten million per year, which I shall never be able to recover." His protests were becoming more and more quarrelsome and petulant, his tone no longer beseeching, for he was demanding that prior agreements be respected and believed that this was his proper due. It seems likely, however, that he cast himself in the role of the sufferer of wrongs, of one practically cheated of his earnings by the sovereign power, to mask what was really tormenting him: the failure of his disastrous final voyage.

At court, he had his eldest son Diego to defend his interests. Diego had a position very close to the throne, first in the queen's personal guard, then in the king's. By age twenty-four he was already an experienced courtier, and skilled at obtaining favors. But he was not bold or impetuous. His father constantly harangued him from Seville, trying to obtain an audience with the sovereigns to address the reparation of his wrongs. He persistently harped on the duties he claimed were owed him on commerce in the Indies, calling them "my tenth, my eighth, my third." Diego was buried under an avalanche of letters and memoranda. But he was unable to obtain what his father desired.

The court at the time resided at Segovia, on the steep slopes of the Sierra de Guadarrama. Unfortunately one of the reasons the sovereigns were not answering Columbus's requests was that Queen Isabella's health had worsened considerably. Added to the grief that had already broken her heart was the hopeless insanity into which her youngest daughter, the only one left, had fallen. Her name was Juana, and she was the wife of the Philip I of Austria and mother of the future Charles V. Everyone already referred to her as *la Loca*, the madwoman. Isabella could not bear the weight of so many misfortunes. She died in Segovia in late November 1504, less than a month after Columbus's return to Spain.

Columbus mourned her death deeply and inconsolably. Isabella in a certain sense had been his lifelong friend, his coeval, a powerful supporter who had always believed in him. If not for Isabella, Columbus would never have crossed the ocean. But their relations had also had their highs and lows. Isabella felt very keenly the majesty of her power. To her, the Columbus adventure had been a kind of concession made to the fascination of the mind, the allure of genius. Later, however, in judging the man in terms of the state's interests, she had become disappointed in him. She nevertheless remained quite cordial to him, though with that tone which one reserves for persons deemed intelligent but awkward, and which implies a kind of pity or indulgence. Columbus, in his presumption, had actually hoped to the very end that the queen, before dying, would reinstate all his privileges and dues. It was a prize that he expected from her. He anxiously awaited news of the will. In December he wrote to his son: "Here people are saying with insistence that the queen had it written that I should be returned possession of the Indies." It was not true. Columbus continued to delude himself.

He spent the entire winter in Seville, since he could not "move his legs because of the great cold." He even considered hiring from the cathedral chapter a magnificent catafalque on wheels that had been used to transport the corpse of the Grand Cardinal of Spain from the monastery of Tentudia to Seville. But it was a senseless idea. The chapter itself had agreed to it, but Columbus's condition was too poor to permit him to travel across Spain, from Seville to Segovia. Thus his personal history was spared the grotesque spectacle of the Admiral of the Ocean Sea riding across Spain on a funeral cart. Yet he seems to have been rather keen on the idea: it would have been yet another expression of his complaint, another display of his gloomy discontent, like the chains and the ragged robe.

He finally managed to leave Seville in May of 1505. He was transported by mule, with the greatest care. After a journey of three hundred miles he arrived in Segovia, where Diego had finally succeeded in arranging for his father an audience with King Ferdinand. Columbus knew that Ferdinand was not at all fond of him, and he dreaded this encounter as much as he desired it. During it, the king listened more than he spoke. He listened courteously and openly, like one who has already made up his mind and has no intention of modifying his conclusions. To speed up the resolution of the discussions, which Columbus was trying to keep open, the king suggested appointing an arbiter in the trust of both men to settle the matter. Columbus suggested Father Deza, who had in the meantime become Archbishop of Seville. Ferdinand agreed to this: what could an arbiter or petitioner possibly do to change what the king, now alone in his authority, had already decided to do?

Deza shrewdly divided Columbus's claims into two groups. The first included all matters concerning income and property, the infamous "tenth, eighth, and third" forever invoked by Columbus as his denied rights. Deza placed his trust in the judgment of several jurisconsults who gave him very useful advice. What exactly did these mysterious fractions represent?

The "tenth" was supposed to have been Columbus's share of the returns on commerce in the newly discovered lands. This was the only remuneration explicitly provided for in the capitulations of Santa Fé. But Deza's counselors were quick to point out that Columbus's tenth was to be applied not to the gross revenue of all the islands across the sea, but to the net amount—that is, to the Crown's share, which was only one-fifth of the whole. Thus Columbus's earnings could only come out of the one-fifth collected by the royal treasury. He was thus to receive one tenth of that fifth, or two percent of the whole. The difference between what Columbus presumed was his due and what he collected in fact was huge. And from it arose a good deal of the controversy.

The "eighth" was to have been the admiral's share of all profits made by the commerce of ships in which he had a direct investment. The sovereigns had granted him this right at Santa Fé, and it is mentioned in the document. But it involved his private affairs, and thus these profits were of no concern to the Crown.

The "third" was pure fantasy on Columbus's part. When he was named Admiral of the Ocean Sea he had wanted the rank to be recognized as equal to that of the Grand Admiral of Castile. He saw it as a question of prestige, and the sovereigns at the time felt compelled to concede the point. The Admiral of Castile, however, enjoyed an old privilege that granted him the right to collect a third of the proceeds on all trade and gains made on those waters under his jurisdiction. It was a real tax, and a personal privilege. Columbus was never granted the same right, and in Deza's consultation it was deemed entirely out of the question.

The second group of Columbus's claims, those concerning the government of the Indies, could not in Deza's opinion be subject to arbitration. Affairs of state could never become a point of contention between a king and his subject, no matter who he might be. Columbus insisted on his right to the titles of viceroy and governor, which he claimed the Santa Fé agreements made "perpetual," whereas in fact no precise indication of duration was made in the text of the document. King Ferdinand considered Columbus's request for reinstatement to the offices from which he had been removed as outright madness, whereas he had never questioned his title of Admiral of the Ocean Sea. The king's advocates explained to Deza, so that he could tell Columbus, that however one might want to interpret it, the Santa Fé contract was invariably subject to the laws of Castile, and that it was fully within the king or queen's power to suspend any or all the privileges granted him therein, if they should deem this to be in the interests of the state. The results of Columbus's governorship had in fact been disastrous. And in any case, the Crown was averse to putting a fief that had grown so large and was so far away from Spain into the hands of a family of foreign origin.

Thus Columbus was defeated all down the line in his final attempt as well. He returned to bed even sicker than before, and more disillusioned. His passion for this last battle had been the main thing keeping him going. He understood that the time had come to surrender. He wrote bitterly to Deza: "Since it seems that His Highness has no intention of keeping the promises he made on his honor and signed in his hand together with the queen, may God keep her soul, I believe that to fight it any longer would be, for me, who am an insect, like flogging a dead horse. It is thus best that I leave it in the hands of the Lord our God, whom I have always found to be rather favorable and sensitive to my needs."

Columbus was offered the appanage of a fief in exchange for a voluntary renunciation of his impossible claims. He would be given the domain of Carrión de los Condes, famous in the annals of Spanish history for having been the theater of the exploits of the Cid Campeador. The fief came endowed with a rather considerable income. But Columbus became enraged at the very suggestion. He could not even bear to hear mention of his renouncing his demands. He was adamant, bound to his bed and more irascible than ever.

Columbus indeed could now afford to refuse such an offer, having become a rich man in spite of everything. In their estimation of his commissions, the Crown's treasurers were very careful to give him his proper due, especially after Bobadilla left Santo Domingo. Carvajal, his confidential secretary, was there in person to verify and collect all revenue from Columbus's personal dealings, which were hardly negligible. True, Columbus had hoped to become even richer. Nevertheless his estate became quite considerable. The legends of his spending his last years in poverty are hagiographic fictions. People don't want rich heroes. The poor hero is more touching. Yet his descendants lived comfortably off his estate for two whole generations before blithely squandering the fortune (the common fate of most inheritances).

At the end of April Columbus, his health deteriorating each day, was transported from Segovia, which was too elevated and too cold, to Valladolid, about sixty miles away. In Valladolid the Columbus family had a house, though it is not known whether they owned or rented it. It was a rather modest abode, only one story high and made of brick. This is not the house today exhibited as Columbus's last dwelling, site of a rather dilapidated museum as well. This house, in which he lived for the brief period before his death, was, however, located nearby. The garden and the fountain atop the boundary wall are perhaps the only remains left. There, in a bed on the first floor, he spent his last days enduring the pain of his gout, arthritis and other ailments. He suffered and fantasized. He escaped his pain by letting his imagination carry him away, just as his caravels had once escaped a storm by letting the wind carry them away. He imagined himself enlisting ten thousand men on horseback and a hundred thousand on foot for the liberation of Jerusalem. He wrote to the king of this idea, assuring him that if given back the earnings that he felt had been stolen from him, in seven years' time he would have the means to finance such an expedition in its entirety. In his delirium, Don Quixote forged on. Columbus's house was in the northern part of the city. In the southern part, less than a mile away, one can still see the house were Cervantes lived a century later. There Don Quixote was born, and there Columbus died. They nearly crossed paths in time; and the city of Valladolid erected monuments to both Columbus and Cervantes in two different squares, each of them a lovely spot shaded by trees.

Columbus passed away on May 20, 1506, Ascension Day, a Wednesday. At his deathbed were his sons Diego and Fernando; his brothers Bartholomew and Diego; Mendez and Fieschi, the two heroes of the Jamaican ordeal; and a few servants. Absent was Beatrice de Harana, of whom nothing more was heard after this time. In the will that Columbus dictated to the notary Pedro de Hinojedo during his last moments, with Bartolomeo Fieschi as witness, he entrusted to his son and heir Diego "the care of Beatrice Enriquez, mother of Fernando, providing for her in such a manner that she may live in dignity, being a person who weighs heavily on my conscience. The reason for this I am not permitted to write here."

Beatrice did not come, nor did anyone from the royal family or the court. The king at the time was staying at the castle of the kings of Aragon in Villafuerte, just a few miles from Valladolid. He did not know that the discoverer of the New World had left the world of the living. It also eluded the notice of the official chronicler of the city of Valladolid, who makes no mention of Columbus's death in the daily register that usually carefully recorded the marriages, births and deaths of prominent families. Until his final hours, Columbus had been in the care of friars from the monastery of St. Francis, which was located near his house.

Composed of only a handful of relatives, friends and monks, the Admiral of the Ocean Sea's funeral procession passed, amid general indifference, through the narrow streets that led to the monastery. Perhaps a few passersby and women at their windows made the sign of the cross. The Mass was celebrated in the monastery itself, after which the body was laid to rest in the crypt beneath the Franciscan abbey. I personally retraced the route of that final procession. From Columbus's house I turned left, passed in front of the lovely church of Santa María Antigua, then behind the Plaza Mayor, once the center of the city. The Franciscan monastery no longer exists. In its place, below the square's colonnades, is the Café del Norte, which has a series of billiard rooms that extend back into the shadows as far as the spot where Columbus was buried nearly half a millennium ago. The rooms are silent, decorated in a long-outdated style, with bulkheads of dark wood on the walls and white sheets extended over the billiard tables. They could be seen as images of oblivion, the oblivion into which Columbus passed from the moment he died, with Bobadilla's chains to keep him company in his coffin. Spain did not even realize that a hero had died.

The boundary between fame and obscurity is a mysterious one. Columbus's oblivion was more than just the incidental neglect of his contemporaries at the moment of his death, the chance absence of great witnesses which deprived that moment of the solemnity that had surrounded other episodes of his life. Columbus's oblivion, unexpectedly, lasted for more than three centuries, from the sixteenth century to the mid-nineteenth century; until recently, in other words. Of all the unusual things he accomplished and experienced, earning the admiration and enthusiasm of the educated and uneducated alike, the most remarkable may well be the fact that his name was forgotten over the course of so many generations, as though lost forever in the depths of the past.

When he visited America in the early nineteenth century, Alexander Humboldt, the famous geographer and universal man of learning, who called Columbus "the modern Aristotle," was saddened not to have found a single stone, across the entire land, erected to the man who had discovered it. Similarly, in 1825, the abbé Mastai-Ferretti, a young delegate to the papal nunciature of Chile, made an extensive voyage through many different North and South American countries and found not a single stone, from Labrador to Patagonia, with Columbus's name on it. Twenty years later, Mastai-Ferretti became pope under the name of Pius IX. He had not forgotten this silence, "history's terrible contradiction." He was the first pope to cross the ocean. He could judge from his own experience the greatness of the man who had crossed it when it was still an unknown realm.

How is it possible for the memory of a protagonist of history to be erased —almost entirely—from the very scene of his exploits? Some have tried to explain it in terms of mass psychology and the image that a hero must have in order to live on in people's memories and to become transformed into legend. Christopher Columbus, a moody, silent man with no real ties of friendship, was never a popular figure. It was easier to hate him than to love him. And there is no such thing as a hero that is not loved. Thus his myth crumbled fast, until it vanished altogether.

There is no doubt some truth to this explanation, but I am not at all convinced that it tells the whole story. Columbus left in his wake a vast reality that changed the world's understanding of itself, among Europeans and all civilized peoples. A rare exception among historians, López de Gómara, in his *History of the Indies* of 1554, went so far as to say that Columbus had achieved "the greatest thing since the creation of the world." Although Gómara was not a contemporary of Columbus, many other writers and witnesses who did know him, and who lived with him and entered his confidence, made a point of expressing their opinion that Columbus was an exceptional person who accomplished extraordinary things. They had no doubt whatsoever that his memory would live on forever. I am referring here to authors with whom the reader is by now familiar, whose names have reappeared repeatedly throughout this account: Las Casas, Bernaldez, Fernando Columbus. But when were these people read? The great Las Casas, who finished his book in 1550, was published for the first time in a "collection of unpublished documents on the history of Spain" in 1875! Bernaldez, the parish priest of Palacíos to whom Columbus opened his heart as he rarely did during his lifetime, was published in 1870! The first edition of Fernando Columbus's *Histories* dates from 1575, when his father had already been dead for three-quarters of a century. After the extraordinary though short-lived interest aroused in Europe after the first voyage, the testimonies of Columbus's contemporaries remained confined to manuscripts that were eventually forgotten. Nobody knew of the fascinating ship's log, which historians attempted to reconstruct when Las Casas's book came to light in the late nineteenth century. Before then, it had never been published. No one read Columbus's writings—correspondences, travel diaries, important letters—because no one knew he had written anything. How then could anyone have really known about him?

Columbus's death was quickly followed by new and major events taking place in the Americas: the conquest of Mexico by Cortes and his soldiers, the subjugation of Peru by Pizarro's army, the exploits of the conquistadors and the galleons arriving in Spain laden with gold. Literature on Columbus, most of which was still unpublished or published late during those years when the memory of his deeds was still alive, remained rather scarce throughout the seventeenth and eighteenth centuries. There was not a single biography of Columbus in the Castilian tongue. Columbus's ocean voyages were mentioned in collections of great travel stories, but were treated as old adventures belonging to a distant past. When Philip II ordered court historian Antonio de Herrera to write a "general history of the Indies," more than a century had passed since the discovery of the New World. The figure of the man was receding more and more into the past; time was destroying it, while in the meantime his negative image, exaggerated by slander, was gaining more and more prominence. As Bacchelli has written: "Christopher Columbus is one of the figures most wronged by history, as often happens with the greatest."

The death of Isabella was certainly one of the major reasons for the declining fortunes of his posterity. With no one to keep it in check, the dislike that King Ferdinand had always felt for Columbus emerged in all its rancor (a terrible sentiment when expressed by a king), and all its cruelty—the cruelty of that kind of power that wants to wipe out all trace of genius, which it never can trust. Columbus had dared to pester the king with his demands for money and redress. That admiral's impudence irritated him no end and combined with other motives to add fuel to his hostility. Columbus had a personality entirely incompatible with his own. To make matters worse, Columbus's son Diego later revived his father's claims and insisted to the king that he should be sent to the Indies as viceroy and governor general, offices which he maintained, through repeated complaints reminiscent of his father's obstinacy, were his by hereditary right. The king answered that Columbus, at the time of his death, was no longer in active service. Diego's demand was rejected because of "groundlessness."

Diego and the king saw each other nearly every day, because of court duties. The young man never stopped pestering and imploring the king. Ferdinand became more and more blunt in his refusals. Diego then suggested that the king allow him to test his claims before a tribunal. The king consented: he wanted to see if there was a single judge in all of Spain who would dare rule against his sovereign authority. In so doing he would be rid of this annoyance once and for all.

Thus began the long, tiresome series of *pleitos,* the petitions brought by Diego Columbus against the Crown of Castile. They lasted for more than half a century, from 1507 to 1563, with yet a few sequels and postludes later on. They involved Diego and his wife Maria de Toledo, niece of the king and a descendant of the "grandest of the grandees of Spain," the Duke of Alba. After Diego's death they were continued by his son Luis, who thirsted more for money than for justice. At one point the Duke of Alba intervened and managed to persuade the king to send Diego Columbus to Santo Domingo as governor, replacing Ovando. The office was granted to him only as a personal and temporary appointment, a concession that did not recognize any hereditary rights to the office and definitively revoked the title of viceroy. But Ferdinand never forgave the Columbus family for forcing him, through politics and parentage, to make decisions against his will. His dislike for Columbus eventually turned into an implacable hatred against the man who had dared to demand money of him as though he, the king, were an insolvent debtor—this man who had the gall to consider himself Spain's "third king," whose memory aroused only resentment in him, much to the detriment of Columbus's posterity. Thus, just as one builds walls around a fortress to render it impregnable, Ferdinand built a wall of silence around Columbus's name. He placed his memory under an interdict, as it were. And with his corps of court slanderers, he turned the *pleitos* into an exercise in the defamation of America's discoverer.

In the diatribes of the inquisitorial lawyers and the testimonies of the surviving witnesses—old sailors from Columbus's expeditions who, because of trial procedures, could answer only yes or no, and whose memories of the events had faded in the twenty or thirty intervening years—Columbus emerged as having discovered nothing. They said he only retraced routes already familiar to the ancients, who had stopped following them because they were too long, thus letting them fall into disuse until they vanished from human memory. Columbus supposedly "rediscovered" them in the knapsacks of a dead man, the "unknown helmsman" who became part of popular legend precisely because of the depositions made in the *pleitos.* The Admiral of the Ocean Sea, stealing from the dead!

At the same time the *pleitos* resurrected a protagonist for the campaign against Columbus's memory, and who could have been better for this role than Martín Alonso Pinzón? To him went the credit for having conceived of the idea, for having persevered in pursuit of its realization, for having possessed the seafaring expertise to overcome Columbus's ignorance in such matters and to suggest, during the last days of the voyage, the shift in course that led to the landing at San Salvador. It was even suggested that half the earnings collected by the Columbus family under the narrow, official application of the capitulations of Santa Fé be given to the Pinzón family. But the heirs of Martín Alonso present at the trial immediately renounced such a claim for the benefit of the Crown. They were Spanish after all, not foreigners!

King Ferdinand died in 1516. He was the last important figure with direct knowledge of the events in question, witness to the truth together with

Isabella and Christopher, whom he now joined for eternity. His successor was Charles V, who came from Austria and had never seen Columbus in his life; he knew nothing about him except that as subjects, he and his heirs had dared to contest the decisions of their king and institute a legal proceeding against the Crown. He immediately revoked Diego's appointment as governor and recalled him to Spain. The name of Columbus was not even to be uttered. A few years later Diego also died, which left the Emperor Charles V face to face with the powerless Luis, Diego's son. It was inconceivable that the emperor would not try to destroy the defenseless young man. Don Luis renounced all hereditary rights in exchange for the title of Duke of Veragua, which came with a moderate income. Then he began to drift. He sold all his grandfather's letters, maps, objects and memoirs. He thus squandered both the patrimony and the memory of his great forefather. He kept only the title of admiral, which cost nothing and earned nothing. The title did not disappear. Even today, in the halls of the Spanish Admiralty in Madrid, one may encounter a distinguished gentleman dressed in navy blue, with the rank, I believe, of sea captain, named Christopher Columbus—Cristóbal Colón. On his visiting card, beside his name and rank, one reads the title that is his by hereditary right: Admiral of the Ocean Sea.

Thus goes the chronicle of a hero's destruction; not a very exciting account at that, but with more than its share of consequences, the first of them being the preposterous story of how America came by its name. It begins in a small city buried in the Vosges Mountains in France, the city of Saint-Dié. In the early 1500s it was part of the duchy of Lorraine, and despite its provincial isolation—though in the heart of Europe, at the crossroads of the emerging nations—it had a special appeal of its own for a coterie of literary men and scientists who kept the fires of culture burning there. One of the more illustrious men of the group was the cosmographer Martin Waldseemüller, who called himself Hylacomylus, in keeping with the Latinizing custom so dear to Humanists of the time. He was a rather obscure man in search of a fame that he never found, but which he served as an instrument.

Amerigo Vespucci, the Florentine who worked for the bank of Giannetto Berardo Berardi in Seville, upon returning from the voyages he made across the ocean some time after Columbus's crossing and in the wake of the admiral's discoveries, did something that had never occurred to Columbus. He published, in Latin and in Italian, a very detailed account of what he had seen. For a long time this text was believed to be the copy of an original report sent to the Gonfalonier of Florence at the time of Columbus, Piero

Soderini. But this belief proved to be erroneous, and thus Vespucci's account should be considered to be of a somewhat later date, a number of years after Columbus's voyages. Vespucci was in any case a very fast and zealous self-promoter. He sent a copy of the account to, among others, the Duke of Lorraine, had editions printed at Strasbourg and Augsberg, and succeeded in calling attention to voyages that he had made as a traveler endowed with a certain degree of culture and a great deal of ambition. The Duke of Lorraine had the account sent to the Saint-Dié coterie, which turned it over to their expert on such matters, Waldseemüller. One important passage that he read in it was the following: "Our ancient forebears thought that there were no continents to the south beyond the equator, only the sea they called the Atlantic . . . My voyage has made it plain that this opinion is erroneous and entirely contrary to the truth. For in those regions I have found a continent more densely populated and abounding in animals than our Europe, Asia and Africa. We may rightly call this continent the New World." The place that Vespucci was referring to was the area around the gulf of Paria, on the Venezuelan coast, where Columbus had landed a few years before him in the course of his third voyage.

Excited by Vespucci's boldness and by the revelations contained in his travel account, Waldseemüller immediately set about writing a *New Introduction to Cosmography*, published the following year, 1507, by the printing office of Saint-Dié. Waldseemüller talked at great length about Vespucci and made the following proposal: "I do not know of any law that would forbid that the land discovered by Amerigo, a man of great wisdom and intelligence, be given his name; and since Europe, Asia and Africa have feminine names, let Amerigo's land be called America." The book, along with the proposal, was sent by the Duke of Lorraine to the Emperor Maximilian. The appellation "America" made its way out of the Vosges and around Europe, where Columbus was either unknown or already forgotten, or at least not remembered by any sovereigns. Within ten years' time the name of America had entered the common speech of the courts, the learned, and the geographers, who defined America, or the New World of Amerigo, as "the fourth part of the globe." The late Columbus's heirs were still grappling with their *pleitos* and with the vengeance of the kings of Spain. No one said a word in protest. Las Casas alone expressed indignation: in his opinion, the only name that could be rightly given to the new continent was Colombia. But in this too, the first Admiral of the Ocean Sea was destined to fail utterly. America remained America.

It should be noted that for another half century the term "America" referred only to what is known today as South America. North America was still represented on maps as a vast peninsula of the Asian continent. Columbus had shared this conviction. He had realized that the lands along the Gulf of Paria could only belong to a new continent. But immediately to the north, in Columbus's mind, lay Asia: the Caribbean islands were Asian islands, Cuba a promontory of Asian terra firma, and the Central American coast from Honduras to Panama an outlying province of China. Between Panama and Paria he tried to find the waterway that in his opinion must divide the Asian continent from that other, unknown one that he had glimpsed at the mouth of the Orinoco. He never did find it, but this did not keep him from believing that it existed. A few years later Magellan, with his extraordinary voyage, set aright the geography of the new lands, which had remained as it were in a state of suspension following Columbus's discoveries.

The world of culture, however, and more particularly that of science, was rather slow to digest these new facts, and it was some time before America became clearly situated within Europe's field of vision. Europe was not prepared for this sudden, radically new development, which threw its knowledge of the world into disorder. Europe's understanding of the world was still solidly anchored to medieval culture, and a long time would pass before it could free itself of these fetters once and for all. Until the late sixteenth century people spoke of the globe on which they lived as if it were still as Strabo or Ptolemy had imagined it. The image of the New World as half Asia, half America—Columbus's own image of it—enabled them to accept the new without breaking entirely with the old.

In the eighteenth century, the century of the Enlightenment and the Encyclopedia, the question of America was examined from a moral perspective and became a problem of conscience, especially during the latter decades. Cornelius DePauw, a Massachusetts industrialist turned philosopher, stated publicly in 1768 that "the discovery of the New World has been the most disastrous event in the history of mankind." He was referring to the resurgence of slavery brought on by the Spanish and started, for all intents and purposes, by Columbus himself. Millions, tens of millions, of human beings had fallen into misery, pain and illness. Rather than progressing, humanity was being wrenched backward. This, according to DePauw, was the fruit of America's conquest.

The French Academy posed itself the same question in the years of the Revolution. In 1792 a competition was given for the best essay in response to the question: "Has the discovery of America been helpful or harmful to humankind?" The winner of the competition made it clear that "the subject is vast and inexhaustible. The more one studies it, the more it grows in size." His conclusion was that America's political and economic effects on Europe were positive, but her moral effect was "dramatically destructive." Europe had a guilty conscience.

Columbus's name began to reemerge at about this time. Madame du Boccage, a friend of Voltaire, wrote the verse epic *La Colombiade,* which the abbé Parini then translated into Italian. Yet even a full three hundred years after the discovery, no one had any precise knowledge about this singular mariner of dubious origin, whose life story remained vague and shrouded in mystery. The best that anyone said of him was that he had been an adventurer. Many believed that he had attempted to steal Vespucci's glory, which had remained intact over the centuries and won him most of the credit for the discovery. On the other hand, no one forgot that Columbus had set in motion the corrupting process of slavery.

With his name under discussion again, there were some who wanted to examine the matter more closely. In 1828 Washington Irving published the first American biography of Columbus, and before long it was being read all over the world. In Spain Philip VII assigned to Martín Fernández de Navarrete the task of collecting all documents concerning Columbus's voyages and discoveries scattered throughout the various archives and libraries. It was then, around 1830, that people's attentions were drawn to the texts of Las Casas and Bernaldez, to Columbus's correspondence with the king and queen, his reports, letters and the remnants of his log.

The Catholic Church made a major contribution toward Columbus's rehabilitation. The New World had no symbol of evangelism comparable to those propagators of the faith who had preached Christ's word throughout Europe in the first centuries A.D. Christopher Columbus was the only figure who might fill this void. As early as the seventeenth century Giovanni Botero, confessor of St. Carlo Borromeo, referred to Columbus as an apostle whose life was not unlike a martyr's. In 1622 the *De Propaganda Fide* confraternity was founded for the purpose of reshaping America's image according to religious ideals and overcoming the distortions caused by the excessively protracted period of conquest and plunder. Columbus fit in well with a providentially oriented interpretation of history: he had been chosen by God to spread the gospel throughout the New World. Thus designated as "God's messenger" (which he himself believed he was), Columbus, by the end of the nineteenth century, was about to be considered for beatification, the antechamber to sainthood. The presence of Pius IX on the papal throne was clearly to his advantage, this pope having already developed an admiration for him when sojourning in America. The beatification proceedings were started in 1866, suspended because of the events of Porta Pia, then resumed under the pontificate of Leo XIII. Many groupings of cardinals, archbishops and bishops supported the postulation of the cause, which was resubmitted in 1891. But there were also fierce opponents. The two great obstacles to beatification were Columbus's concubinage with Beatrice de Harana and his introduction of slavery into America. Hundreds of Indians captured by Columbus had been sold at the market in Seville. The "black legend" of the Spanish conquest had begun with him.

Opponents also had not forgotten Rodrigo de Triana, the poor sailor who had been the first to sight land at the end of the crossing that first brought Europeans to America. He rightly should have received the lifelong pension of ten thousand maravedis yearly, but Columbus took it for himself and used it to support Beatrice de Harana in Córdoba. Thus he sinned on top of a sin. This was not the conduct of a holy man. When the Church tribunal took its final vote, only one ballot was cast in favor of Columbus's beatification. The postulation was rejected.

This time, however, failure benefited Columbus. True, he was not beatified, nor should he have been. But no one questioned any more that he really had discovered America, for better or for worse. With the fourth centenary of the landing at San Salvador, which was celebrated in 1892 across the world in cities having some connection to his life (Genoa, Lisbon, Córdoba, Seville, Santo Domingo, and many others), the figure of Columbus was at last resurrected from oblivion. The Church's interest was seconded by historical and scientific investigations. All available documents were published; written works on Columbus numbered in the hundreds, not all of them in praise of him. Yet the very tenacity of the detractions, accusations and equivocations that had accompanied his exploits four hundred years earlier was itself a sign of the rediscovered hero's vitality. Claims for his greatness, genius and incomparable imaginative power were finally recognized. But the virtue that stood out most prominently and evoked the most admiration in this belated return to triumph was his boldness. As Victor Hugo said so succinctly of Columbus: "Columbus's glory lies not in having arrived, but in having weighed anchor."

I shall end my account in the city where Columbus's life came to an end, Valladolid. His mortal remains, laid to rest in the crypt of the Franciscan monastery in 1506, were supposedly transferred at some unspecified time between 1509 and 1514 to the Carthusian monastery of Las Cuevas, at the gates of Seville. Many years later Columbus's daughter-in-law Maria de Toledo, already a widow, and her son Don Luis, the third Admiral of the Ocean Sea, asked Charles V permission to transfer the body to the Cathedral of Santo Domingo in America, a request promptly granted. This happened in or around 1537. The bishops of Santo Domingo refused to bury Columbus's remains (as he was a "layman and foreigner") in the mortuary chapel of the high altar, as the high office of the deceased should have dictated. The coffin was placed in the underground chambers beneath the cathedral, where it remained for three years, as long as the bishop refused to obey the repeated orders of Charles V. The remains of Columbus's son Diego were later buried in Santo Domingo as well, alongside those of his father. They were joined in time by Don Luis, his brother Christopher the second, and the *adelantado* Bartholomew.

Their bodies are said to have remained in the Cathedral of Santo Domingo for two centuries. In 1795 France occupied the entire island of Hispaniola and the city of Santo Domingo with republican troops. The Spanish authorities did not want Columbus's remains to fall into French hands. His coffin, dug up in haste from below the high altar, was transferred to Havana. When Cuba proclaimed independence in 1899, the admiral's beleaguered corpse once again crossed the Atlantic and was laid to rest in the Cathedral of Seville, where today it lies at the foot of the marble monument built in his honor.

But is it really there? This is the last of the many mysteries of Columbus's life, the mystery of his burial. When his remains supposedly still lay underground in Havana, some restorers working in the cathedral of Santo Domingo came across, to the right of the high altar, a lead coffer containing bones and ashes and marked in such a manner as to lead one to conclude that these were Columbus's remains. But they could not be in Havana and Santo Domingo at the same time. The Spanish government assigned the historian Manuel Colmeiro to look into the problem. He came to the conclusion that the remains lying in Santo Domingo belonged to Don Diego. Colmeiro's findings, which were officially accepted at the time, were later contradicted and contested after further researches were conducted in the Cathedral of Santo Domingo. The remains transferred to Havana and later to Seville were said to belong not to Christopher but to his son Don Diego. Thus, according to this thesis, which the current Archbishop of Santo Domingo told me was "irrefutable," Columbus lies not in Seville, but in Santo Domingo.

This gives Columbus two tombs. The one in Santo Domingo is also graced with a monument, though in all honesty it is hardly the most beautiful of memorials, surrounded as it is by inscriptions in wrought iron, hosanna scrolls of a sort, which were set forever flapping on the funerary marble in 1892, on the occasion of the fourth centenary of the discovery. The thesis that places Columbus in Santo Domingo was corroborated by the English historian Thacher and the Cuban A. Álvarez Pedroso, the latter in a work from 1944. The contrary thesis, which considers the remains in Seville to be the real ones, is upheld by Antonio Ballesteros in a long document submitted to the General Academy of History in Madrid in 1946 and approved by a consensus of Spanish historians.

And so? In 1960, Professor Charles Goff, an illustrious orthopedic surgeon from Yale University, obtained permission to have Columbus's alleged tomb in Santo Domingo opened up, and thus had the opportunity to measure and photograph every fragment of skeleton over a period of several weeks. The remains were judged to have belonged to a man 5'8" in height, who had a large head and traces of arthritic deformities, and who died when he was between fifty and sixty years of age. Are these data sufficient to allow one to identify the deceased as Christopher Columbus? According to Professor Goff, they are not. Many parts were missing from the coffin, others seemed not to fit with the rest of the skeleton. In the American surgeon's opinion, the bones he examined belonged to two different bodies, whose skeletons are divided between Santo Domingo and Seville. He believes they belong to Columbus *and* to his son Diego, and that the mix-up may have occurred in 1795, during the hasty and careless efforts to move Columbus's alleged corpse from Santo Domingo to Havana.

I have my own idea on the matter, which was actually suggested to me when visiting Valladolid, and which since then I have grown to like because it seems to me more in keeping with Columbus's character than any of the other arguments regarding his place of burial. At Valladolid, a young scholar associated with the university frequently accompanied me on my Columbus-related visits to different parts of the city. He was both passionate and cynical. He did not believe many of the official verities built around the figure of Columbus "to fill," he said, "the gaps in his life about which we know nothing and quite likely will always know nothing." He told me about a little book published by some Andalusian historians in 1949, in which they assert that Columbus's corpse never left Valladolid.

"How is that possible?" I asked. The young man made a vague gesture, very Spanish, as if to say that everything is possible when there is no definite proof.

I pursued the matter. "Well then what was it that was transported to Las Cuevas, to Santo Domingo, to Havana, and finally to Seville? Whose corpse was it?"

He answered me with a question. "Do you think that the Franciscans, the unbending Franciscans of those days, would ever have handed over to others an exquisite corpse of their own? For Columbus was one of them, of the Franciscan faith; he had worn their habit. He had discovered America thanks to the Franciscans and their support. People said he was a messenger of God, but the intermediary between the two was St. Francis. And you think the Franciscans would have relinquished possession of his body?"

I continued to weigh the pros and cons. All things considered, it still seemed to me that if nothing else, the first transferral, the one from Valladolid to Las Cuevas, had to have taken place. We have the testimonies of Fernando Columbus, Las Casas and Bernaldez, all of whom were living at the time. And if this first transferral did take place, than all the corpse's other voyages also appeared possible. In any case, if it left Valladolid, it certainly could not be lying there now. The young man shrugged. "Yes, I see what you're saying. But you would have to know just what the Franciscans pulled out of their underground vaults. As far as I know the body was never identified. The coffin was never opened for the transferral."

I still had my doubts. But as we were walking from Columbus's house to the Plaza Mayor, my companion took me by the arm and stopped me. "But even admitting that they did let him get away the first time, who's to say that they didn't go to Santo Domingo to retrieve him, during the three years when the body was sitting in the cathedral's cellars? Of course, I'm not saying they would have done it themselves, robes and all. Rather, they could have hired people to do the job. In those days they did those sorts of things and more. Don't forget that the cathedral belonged to the Dominican order, their great adversaries. Would they have allowed a fellow Franciscan to be buried in enemy ground?"

He released my arm, and we continued our walk. We came to Plaza Mayor, to the spot where the monastery of St. Francis once stood. We entered the Café del Norte, which I described earlier. There was that same shadowy, silent atmosphere. In the old café's inner rooms there reigned an almost metaphysical feeling of solitude. When we entered the billiard room the young professor stamped his foot on the wooden floor, which seemed to spring up under the force. "Here," said my companion in a low voice, as though telling me a secret. "In my opinion he is buried right here, in the monastery crypt, which no longer exists but used to be right below us. Everything is gone now. All that remains are the bones of the dead, the bones of heroes."

"Beneath the billiard tables?" I asked.

"Yes, beneath the billiard tables. Christopher Columbus, America's discoverer, lies buried beneath the billiard tables."

As a final resting place it seemed to me rather bizarre. It reminded me quite a bit of the story of Columbus's request to use that cardinal's catafalque to travel across Spain to Segovia. Thinking back on Columbus's life, I realized that he never had a clear sense of death. Everything about him bespoke vitality, and nothing was ever clear. It began to seem almost logical that his burial also should remain unclear. Arguing over this question became just as useless as arguing over his place of birth. Wherever he was born or buried does not alter the fact of his pride and courage, his flashes of genius and imagination sparked by that touch of madness that enabled him to overcome all obstacles with an unconscious temerity.

But is a grave beneath the Café del Norte's billiard tables a proper, fitting grave? In my opinion it is, at least for Columbus. Cervantes, in the chapter on the death of Don Quixote, which takes place in Sancho Panza's native village, recounts that there were some who wanted to transport "his tired and moldering bones" to Old Castile, "contrary to all the laws of death." Numerous times in this book I have hinted at the affinities between the figures of Don Quixote and Columbus, even though one is a literary creation and the other a real historical personage. Why not then point out their similarities in death as well? "Contrary to all the laws of death," some people wanted to transport Christopher Columbus's "tired and moldering bones" far and wide across the seas and continents. But death's laws are intangible. This is why I believe that the man who discovered America lies beneath the billiard room of an old café in Valladolid—and that this is proper and fitting, for him and for us.

Bibliography

(after Cervantes)

Whenever the moment comes to write a bibliography of works consulted I always fall prey to the suspicion that it serves no purpose, or little purpose, as far as the reader is concerned; and that all it really does is give the book—and above all its author—a patina of scholarly authority. In the Prologue to *Don Quixote* Cervantes pokes fun at people who compile long bibliographies at the end of their works, dense and detailed lists much like the endless pages suffixed to the countless books that have been written about Christopher Columbus and his exploits. Labyrinths within labyrinths.

For those who must have a bibliography at all costs, Cervantes advises: "You have but to look up some book that has them all, from A to Z, and transfer the entire list as it stands. What if the imposition is plain for all to see? You have little need to refer to them, and so it does not matter; and some may be so simple-minded as to believe that you have drawn upon them all in your simple unpretentious little story." (Tr. S. Putnam, *Don Quixote,* Viking N.Y. 1949.)

I shall not try to imitate that great writer. I shall only say that I came to know Columbus through reading what his contemporaries (Las Casas, Bernaldez, Oviedo, his son Fernando) wrote about him, and what I was able to find in other documents and fragments of the time, such as the records of the *pleitos.* The countless books of Columbus scholarship are all derived from this material. In our day Columbus's deeds have been described with passion and great diversity by three different scholars, whom I have chosen from a forest of useless books. It is perhaps no accident that one is Spanish, the navigator's adopted nationality; one is American, from the land he discovered; and one is Italian, from the country and city that in all likelihood spawned him (the author is Genoese). The Spaniard is Salvador de Madariaga, more a writer than a scholar, whose excellent book on Columbus survives his stubborn attempt to prove that Columbus was descended from Spanish Jews. The American is Samuel Eliot Morison, Admiral in the U.S. Navy, who sailed to the same places that Columbus did and reconstructed in graceful prose the discoverer's perceptions, adventures and arts. The Italian is Paolo Emilio Taviani, who devoted half a century of his life to Columbus. Of living Columbus experts, he is the one who knows the most about the man.

Yet other names from my reading and research also stand out in my memory, names of people who are not specialists or scholars. They are poets and writers, creators of images, explorers of men's lives and their mysteries. And since what I wanted to recount in my book was the story of a man's life, I found their ideas more illuminating and inspiring than all the lifeless lists of facts, with their plethora of dates, references and quotations. The writers I am referring to are: Lope de Vega and his drama *Columbus,* buried amid dozens of other plays of his; Paul Claudel and his *Christophe Colomb;* Jakob Wassermann; Riccardo Bacchelli; Massimo Bontempelli; and the Cuban Alejo Carpentier and his *La harpe et l'ombre.* None of them claimed to have discovered anything new about Columbus's undertaking or his life. Yet they understood him as a man and succeeded in going beyond the concatenation of events and into the protagonist's mind. Often one line of theirs told me more than a hundred scholarly books. The imagination has qualities that no amount of learning can produce. On its wings these writers have retraced Columbus's steps. And was it not poetry and the imagination, more than learning, that moved Columbus to alter the world's identity? You see, it all works out, even in terms of bibliography.

Index

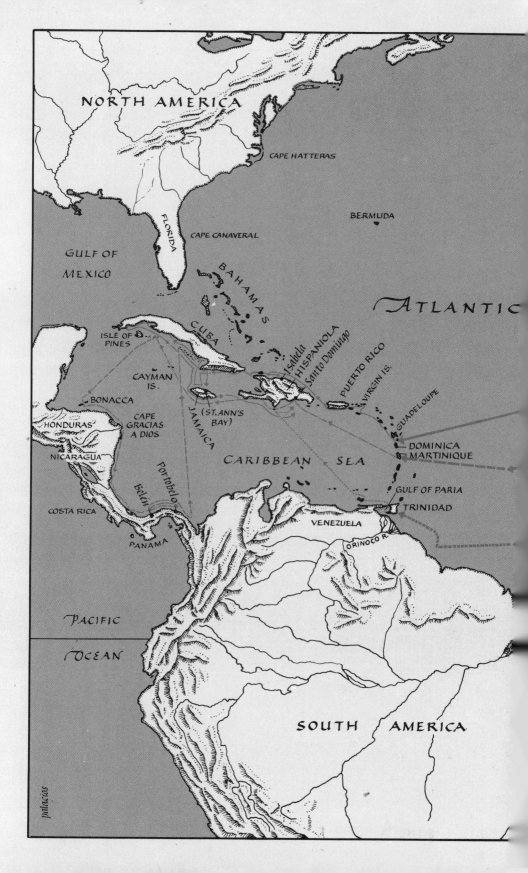

NORTH AMERICA

CAPE HATTERAS

BERMUDA

FLORIDA

CAPE CANAVERAL

GULF OF
MEXICO

BAHAMAS

ATLANTIC

CUBA

ISLE OF
PINES

Isabela
HISPANIOLA
Santo Domingo

PUERTO RICO

VIRGIN IS.

CAYMAN
IS.

GUADELOUPE

BONACCA

(ST. ANN'S
BAY)

HONDURAS

CAPE
GRACIAS
A DIOS

JAMAICA

DOMINICA
MARTINIQUE

NICARAGUA

CARIBBEAN   SEA

GULF OF PARIA

Portobelo

Belén

TRINIDAD

COSTA RICA

VENEZUELA

PANAMA

ORINOCO R.

PACIFIC

OCEAN

SOUTH   AMERICA

palacios